T0326569

The Buy or Lease Decision

Value-Added Management

Edited by Hans-Dietrich Haasis

Volume 10

PETER LANG

Frankfurt am Main · Berlin · Bern · Bruxelles · New York · Oxford · Wien

Michael Wehrheim

The Buy or Lease Decision

An Enhanced Theoretical Model Based on
Empirical Analyses with Implications for the Container
Financing Decision of Shipping Lines

PETER LANG

Frankfurt am Main · Berlin · Bern · Bruxelles · New York · Oxford · Wien

Bibliographic Information published by the Deutsche Nationalbibliothek
The Deutsche Nationalbibliothek lists this publication in the Deutsche Nationalbibliografie; detailed bibliographic data is available in the internet at http://dnb.d-nb.de.

Zugl.: Bremen, Univ., Diss., 2011

Cover Design:
Olaf Glöckler, Atelier Platen, Friedberg

D 46
ISSN 1863-169X
ISBN 978-3-631-61593-5

© Peter Lang GmbH
Internationaler Verlag der Wissenschaften
Frankfurt am Main 2011
All rights reserved.

www.peterlang.de

Preface

After having worked in container leasing for several years, I decided to write this doctoral dissertation to supplement my practical knowledge with academic analysis.

With professor Dr. Haasis I found an excellent advisor. As head of the Institute of Shipping Economics and Logistics (ISL) and full professor at the Bremen University he has a solid background in both shipping and economics. I would like to take this opportunity to thank him for his valuable advice and clear feedback.

I would also like to thank Prof. Lemper for his advice and other staff members of ISL for their help to collect the necessary data and literature.

My special thanks go to several professors at American University in Washington DC. The classes of Prof. Golan and Prof. Langbein provided the necessary foundation regarding econometrical methods for this thesis. Prof. Lumsdaine helped with expertise in international finance aspects.

Many industry experts gave valuable input. To mention only a few: Andrew Foxcroft (Containerization International) provided critical data for the empirical analysis. Patric Hicks (Container Owners Association) gave excellent feedback and established new contacts. Detailed industry knowledge was gathered in interviews with Mark Weidemann (Hapag-Lloyd), Guenther Kochan (Hamburg Sued), Peter Pilgaard (Maersk), Mark Wilkinson (OPDR), Philip Brewer (Textainer) and others.

I would also like to thank my former colleagues of Capital Lease for their input. Most important were Ian Karan, Claudio Paiva, Navina Karan and Marc Schumann. Next, I owe thanks to all industry practitioners who participated in the online survey conducted in April / May 2010.

Last, but most important I would like to thank my beloved wife Ines Schlotter, my daughter Selma and son Nils for their support. Especially in times when problems had to be solved and the path going forward was unclear, they encouraged me greatly.

Table of Contents

List of Tables

List of Figures

Abbreviations

Abbreviation	Description
20 DV	20 foot standard dry van cargo container
40 DV	40 foot standard dry van cargo container
40 HC	40 foot high cube standard dry cargo container
CPI	Consumer price index
IMF	International Monetary Fund
IRR	Internal rate of return
NAL	Net present value advantage of leasing
NPV	Net present value
OLS	Ordinary least square – standard type of regression analysis
reefer	Refrigerating container
TEU	20 foot equivalent unit – a container that is 20 feet long
USD	United States Dollars
VIF	Variance inflation factor – a measure for collinearity
WACC	Weighted average cost of capital

1 Introduction and thesis plan

1.1 Motivation

The container industry has seen dramatic growth since its early days in the 1960s. Both the total shipping volume and the share of containerization have appreciated rapidly since then. In 2008 the total container volume exceeded 18 million units or 26 million TEU (twenty foot equivalent units). In the years 2002 to 2007, the container volume increased about 10% per year due to rising global trade (Foxcroft, 2009b, p. 402). According to the industry journal *Containerization International* more than 90% of the worldwide container fleet is used for seaborne transportation (Foxcroft, 2009b). Therefore this thesis focuses on maritime containers.

The industry differentiates between standard and special containers. Standard containers are 20 feet (20 DV – dry van) or 40 feet (40 DV) long. The 40-feet long container also exists as high cube (40 HC), which means that the container is one foot higher. The special containers include reefers, tanks, bulk, open tops, flatracks, side doors, pallet wides and others. Standard equipment accounts for 89,6% of the total maritime container fleet. Refrigerating containers (reefers) account for 6.2% and special dry freight containers for 3.5% of the total container fleet. The remaining 0.7% are tank containers (Foxcroft, 2009a, p. 8).

The following chart provides an overview of the price development of a new 20 DV container as well as its resale price (after about 12 years) and its daily rental rate (Foxcroft, 2009b).

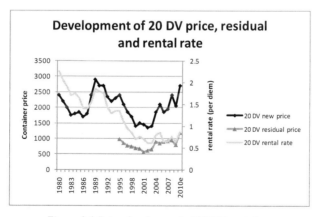

Figure 1-1 Price development of 20 DV container

Figure 1-1 shows the decline in container prices from about 2900 USD in 1990 to about 1500 USD in the year 2000. In this period nearly 100% of the container production was transferred to China. The lower labor costs in China resulted in lower prices. Due to rising steel costs in recent years the container price went up again. Resale prices follow the trend of new containers to some extent but remain between 500 and 1000 USD. The per diem rental rate follows the new container price very closely but combined with a downward trend. This trend might be the result of better refinancing possibilities of lessors (e.g., asset-backed securities, bank loans) and increasing competition.

The container shipping industry is one of the most global industries. There are a number of very big players that connect the main ports worldwide. The following table presents and overview over the top 100 shipping lines (Alphaliner, 2010).

Table 1-1 Top 100 shipping lines

Alphaliner - Top 100 : Operated fleets as per 26 May 2010									
		Total			Owned		Chartered		
Rnk	Operator	TEU	Ships	market share	TEU	Ships	TEU	Ships	% Chart
1	APM-Maersk	2,059,135	549	15.6%	1,118,663	207	940,472	342	45.7%
2	Mediterranean Shg Co	1,646,213	417	12.5%	858,591	202	787,622	215	47.8%
3	CMA CGM Group	1,101,793	382	8.3%	343,351	85	758,442	297	68.8%
4	APL	595,650	148	4.5%	170,373	45	425,277	103	71.4%
5	Evergreen Line	557,456	153	4.2%	319,263	87	238,193	66	42.7%
6	Hapag-Lloyd	543,743	123	4.1%	292,613	60	251,130	63	46.2%
7	COSCO Container L.	496,156	132	3.8%	276,405	88	219,751	44	44.3%
8	CSAV Group	477,519	130	3.6%	41,410	8	436,109	122	91.3%
9	Hanjin Shipping	448,051	98	3.4%	104,068	19	343,983	79	76.8%
10	CSCL	440,236	122	3.3%	250,099	71	190,137	51	43.2%
11	NYK	364,941	95	2.8%	285,301	55	79,640	40	21.8%
12	MOL	364,484	95	2.8%	157,974	28	206,510	67	56.7%
13	OOCL	351,726	77	2.7%	259,346	43	92,380	34	26.3%
14	Hamburg Süd Group	337,748	108	2.6%	142,326	38	195,422	70	57.9%
15	Zim	324,582	98	2.5%	168,035	36	156,547	62	48.2%
16	K Line	321,017	82	2.4%	205,677	38	115,340	44	35.9%
17	Yang Ming Marine Trans	317,197	77	2.4%	187,201	45	129,996	32	41.0%
18	Hyundai M.M.	271,604	52	2.1%	74,325	12	197,279	40	72.6%
19	PIL (Pacific Int. Line)	230,071	127	1.7%	143,537	83	86,534	44	37.6%
20	UASC	199,082	50	1.5%	113,596	27	85,486	23	42.9%
	Top 21 to 100	1,763,211	1,474	13.3%	738,613	703	1,024,598	771	58.1%
	Total	**13,211,615**	**4,589**	**100.0%**	**6,250,767**	**1,980**	**6,960,848**	**2,609**	**52.7%**

Table 1-1 shows that the top 20 shipping lines account for 87% of the shipping capacity. The ship capacity of the biggest 5 players are Maersk (Denmark), MSC (Switzerland), CMA (France), APL (Singapore) and

Evergreen (Taiwan) adds up to 45%. The industry is dominated by the big players that operate on a global basis.

Container leasing is provided by firms specializing in container equipment. The reason for the specialization is obvious. Besides the financing function, container lessors provide some logistical services. Containers can be leased and returned at many destinations worldwide. Lessors partner with depots around the globe that provide repair and storage services. Lessors have to coordinate the repair process, new leases, container relocations and second hand sales. The following table provides an overview of the top container leasing firms (Foxcroft, 2009b):

Table 1-2 Top container lessors

Top container lessors		
Company	TEU (in 1000)	Market share
Textainer Group	2069	18%
Florens Container Leasing	1632	15%
Triton Container	1478	13%
TAL International	1034	9%
GESeaCo	946	8%
CAI International	786	7%
Seacastle Container Leasing	566	5%
UES International HK	491	4%
Gold Container	480	4%
Cronos Group	446	4%
Capital Intermodal-Xines	193	2%
Amficon Leasing	148	1%
CARU	92	1%
Blue Sky Intermodal	92	1%
Beacon Intermodal Leasing	76	1%
Waterfront Leasing	74	1%
Other	629	6%
Grand total	11,229	100%

Table 1-2 shows the market dominance of the top 5 lessors. These include Textainer Group (USA), Florens Container Leasing (Hong Kong), Triton Container (USA), TAL International (USA) and GESeaCo (USA). Their total market share adds up to 64%.

The shipping line business is very capital intensive, because the ships cause high investments. The increasing need for containers adds further high investments. In 2008 containers in the value of 4 billion USD (2007: 5.4 billion USD) were bought. How are these containers financed? The following chart presents the development of containerization (Foxcroft, 2009b) and the share of owned and leased containers.

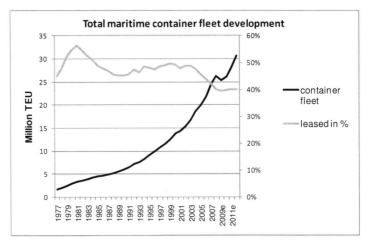

Figure 1-2 Development of leased and bought container volume

Figure 1-2 shows that on average, about 45% of the containers are leased and the remainder are owned by the shipping lines (financed by debt and equity). The leasing share reduced in recent years to about 40%.

The chart below shows the percentage of leased and bought containers in each year (Foxcroft, 2008).

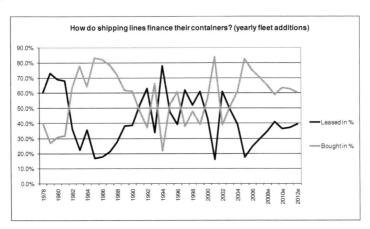

Figure 1-3 Development of share of leased and bought containers per year

Figure 1-3 shows that the annual share of leased and bought containers varies greatly—in some years 20% and in others 80% of the annual demand for containers is leased.

1.2 Problem to be solved within this thesis

There are a number of resulting interesting questions:
1. What are the arguments for or against leasing containers? How important are these criteria for the decision process?
2. What influences the aggregated share of bought and leased containers in practice?
3. Which variables/criteria have an impact on the buy or lease decision of an individual shipping line?
4. What are the leasing strategies of the shipping lines and how did they change over the years?
5. How should shipping lines evaluate leasing versus buying? Which theoretical model should be used?

The target of this thesis is to find answers to these questions.

The problem to be solved within this thesis can be summarized as follows: Which theoretical model should be used to evaluate the buy or lease decision, taking into account econometric analyses of empirical data regarding shipping containers?

1.3 Approach

First, for this analysis, the relevant literature has to be taken into account. Existing literature was found at the libraries of Bremen University, the Institute of Shipping Economics and Logistics, American University, U.S. Congress and Google Scholar. Many articles are available online at JSTOR and other databases.

There is a large amount of literature regarding the general buy or lease decision. Literature about the theoretical concept as well as empirical analyses can be found. The theoretical literature focuses on mathematical decision models for the buy or lease evaluation. The net present value (NPV) of the future cash flows of the lease and the purchase (loan) alternative are compared. The difference is called the net present advantage of leasing (NAL). Even if other reasons for leasing are mentioned, they are not covered in the suggested evaluation models. This thesis shall first find the empirically relevant variables with impact on the buy or lease decision. Based on the results, the theoretical model will be enhanced by integrating additional decision criteria.

The existing empirical literature focuses on the econometrical analysis of potential variables with impact on the buy or lease decision. Interestingly, the theoretically most important variable, the relevance of the NPV or NAL in practice, has never been analyzed using econometrical methods. This thesis will analyze the empirical effect of the NAL on the buy or lease decision for the first time.

Additionally, regression analysis has never been used to examine the buy or lease decision for shipping containers. This thesis will provide the first regression analysis based on a macroeconomic and a microeconomic dataset which has never been used for academic purposes before.

The existing literature includes two relevant surveys. One focuses more generally on leasing and one targets specifically shipping containers. The container survey is outdated because it was performed in 1987. An updated survey will be presented in this thesis. The purpose of the survey is to find out which variables industry practitioners find important for the decision. The direction and intensity of the effect on the lease share shall be analyzed. For the first time, survey data regarding the buy or lease decision of shipping lines regarding containers shall be analyzed using regression analysis.

The following chapter gives a detailed overview of the existing literature and the literature gap.

The organization of the remaining thesis is presented in the chart below:

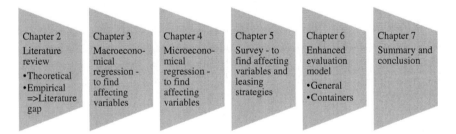

Figure 1-4 Organization of thesis

Chapter 2 lays the fundation for the rest of thesis by summarizing the existing theoretical as well as empirical literature in general and specifically for the container shipping industry. The resulting literature gap is presented and analyzed. Furthermore answers to the first part of question one shall be found: A summary of all reasons for or against leasing shall be developed. The importance of these criteria in practice shall be analyzed in chapters 3–5.

In chapters 3, 4 and 5, the current situation will be analyzed using academic regression analysis. The target is to find out, whether the suggested theoretical model in the existing literature is used by industry practitioners and if it needs enhancements.

Chapter 3 includes an empirical time series (30-year) analysis with NPV and other independent macroeconomic variables. The evaluation is based on aggregated industry data. It checks the empirical relevance of the NPV analysis for the first time using regression analysis. This chapter mainly delivers answers to question number two as well as the second part of question number one—the importance of the criteria in practice.

Chapter 4 describes the empirical model, data and result of a regression analysis using panel data from the top 20 shipping lines. In contrast to chapter 3, the focus is on microeconomic data of individual shipping lines. Again, the impact of the NPV / NAL analysis and other variables is verified. Chapter four mainly gives answers to question number three as well as the second part of question number one—the importance of the criteria in practice.

Chapter 5 presents the design and results of a shipping line survey performed in 2010. The relevance of several criteria, including NPV, is questioned. Besides individual and ranking analysis, the data are evaluated using a linear regression model. The survey also asks about the leasing strategies of the shipping lines. The results are compared with past surveys to find industry changes. Chapter 5 provides answers to question number four regarding leasing strategies as well as the second part of question number one—the importance of the criteria in practice.

Based on the knowledge of the existing literature summarized in chapter 2 and the results of the empirical analysis in chapters 3–5, a general extended theoretical model for the buy versus lease decision will be developed in chapter 6. Furthermore, by including industry specific arguments for and against leasing found in chapters two to five an evaluation model for shipping containers will be developed. In addition a numerical example with up-to-date assumptions shall be given, which uses the new model. This chapter gives answers to question five.

Finally, chapter 7 provides conclusions and suggests future research areas.

2 Status of research

This chapter summarizes the existing literature regarding the buy or lease decision for shipping containers. It is organized as follows. The first section provides an overview of the theories in general and those with a focus on containers. The second section looks at the empirical literature in general and regarding containers. Within these two sections, the literature is summarized by topic. The third section tabulates variables and their impact on the buy or lease decision. The last section summarizes the literature gap and the lessons learned.

2.1 Theories of Leasing

2.1.1 General (non-industry specific) buy or lease theories

Schallheim (Schallheim, 1994) summarizes the essence of leasing as

> "customized financing with potentially unique tax features".

He adds that there would be no reason to lease if the capital markets were perfect. Perfect markets imply (1) no taxes; (2) no transaction costs, floatation costs, contracting costs or brokerage fees; and (3) no single firm that can affect the market price.

Bower (1973) advises separating the financing decision (buy with a loan or lease) from the decision to acquire (capital budgeting decision[1]). Pritchard & Hindelang (1980) provide examples that include cash flow from operations in the analysis. They conclude that leasing can be cheaper than loan financing and therefore affect the decision whether an asset should be acquired. Even if the NPV analysis of the purchase alternative is negative, a beneficial leasing alternative can salvage a project. The focus of this dissertation is on how an asset should be financed (e.g., leasing, loan). It is assumed that the capital budgeting decision on whether the asset is to be acquired already has been made.

Brealey, Myers & Allen (2008, p. 699) list sensible and "dubious" reasons for leasing. Their sensible reasons include the following: Short-term leases are convenient, cancellation options are valuable, maintenance is provided, the administrative and transaction costs are low, leasing is less time consuming because of standardization, tax shields can be used, leasing is advantageous in financial distress, and leasing avoids the U.S. alternative minimum tax. Their so-called dubious reasons include the avoidance of capital expenditure approvals / controls, preserving capital / 100% financing, off-balance sheet financing, and the effect on book income. Schierenbeck (1989, p. 402) adds another "dubious"

---

1   For details regarding the capital budgeting decision see (Kruschwitz, 2010a).

reason: The lessor overtakes the risk of obsolescence and economic depreciation. All the listed "dubious" reasons might have a real effect. Some of them have been empirically confirmed. For example, Eisfeldt (2007) shows that preserving capital / 100% financing is a real advantage of leasing for financially constrained firms (see Eisfeldt (2007) below). Furthermore, if no internal approval is necessary for leasing, whereas it is necessary for purchasing; leasing is an attractive option for the employee in charge. Next, the accounting treatment of leasing differs from loan financing in some countries, leading to better debt ratios, book profit in early years, and profits to assets. As Brealey et al. (2008) write, this will not have an effect on valuation or rating upon a detailed financial analysis. In the case of a less detailed analysis or manager incentives based on these figures, it might be advantageous for the firm or the management (see empirical results of Lim (2003) below). Lastly, Smith, Wakeman & Hawkins (1985) mention that management compensation plans based on return on invested capital provide an incentive for leasing. If a lessee is not familiar with the market of the needed asset, it might make sense to lease the equipment to hedge the risk of obsolescence.

In the 1970s, Lewellen, Long & McConnell (1976) argued that in an ideal competitive environment, there is no reliable rationale for leasing. They show in a market-value model of both lessees and lessors, there can be a benefit from leasing if the lessor can (a) purchase or (b) sell the equipment better, (c) depreciate faster, (d) use a greater leverage than the lessee or (e) if they have different tax conditions[2]. Differences in the circumstances of the lessee and lessor generate a market valuation benefit that can make leasing attractive.

Myers, Dill & Bautista (1976) present a formula for the buy or lease decision in the Modigliani-Miller[3] environment, where firms are indifferent toward leasing and buying when they have the same tax rate. They show that leasing may be beneficial for a firm with a low tax rate that has a higher discount rate because interests are tax deductible. Leasing generally has lower cash outflows in the early years but higher cash outflows in the later years. The higher discount rate of the low tax rate firm leads to better results for leasing compared with the high tax rate firm.

Schallheim (1994) describes three approaches to compare leasing to borrowing. To calculate the debt equivalent, he proposes (1) borrowing the total asset costs of the lease, (2) using the same debt-to-equity ratio that the firm uses to

---

2   Also see (Dietel & Heinen, 1991) for tax related reasons to lease equipment

3   Franco Modiliani and Merton Miller (MM) received the Nobel Price for their theory (MM-Theory, 1958) where they show that the capital structure of the firm is irrelevant to the total value of the firm under the assumption of perfect capital markets.

finance its existing assets or (3) determining a schedule of loan payments that matches the lease schedule. He prefers the third approach, which is equivalent to discounting the cost of leasing at the after-tax borrowing rate.

Robichek (1965) mentions the impact of expected inflation on the debt/equity decision. As debt contracts fix the nominal rather than the real interest rate, high expected inflation is a driver for debt and leasing. Schallheim (1994) adds that the optimal capital structure depends on both personal and corporate taxes, non-debt tax shields (such as depreciation) and costs of financial distress and bankruptcy.

Chemmanur & Yan (2000) analyze the effect of asymmetric information of manufacturers and buyers/lessees regarding a product with an equilibrium model. They find that newer as well as higher quality products are more likely to be leased whereas lower quality products will be sold. Hendel & Lizzeri (2002) and Johnson & Waldman (2003) analyze the role of adverse selection in the car leasing market. Adverse selection refers to a market process in which "bad" results occur when buyers and sellers have asymmetric information (i.e., access to different information). For example, some customers do not receive loans or receive loans with unusually high interest rates. They conclude that leasing reduces the adverse selection problem in the used-car market because lessees must follow the standard restrictions found in lease contracts, such as maximum mileage.

The effects of transaction costs on the short-term leasing decision have been analyzed by Flath (1980). It is shown that leasing can reduce the transaction costs, including costs of assuring quality. The effects of transactions defined as

"Ownership changes, incentive changes, and governance structure changes"

have been analyzed by Williamson (1985, pp. 388 - 393). Transaction costs include ex ante ("drafting and negotiating agreements"), and ex post ("set up and running costs of governance structure to which monitoring is assigned and to which disputes refer and are settled"). Krishnan & Moyer (1994, p. 35) expect that transaction costs of leasing are higher than that from secured borrowing. If a lessee wants to terminate the lease during the term or sublease the equipment because the asset is no longer needed, negotiations with the lessor are unavoidable. They conclude that

"transaction cost elements are expected to dominate in the lease-borrow analysis when a firm has a low probability of firm failure".

In container leasing, transaction costs are comparatively small because the product and leasing contracts are standardized. The impact of maintenance and repair issues at redelivery will be analyzed in detail in chapter 6.2.2.

The short-term buy or lease decision has been analyzed by several authors, including Flath (1980), as a portfolio choice problem (taking into account risk and return of an investment), especially for the housing market. Flath argues that short- term leasing and selling would be nearly perfect substitutes in the absence of transaction costs, including the costs of identifying, assuring and maintaining quality, search costs and the costs of risk bearing. The lessor takes over the responsibility to inspect new containers, which reduces the costs and responsibility for the lessee. Flath argues that transaction cost gains of leasing rise with reducing usage time of a good. The short-term lessor has an incentive to provide high-quality products to maintain his image for returning customers, which reduces transaction costs. Lessors have a long-term interest in the equipment and therefore maintain the object better and more economically than a sequence of changing owners. If the users are responsible for the maintenance, the opposite might be the case because of "moral hazard". The user could perform minimum maintenance because he has no financial long-term interests in the product. Search costs are reduced by leasing because the best price-offering partner has only to be found once whereas twice (for buying and selling) at the purchase alternative. Lessors take the risk of obsolescence and pool risks (e.g., redelivery repair costs) comparable with insurance companies.

Klein, Crawford & Alchian (1978) argue that transaction, information and enforcement costs as well as the possibility of opportunistic behavior of lessees lead to intrafirm (purchase) solutions if equipment is more specialized. Opportunistic behavior of a lessee (rental reduction negotiation after signing) could happen if the equipment is very specialized (or the transfer is expensive) and alternative lessees would pay less. This aspect is of minor importance with standardized containers because they can be used by many shipping lines, and transfer costs are relatively low.

The effects of down payments on the buy or lease decision have been studied by several authors, including Engelhardt (1996). Engelhardt finds that personal consumption is reduced by saving for the down payment when a home purchase is planned. Down payments are necessary to receive a loan in most cases (equity share) and therefore create credit market imperfections that have an impact on the buy or lease decision. Down payments or deposits are often lower or not needed when equipment is leased. Therefore, leasing is an attractive option for firms with capital constraints.

Eisfeldt (2007) developed an equilibrium model, focusing on debt capacity / financial constraints. The more restricted the available funds, the more advantageous leasing is for the firm. Eisfeldt stresses the repossession advantage of leasing compared to debt financing. Because of different legal treatment (e.g., the U.S. bankruptcy code), a lessor can repossess equipment more easily than a lender. This allows the lessor *ceteris paribus* to lend more than a lender, which makes leasing valuable for financially constrained firms. On the other hand, leasing involves the separation of ownership and control, which increases its costs due to agency problems. A lessee has less incentive to care for the asset. There is a tradeoff between maximizing financing (leasing) and minimizing agency costs (owning). The mentioned agency costs regarding maintenance of the asset should be less relevant with container leasing because shipping lines normally do not distinguish between leased and owned equipment (including maintenance and usage) during the lease term.

Dasgupta (2007) finds that maintenance costs with newer cars are lower than for older ones. Therefore, equipment leasing (which implies younger equipment) has lower maintenance costs. At the end of the lease term, container leasing maintenance costs (repair costs) differ substantially between leased and owned equipment. The impact of repair costs will be discussed in detail in chapter 6.2.2.

Brealey (2008, p. 705) formulates a general buy-or-lease rule for businesses:

> "Buy it if the equivalent annual cost of ownership and operation is less than the best lease rate you can get from an outsider".

He provides the following formula for the net advantage of operating leasing to the lessee. The formula, which is similar in many other corporate finance textbooks (Van Horne, 1998); (Brigham & Gapenski, 1990, p. 557), is based on the model of Myers, Dill & Bautista (1976). It is assumed that the firm pays taxes and can make use of tax shields:

$$\mathbf{NAL} = \mathbf{D_0} + \sum_{t=1}^{N} \frac{-L_t(1-T)-D_tT+O_t(1-T)}{[1+r_d(1-T)]^t} - \frac{S_N}{[1+r_d(1-T)]^N} \qquad \text{Equation 2-1}$$

Where:

NAL	= net advantage of leasing [currency]
D_0	= initial financing provided (debt amount received) in t_0 [currency]
N	= length of the lease in years [-]
L_t	= lease payment in period t [currency]
T	= marginal corporate tax rate [%]
D_t	= depreciation in period t [currency]
O_t	= operative costs incl. in lease (e.g. maintenance, insurance) [currency]
S_N	= after tax salvage value (terminal value) of the asset at time N [currency]
$r_d(1-T)$	= discount rate (risk equivalent opportunity costs/after tax cost of debt) [%]

The lost interest tax shields of displaced debt are implicitly recognized in the adjusted discount rate. If the net value of leasing is positive, the firm should lease; otherwise the firm should buy and borrow the asset. Schallheim (1994, p. 115) emphasizes that the presented calculation is the same as calculating the NPV of the lease and the NPV of the loan option and comparing them, since the NPV of the loan repayment cash flows equals the loan amount if

> "the total cost of the asset is borrowed and the discount rate is the after-tax cost of debt".

The assumption regarding the borrowing of the total costs is not realistic in many cases because deposits (in the leasing alternative) and advances (equity share in loan financing) have to be taken into account. Because advances and deposits play an important role in the buy or lease decision, the model provided above will be extended by integrating advances and deposits in chapter 6.1.2.

Brealey (2008) concludes that firms planning to use the asset for longer periods usually should buy because the annual costs of owning are lower than the operating lease rate. The lessor has to add a markup for negotiating, administrating, and off-hire times. If the lessor is able to generate economies of scale when buying and selling the asset but the lessee is not, or if the lease contains useful options (e.g., purchase of the equipment), leasing might be a good long-term decision. Such options or short-term leases can be seen as insurances which lessors can sell at a profit based on their market knowledge.

Schallheim (1994) and Brealey (2008) use the after-tax borrowing rate to discount leasing cash flows. To the contrary, Weingartner (1987, p. 8) argues that the discount rate should be the firm's or project's weighted average cost of capital (WACC) because a project has to be financed "with the target mix of debt and equity"[4] and banks take more than the value of the collateral into account. Olsen (1978) explains part of the confusion regarding the discount rate. In a lease versus purchase analysis, the WACC has an important role, whereas in a lease versus borrow analysis the debt interest rate is of higher importance. Schallheim (1994, p. 159) emphasizes that the discount rate for the operating costs and the residual value should reflect the uncertainty. Regarding the residual value, he suggests using the discount rate

$$r = r_f + \beta(r_m - r_f) \qquad\qquad \textbf{Equation 2-2}$$

Where:

r	= discount rate for residual [%]
r_f	= risk-free interest rate (on government bonds) [%]
r_m	= market return (market wide index of stocks) [%]
β	= Beta, measure of systematic risk [-]

---

4   See also Schallheim (1994, p. 115) for a discussion of the appropriate discount rate.

To calculate the beta, he proposes:

> "Measure a time series of prices for used equipment, and then correlate the returns from this time series with the time series of returns from a market wide index".

Weingartner (1987) adds that the uncertainty should be reflected in the NPV calculation by using the expected values (e.g., using probabilities for terminal value scenarios).

Myers et al. (1976) introduce a discount factor based on the weighted average cost of capital concept invented by Modigliani-Miller

$$r = r_d(1 - T * \lambda) \hspace{4cm} \text{Equation 2-3}$$

Where:

r_d = before tax interest rate on debt [%]

T = corporate tax rate [%]

λ = debt-to-assets ratio [%], the debt displaced by leasing

Since firms are not 100% debt financed, they conclude that λ should be less than one. Bower (1973) summarizes the (dis)agreement of several authors regarding the discount factor to be used (after-tax cost of capital, pre-tax cost of borrowing and the after-tax cost of borrowing). The appropriate discount factor is a major issue that will be discussed in more detail in chapter 6.

Nevitt & Fabozzi (2000) mention that in addition to the previously covered aspects above, the timing of the lease, tax payments and any guarantee of the residual value and advances or deposits of the lease have to be taken into account. They use the after-tax borrowing rate for discounting. An advance rate (equity share) needed for the purchase alternative is not taken into account. They emphasize that the marginal tax rate can change over time (for example, if a company generates a low profit but expects higher profits going forward). If this is the case, the tax payments based on the tax benefits carried forward have to be built into the model. The effect of the forecast tax position including carry forward allowances on the NPV was also shown by Franks & Hodges (1978). Franks & Hodges (1987) analyzed the effect of scarce taxable earnings on the NPV of a lessor.

Besides the above described NPV model, Nevitt & Fabozzi (2000) show two further alternative calculation methods to analyze the buy-or-lease problem. First, the internal rate of return (IRR)[5] method calculates the interest rate of the lease that delivers a zero NPV and compares it with the after-tax borrowing rate. If the IRR of the lease is less than the after-tax borrowing rate, the lease is bene-

---

5   For IRR calculation methods, see (Kruschwitz, 2010b).

ficial. The NPV method is preferred, as the IRR method has weaknesses when comparing cash flows with positive and negative amounts. Second, the equivalent loan method constructs a loan that rebuilds exactly the same cash flows as the lease. The net cash flow in Period 0 is the NPV advantage. This result and the NPV method result are the same, but the NPV method is simpler to calculate. They conclude that the NPV method should be used.

Smith et al. (1985) stress that the effect of taxes, contracting costs and production/investment incentives have to be included in the valuation of lease agreements.

Schallheim (1994) emphasizes the necessity to take the value of options into account. Mainly, there are options to purchase the asset and to renew and/or cancel the lease. Based on the Black-Scholes model, the value of a purchase option can be calculated as follows:

$$C = \lambda^t A\, N(d_1) - Ee^{-rt}N(d_2) \qquad\qquad \textbf{Equation 2-4}$$

with

$$d_1 = [\ln\left(\lambda^t \tfrac{A}{E}\right) + \left(r_f + \tfrac{\sigma^2}{2}\right)t]/\sigma\sqrt{t} \qquad\qquad \textbf{Equation 2-5}$$

$$d_2 = d_1 - \sigma\sqrt{t} \qquad\qquad \textbf{Equation 2-6}$$

$$\lambda = [\tfrac{1-d}{1+r_f}]e^{\sigma_{ly}} \qquad\qquad \textbf{Equation 2-7}$$

Where:

C	= call option value [currency]
$N(d)$	= cumulative normal probability density function [-]
$\lambda^t A$	= depreciating asset price [currency]
E	= exercise price of the option [currency]
r_f	= annual, continuously compounded, risk-free rate of interest [%]
t	= time to maturity or expiration date in years [-]
σ^2	= variance of the asset price in one year [-]
d	= expected rate of economic depreciation [%]
$e^{\sigma_{ly}}$	= adjustment for the covariance between economic depreciation and the market factor [-]

Miller (1976) provides an explanation of the depreciation adjustment tor $e^{\sigma_{ly}}$. If the depreciation is independent from the state of the economy, the covariance term is zero. If boom times stimulate technologic development (falling residual values), the covariance term is positive, and the adjustment term will be therefore higher.

Smith et al. (1985, p. 906) argue that purchase options

"reduce the perverse use and maintenance incentives for the lessee",

because the value of the option is a positive function of the terminal value. Copeland & Weston (1982) provide a calculation solution for cancelable leases. They consider the cancelable operating lease to be a combination of a non-cancelable lease and a put option with an exercise price equal to the market value of the depreciating asset. The value of the option can be calculated using a binominal option pricing method.

Grenadier (1995, p. 324) develops an equilibrium model for the pricing of leases, including various option components such as forward leases, cancellation renewal and insurances.

"The analysis implies a downward-sloping term structure for lease rates in markets in which supply has recently been added; similarly, the model predicts an upward-sloping term structure for makets in which the economic fortunes of active firms are severely depressed,"

according to Grenadier. This structure cannot be observed in the container leasing market. Long-term leases have always been less costly than master leases.

The general buy or lease theory literature can be summarized as follows. There are many publications about the topic with diverse focus. Many propose a NAL calculation for decision making. The given formula is incomplete because many relevant decision criteria are not included.

2.1.2 Theories with a focus on container leasing

Temple (1987) describes the flexibility advantages of container: Container leasing minimizes inventories, avoids repositioning and enables redelivery of unused boxes resulting from trade, seasonal and peak imbalances. Furthermore, Temple states that leasing provides marketing flexibility (e.g., access to equipment with limited lead time, improved efficiency through global coverage and rationalizing equipment fleets between carriers). In addition, leasing can hedge the risk that the equipment becomes obsolete. Another advantage is financial flexibility. It conserves cash that can be used for other immediate needs. Next, it provides off-balance sheet financing that improves the balance sheet compared with loan debt financing. Lastly, he stresses the advantage that leasing improves after-tax profit as lease payments are normally lower than depreciation plus interest in the first few years.

Palmer (1991, p. 19) states that

"very few shipping lines have trades that are geographically or seasonally balanced and the ability to on-hire and off-hire to suit these changing requirements has been an important factor in maintaining their efficiencies. The job of the rental company is to provide specialized equipment which individual customers could never justify owning themselves."

He also states that shipping companies lease in uncertain times to reduce capital expenditure and conserve cash. Leasing also reduces risk when the life of the asset exceeds the user's need for it. According to several shipping line experts, lessors cannot balance geographically and seasonally unbalanced trades. Therefore, large shipping lines with a global presence cannot balance their container flows by using leasing. Nevertheless, this advantage of container leasing remains valid for smaller shipping lines. Lessors might be able to balance their volumes by releasing/repositioning equipment to other shipping lines.

Tan (1983) emphasizes the cash flow advantage of leasing. Other use of cash may outweigh the additional costs of leasing. Leasing provides 100% financing that is fast, flexible and less restrictive than loans. It extends the length of financing compared to loan financing. Leasing is often the only option if the company's capitalization cannot be further increased. It also conserves existing credit and does not restrict the company's borrowing capacity in most cases. Long-term leasing provides a hedge against inflation because the lease payments are fixed. However, some contracts allow for early termination (at additional costs), renewal or subsequent purchase. Packaging a series of legal, administrative, tax and other expenses (acquisition cost, sales tax, inspection and delivery) and adding them to the price of the lease results in more than 100% financing. Leasing provides the possibility to explore the feasibility of new routes without the long-term commitment of buying the asset. Master leases place the problem of supplying the right container, in the right condition and at the right location to the lessor. Due to the lower overall risk exposure of a lessor, the cost of funds (debt and equity) may be significantly less than to an operating company (lessee).

World Cargo News (WCN, 2000) mentions the cash flow advantage of leasing during the contract term. Banks favor straightforward loan repayment within a few years without an awareness of high resale values. This leads to higher cash outflow than in the leasing alternative.

"When the market turns down, banks tend to overreact and perhaps look to escape their commitments too quickly" (WCN, 2000, p. 42).

They add that hybrid leases have been developed over time to increase the flexibility of the lessee. Some leases contain options to purchase the equipment after the initial lease term, extend the lease period, or return the equipment. Flexible long-term leases are another possibility where the lessee has the option to return the equipment during the term. In the case of early redelivery, the lessee retroactively pays a higher per diem for the flexibility.

Drewry (2002, p. 19) states that shipping lines make extensive use of (short-term) leasing

> "to cope with operational contingencies and emergencies, such as ship breakdowns, industrial disputes and natural disasters".

Stricter inspection requirements can lead to extended cargo transit times and therefore additional container leasing demand.

Temple (1987) mentions the tax advantage of owning containers (tax depreciation/allowance of container plus interest on debt are higher in the first years than with leasing) when a company's marginal tax rate is high and the company has sufficient earnings before taxes to offset the allowances.

Tan (1983) states that leased assets do not appear on the balance sheet of a lessee as fixed assets, which may have an undervalued effect. He describes the disadvantage that leased assets cannot be used as collateral in order to secure loans. Tan adds that bankers and trade creditors may take a view that companies with a substantial proportion of leased equipment are in a weaker financial position than companies owning the assets. These disadvantages are not convincing because leasing already provides 100% financing (minus deposits) of the containers and detailed valuations take off-balance sheet assets into account (see Lim, (2003). Lim even shows that off-balance sheet financing might improve credit ratings[6] compared with on-balance sheet financing, which leads to an advantage for leasing.

Tan (1983) argues that long-term leases with fixed commitments can be a burden on the cash flow of a company—especially in an economic recession—which can lead to a default in payment and the lessor withdrawing the equipment. Long-term leases may lead to a currency risk because rental payments are in USD, whereas the revenue might be in a different currency. Heavy penalties for early cancellation of long-term leases or non-cancelable leasing obligations may sometimes deceive bidders who are attempting a takeover of the company. The lessor cannot transfer his obligations under the health and safety at work legislation. Therefore, lessors need separate liability insurance.

---

6   For a detailed description of how banks handle credit ratings see (Hartmann-Wendels, Pfingsten, & Weber, 2007).

Tan (1983, p. 10) states that

"it is common practice for a substantial proportion of the disposal proceeds of an asset, after the end of a lease term, to be paid over by the lessor to the lessee by way of rebate of rentals."

In container leasing (master leases and long term leases), lessees do not participate in the disposal proceeds. This is in fact a major disadvantage of leasing as owners are in the position to sell secondhand equipment at attractive prices. According to Foxcroft (2008), the average price of a new 20-foot standard container was 1761 USD from 2000 to 2008, whereas the secondhand price average was 783 USD. Therefore, owners were in the position to achieve about 44% of their original investment when selling the equipment after 12 to 13 years.

Deziel (1981) provides an equilibrium model for the container transportation market with trade imbalances for owned and leased container equipment. The model calculates equilibrium one-way (from port to port) rental rates as well as pick-up and drop-off charges that result from exceeding container inflow (bad locations) or exceeding container outflow (good locations). Deziel's dissertation shows that one-way leasing helps to balance transportation demand differences between carriers but not general imbalances between locations.

Tan (1983) focuses on NPV calculations taking the tax aspect into account. The alternative with the lowest NPV of the costs is said to be optimal.

The NPV of the purchase alternative is calculated as follows:

$$NPV_{Purchase} = \sum_{i=1}^{12} \frac{(DS_i - TR_i)}{(1+r^*)^i}$$

Equation 2-8

Where:

DS_i = debt service (repayment and interest) [currency]

TR_i = tax relief in the i_{th} year [currency]

r^* = net of tax borrowing rate which is used as discount rate [%]

The net of tax borrowing rate is calculated as

$$r^* = r - \frac{rT}{(1+rT)^n}$$

Equation 2-9

Where:

r   = debt interest rate [%]

T   = corporate tax rate [%]

n   = tax payment delay in years [-]

The NPV of the lease alternative is calculated as follows:

$$NPV_{Lease} = \sum_{i=0}^{11} \frac{(LR_i - TR_i)}{(1+r^*)^i}$$

Equation 2-10

Where:

LR_i	= annual lease payment [currency]
TR_i	= tax relief in the i_{th} year [currency]
r^*	= net of tax borrowing rate as defined above [%]

This approach is very similar to the general formula presented in 2.1.1. Tan (1983) compares the NPV of the lease and the loan alternative whereas the general formula calculated the NAL as the difference between the NPV of the leasing and loan alternative. These two approaches lead to the same result. There is only a minor difference regarding the discount rate because Tan incorporates a delay in tax payments whereas the general formula assumes immediate tax payments. If the tax delay is set to zero, the general and Tan's formula are the same.

The conclusions of Tan (1983) are also similar to the ones in the general theory section (see 2.1.1). A purchase with cash is not recommended if a loan with an interest rate below the used discount rate is available. If profits are sufficiently high to make beneficial use of allowances, the purchase with a loan becomes a good option. For companies unable to take immediate and full use of tax allowances because of low profits, a 50-50 purchase with a loan and lease alternative is preferable. Master leases are preferable (instead of long-term leases) because flexibility increases the NPV. Tan concludes that operators on unbalanced routes with high box-slot ratios should look into master leases.

Besides tax implications, Temple (1987) analyzes the following industry-specific problems, which have an effect on the buy-or-lease decision: unbalanced trade, growing market with minimum purchase container volume, local imbalance scenario and irregular demand. The models show the advantages of short-term leasing.

The assumptions used by Tan and Temple are summarized in the following table.

Table 2-1 NPV calculation assumptions

Assumption	(Tan, 1983)	(Temple, 1987)
General		
Economic life	10 years	More than 7 years
Corporate tax rate	52%	34% / 0%
Capital allowance	100% in first year	Decreasing over 5 years
Tax lag	24 months	none
Discount rate	Net of tax borrowing rate	15%
Leasing		
Lease duration	10 years	5 years
Lease rental (per diem)	1.45 USD	1.00 USD
Reduced rental (per diem) after first lease term	Not covered	Not relevant
Lease payment	At beginning of year in advance	In same period
Drop off charges	Not covered	Not covered
Redelivery repair costs	Not covered	Not covered
Purchasing		
20-foot container cost	2500 USD	1700 USD
Residual value	Zero	500 USD after 7 years
Before tax borrowing rate	14%	10%
Annual repair costs	Not covered	Not covered

Temple argues that the lowest NPV might not lead to the best option if leasing is the only financing option available. This can be especially relevant for smaller companies or ones with a higher level of gearing (debt/equity). Companies with a high gearing ratio have less room for additional debt that might be needed in situations with weak cash flows. The risk attached to financing containers by loan or leasing instead of retained profits (i.e., committed long-term payments might lead to financial distress) are not reflected in the NPV calculation.

Literature that addresses the container-specific buy or lease theory can be summarized as follwows. There are only two theoretical container specific publications available: Tan (1983) and Temple (1987). Their models are based on the general NAL for decision making presented above. The given formula is incomplete because many relevant decision criteria are not included. Furthermore the assumptions made do not reflect the current situation on the container leasing market.

In chapter 6, the existing general as well as container-specific model will be enhanced by including more relevant decision criteria. Furthermore sample calculations based on updated assumptions will be presented.

2.2 Empirical studies

2.2.1 General (non-industry specific) empirical studies

Sorensen & Johnson (1977, p. 37) performed an empirical study based on a regional sample of 520 financial lease contracts. They found a very high average lease contract IRR of 25% before taxes and 18.7% after taxes (50% tax rate). Their multiple regression analysis shows that the IRR is mainly dependent on the duration of the lease (negative relation), collateral (negative relation) and prepayments (positive relation). They explain that the positive relation to prepayments might be

> "a mechanism for adjusting for the risk class of the lessee".

The missing credit rating data might have an effect on the results. Their analysis does not provide insights as to why lessees choose this rather expensive financing option instead of purchasing.

Graham, Lemmon & Schallheim (1998) find evidence that firms with lower tax rates as well as high financial distress risk (measured by lower rating, negative book value and higher earnings volatility) use operating leases (treated tax wise as true leases) more. They argue that non-true leases (often financial leases) receive the same tax treatment as loans. They find a positive relation between debt levels and the before financing measure of the marginal tax rate. Therefore, they argue that the volume of finance leases (comparable to debt) should rise with the marginal tax rate, whereas the volume of operating leases should decline with the marginal tax rate.

Krishnan & Moyer (1994) study the impact of financing constraints on finance lease decisions using a regression analysis. They find with statistical significance that firms with lower retained earnings to total assets, higher growth rates, lower coverage ratios, higher debt ratios, higher operating risk and lower ratings use finance leases more frequently. They conclude that leasing becomes increasingly attractive when a company has higher bankruptcy potential. Krishnan & Moyer also analyze the impact of the industry. When analyzing what percentage of firms lease and what percentage of assets is leased, they find the following: transportation firms (40% of firm lease; 12% of assets leased), services (10%; 9%), wholesale (23%; 5%) and retail trade (58%; 5%) are more likely to use leasing. They conclude that leasing is more attractive for assets that are not firm-specific. The high ratios in transportation are in line with the high lease share observed for container equipment.

Sharpe & Nguyen (1995) find that the finance and operating lease share increases when firms pay no dividend, have lower earnings to sales, have lower credit ratings and are smaller. In addition, there is empirical evidence that firms with lower tax rates and higher tax losses carried forward lease more. Finally, the variance of revenues shows no significant impact on the leasing share. They conclude that leasing is more attractive for financially constrained firms with high financing costs. Because of information asymmetries, smaller firms are likely to face higher external funding costs. Sharpe & Nguyen suggest that leasing mitigates these information problems, which leads to a negative relationship between firm size and usage of leasing.

Ang & Peterson (1984) use a Tobit regression to analyze the debt ratio of about 600 firms between 1966 and 1981. They conclude that there is a leasing puzzle because theory suggests that leasing and debt are substitutes, whereas they find that more debt is associated with more leasing. This would mean that leases and debt are complements. In addition, they find that the lease ratio rises statistically significant with increasing sales variability. Furthermore, the lease ratio increases with decreasing operating leverage (operating earnings to sales), lower profitability and higher liquidity. Expected growth (price earnings ratio) and size show no clear impact. However, Adedeji & Stapleton (1996) criticize that the debt ratio coefficient is only statistically significant in one of six analyzed years and book value of equity was used as denominator of the lease as well as debt ratio instead of total assets. Lastly, they suggest including controls for debt capacity and tax effects. Bayless & Diltz (1986) measure the debt displacement (substitution) effect of leasing using a banking survey. They find that leasing displaces 10 to 26% more debt capacity than debt financing.

Lewis & Schallheim (1992) provide a theoretical solution for the puzzle: The tax treatment of leasing and lending is not the same. Leasing allows the transfer of tax shields to lessors who can use the tax benefit to reduce lease rates. Because of the reduced tax shields, loan financing subsequently becomes more attractive for the lessee. They conclude, based on their theoretical model, that leasing and debt are complements as shown by Ang (1984). Deloof, Lagaert & Verschueren (2007) provide strong support for the substitution hypothesis (without tax interference) using Belgian medium-sized company data. In Belgium, leases and loans are treated equally in taxes. They find that more debt is associated with fewer leases. Furthermore, they find that the lease ratio is significantly negative related to profitability and positive with growth. This is consistent with the pecking order theory of Myers & Majluf (1984): Firms with higher profits need less external financing and therefore have lower debt ratios. Because of asymmetric information (managers know more than investors), corporations go for internal financing first (retained earnings), then they use debt (or leasing) and finance with equity as a last resort.

Adedeji & Stapleton (1996) find evidence of the substitution theory (more leases are associated with less debt) using a Tobit regression on UK-listed corporation data when they exclude companies that do not lease. Their results suggest that one pound in finance leases displaces less than one pound of debt. Furthermore, they find that finance leases rise with a shortage of taxable capacity (higher tax rate) and inadequate access to debt capital markets (e.g., low price earnings ratio, low liquidity and small size). Using their full dataset leads to an unclear picture. Their results could be biased because they only focus on finance leases and listed companies in UK.

Adams & Hardwick (1998) also use a UK dataset of listed firms to find a positive relation between leverage (long term debt to assets) and lease share. Eisfeldt (2007) has a similar argument and suggests the following resolution to the leasing puzzle: Financially constrained firms rely on both leasing and secured loans more heavily as sources of costly equity. The data shows that the lease share decreases with the size of the firm. Dividends to assets show a negative relationship to leasing. This reflects the general idea that cash-constrained firms lease more.

Yan (2006) reexamines the substitution (versus complementary) theory because previous empirical analysis gave a mixed picture. He separates the true relation from the effects on both leasing and debt by using the generalized method of moments. He finds evidence that debt and leases are not complements but substitutes. Additionally, the substitution effect is higher (i.e., the cost of debt increases with more leases) in firms with more investment opportunities, higher marginal tax rates and companies that pay less dividends. His results are consistent with the agency cost hypothesis, the tax hypothesis and the asymmetric information hypothesis, respectively.

Eades & Marston (2002) analyze a large sample of U.S. lessees and lessors and find little evidence that either taxes or financial contracting motives (cost of capital, access to capital) control the leasing decision. Ten firms were found among the 100 biggest lessors also as lessees. They argue that it is not likely that firms show up on both sides if their decision would be tax- or cost of capital-driven. They find support for Smith and Wakeman's (1985) assertion that non-firm specific assets are more attractive for leasing and that real options as modeled by Grenadier (1995) are a likely incentive for leasing because of their high frequency of use. The limitation to the top 100 lessees could bias the results, as small companies with a relatively bad rating are not included in the sample. Furthermore, a comparison of means was tested instead of a regression analysis with control variables such as size. Therefore, cost of capital and access to capital could nevertheless be valid reasons for leasing, especially when firms are small.

Baker & Hubbard (2003) analyze the impact of technological development on the buy or lease decision in the trucking market. They find evidence that on-board computers that provide location information and real-time communication increase the leased share because they enhance the utilization. On the other hand, they find that increased monitoring with trip recorders (and the attendant improvement in incentives) leads to more ownership. These results are not yet relevant for standard container leasing because GPS systems are still too expensive to be applied. Lessees are not willing to pay additional rental fees because the conventional method of registering and electronically providing all terminal and depot gate in and out transactions are detailed enough for shipping lines. For lessors, GPS functionality could be of interest in the case of default and lost boxes (e.g., in Africa). Currently, the extra investment for this technology is not worthwhile.

Baker & Hubbard (2003) also analyze the impact of transaction costs. Owners of equipment can require that the equipment waits until it will be used, whereas lessees have to negotiate if the waiting time exceeds the time specified in the contract. This effect is also relevant regarding container leasing. Container leasing contracts specify pickup locations, volumes and timing. Contracts normally also specify redelivery schedules specifying the allowed volume in a certain timeframe per location. Furthermore, drop-off charges apply, reflecting the supply and demand situation for containers per location. These aspects of higher transaction costs related to leasing should have a negative impact on the share of leased containers.

De Bodt, Filareto & Lobez (2001) analyze agency cost effects of leasing decisions in an empirical study of 817 Belgian companies. They highlight three types of agency costs. First, existing creditors do not participate in the additional asset which they would if the asset was financed with same rank debt. Second, agency gains are realized by existing creditors through the limitation of the substitution risk (i.e., risk manipulation—assets could be sold and replaced with more risky ones). Third, agency costs due to the lack of operating flexibility (the sale of leased assets no longer needed is not possible) may occur. They analyze the impact of additional leasing on the interest charged and collateral needed. They find that creditors increase the collateral level if firms lease more. However, the interest rate is adjusted only for firms with a small leasing share. They conclude that leasing decisions are not neutral for unsecured creditors.

Lim, Mann & Mihow (2003) analyze the empirical impact of leases that are reported off-balance sheet (true/operating leases have to be reported only in the notes to the balance sheet). They find that credit ratings change relatively more often when debt is added compared to off-balance sheet leases. On the other hand, the data show no significant differences in newly issued bond rates comparing existing on- to off-balance sheet debt. Therefore, they conclude that it might be useful to move debt off-balance sheet to maintain higher debt ratings. Bond yields reflect off-balance sheet obligations in the same manner as on balance sheet debt. The reduced credit rating effect of off-balance sheet financing can be a valid reason for using long-term operating leases.

According to a survey conducted by Anderson & Martin (1977), firms mainly used an IRR approach in the 1970s. O'Brien & Nunnally (1983) sent a survey to the first 195 of the Fortune 500 firms. They found that 75% of the firms incorrectly analyze the leasing approach only when an asset is profitable on a purchase basis. Most practitioners use the NAL calculation for decision making. Seventy seven percent of them use the cost of debt as discount rate. Only 18% use the WACC for discounting. Anderson & Martin did not use regression techniques to analyze their data.

Mukherjee (1991, p. 105) updates and enhances the survey done by O'Brien & Nunnally. He finds that 88% of the answering firms treated leasing as a financing decision. Seventy three percent of all firms use the after-tax debt rate for discounting. Most firms do not analyze the lease option if the purchase alternative has a negative NPV. Eighty two percent of the firms mention "avoiding the risk of obsolescence" and "cheaper than borrowing" (57%) as important advantages of leasing. The "length of the lease period" (5%), "tax deductibility of lease payments" (5%), "off balance sheet financing" (4%) and "avoidance of expenditure controls" (2%) seem to be less important reasons for leasing. Regression techniques were not used to analyze survey data.

The general empirical literature regarding the buy or lease decision can be summarized as follows. There are many publications showing the effect on a firm's financial situation including taxes, debt ratio and rating on the lease share. None of the empirical regression analyses includes the most relevant variable according to the theoretical literature: the NAL. In chapters 3 and 4 the first regression analyses with NAL as an independent variable are presented.

The existing surveys confirm the relevance of the NAL calculation in practice. However, the survey data has never been analyzed using regression techniques. In chapter five an updated survey with regression analysis will be presented.

2.2.2 Empirical studies with a focus on container leasing

Temple (1987) conducted a survey of 15 shipping lines of different sizes. First, they found a declining lease share with the size of the firm. Second, 82% of the shipping lines answered that that the flexibility in equipment availability is an advantage of container leasing. Third, 38% of the survey participants thought that leasing is more expensive than owning. Fourth, the strategies regarding leasing of container equipment differed greatly (8–100% of the container fleet was leased). Fifth, the future lease target was in many cases lower than the current level. Sixth, most of the shipping lines planned to reduce the number of lessors they work with. Last, only a small group showed interest in working with other carriers to form equipment pools.

Important factors for the development of container leasing are summarized by Temple (1987). First, the overall growth in the demand for container transportation (measured by degree of containerization, world trade and GDP) has an impact. Second, the world slot capacity and world container movements can affect leasing. Third, Temple mentions the effect of container flow imbalances on leasing. Fourth, changes in the structure of the container shipping industry (e.g., larger players, consolidation) might affect leasing. Fifth, the financial condition of container carriers as measured by company profits has an impact on leasing. Lastly, changes in equipment types and sizes can play a role.

World Cargo News (WCN, 2000) mentions that some shipping lines have taken advantage of a lower container price and the availability of low-cost credit to increase their percentage of owned equipment. Prices for used equipment have remained at a good level, leading to balance sheet gains when containers are sold (after approximately 12 years). High secondhand prices are thus a trigger for buying equipment.

Lemper (2008) describes the influence of oil prices on container shipping. Because of increased oil prices in 2008, shipping lines reduced the speed of their ships, which reduced transport capacity (more ships and containers needed for the same transportation volume). The world trade growth (driven by world GDP growth and globalization) — especially on long routes between China and Europe / North America — increased the demand for ships and containers. The number of used containers per containership slot declined over the last 13 years from 3.5 to 2.4. This means that for 1 TEU, additional containership capacity 2.4 TEU containers are necessary. Furthermore, limited port and waterway capacity increases waiting times of ships, which in turn increases the number of ships and containers needed for the same transportation volume (ISL, 2007; Lemper, 2007).

In the 1980s, an oligopolistic trend among lessors emerged. The dependence on lessors can be a disadvantage of leasing (Lloyd's, 1989), therefore reducing the leasing volume.

In recent years, the total share of leased containers reduced. ISL (2007) gives two reasons: First, the financial resources of the shipping lines have improved. Second, lessors have limited their container purchases and therefore have reduced container leasing supply. Drewry (2002) argues that history shows that lessors tend to lose out when equipment prices are low. In 2002, new container prices were highly competitive but increased in the years thereafter because of rising steel prices. Other mentioned reasons include the reduction of the number of lessors and tightened inventory control. There is a trend to use fewer master leases (duration of less than 3 years) in favor of long-term leases. Some lessors dislike the master lease business, because of the low profitability and high fixed costs associated with it. Some lessors spend tens of millions of dollars to reposition empty containers to locations where they can be leased out again.

The container-specific empirical literature regarding the buy or lease decision is very limited. There are no empirical regression analyses available. Only one survey was conducted by Temple (1987). This survey does not include the theoretically most important variable: The NAL. Other important decision criteria were not incorporated, and the data were not analyzed with regression techniques. Additionally, the number of participating shipping lines is very limited and the survey is more than 20 years old.

In chapter 5, an updated container buy or lease survey will be presented that includes NAL and other additional decision criteria. For the first time, buy or lease survey data will be analyzed using regression analysis.

2.3 Summary of variables affecting the buy or lease decision

The following table summarizes the variables mentioned in section 2.1 and 2.2 by category with their theoretical and empirical impacts on the buy or lease decision (finance and operating leases). A + (-) signals a positive (negative) effect on the lease share, whereas a 0 signals no statistically significant relation. If different impacts by several authors are found, they are all displayed. This summary lays the foundation for the following chapters, because it shows the literature gap and therewith the problems to be solved in this thesis. Furthermore the listed variables provide a basis for the empirical analysis presented in the following chapters. In turn, the results of the empirical analysis are the foundation for the extension of the theoretical model.

Table 2-2 Variables affecting the buy or lease decision

Criteria category	Variable	Theoretical impact	Author	Indicator	Empirical test result	Author
Corporate financials	Tax rate	Lower tax rates / excess tax shields imply more leasing (transfer of tax shields)	(Lewis & Schallheim, 1992)	Tax rate	-	(Adedeji & Stapleton, 1996; Graham, et al., 1998; Sharpe & Nguyen, 1995)
				Tax loss carried forward	+	
Corporate financials	Financial condition / constraints / asymmetric information (Leasing provides 100% financing, saves cash and credit lines)	Capital constrained firms (high financial distress risk) have limited access to debt and therefore lease more. Lessors are privileged in case of bankruptcy	(Eisfeldt, 2007)	Firm size	-	(Deloof, et al., 2007; Eisfeldt, 2007; Graham, et al., 1998; Krishnan & Moyer, 1994; Sharpe & Nguyen, 1995)
				Dividends/assets	-	
				Liquidity	-	
				Rating	-	
				Negative book value	+	
				Earnings volatility	+	
				After tax profits	-	
				Earnings/sales	-	
				Variance of sales	0, +	
				Retained earnings to total assets	-	
				Growth rate	+	
				Expected growth (price/earnings)	0, -,	
				Coverage ratios	-	
				Operating risk	+	
Corporate financials	Debt ratio	Substitution theory: more leases are connected to less debt	(Ang & Peterson, 1984)	Debt/equity	+ (Leasing puzzle)	(Ang & Peterson, 1984)
				Debt/assets	-	(Adedeji & Stapleton, 1996; Deloof, et al., 2007) (Yan, 2006)
Corporate financials	Agency costs	additional leasing should affect future collateral and interests on debt	(De Bodt, et al., 2001)	future collateral	More collateral needed	(De Bodt, et al., 2001)
				future interests on debt	No effect / + with small leaseshare	

Criteria category	Variable	Theoretical impact	Author	Indicator	Empirical test result	Author
Corporate financials	Off-balance sheet financing	Theory suggests no difference between on and off balance sheet financing	(Brealey, et al., 2008)	Impact of additional on balance versus off- sheet debt on credit rating	Credit rating is less effected by off-balance sheet rating	(Lim, et al., 2003)
				Impact of additional on balance versus off-sheet debt on bond rating	Same effect	
Corporate financials	Availability of low-cost credit	If debt is easier and cheaper to access, buying is advantageous		Credit margin (debt cost over Libor or Treasury notes)	- (no regression)	(WCN, 2000)
Financing evaluation	NAL	If the NAL is positive, firms should lease; otherwise, purchase	(Brealey, et al., 2008)	Asset price	- (no regression)	(WCN, 2000)
		Lease payments are negative in NPV formula		Lease rate (per diem)		
		Residual value is neg. in NPV formula		Residual value at end of lease period	- (no regression)	(WCN, 2000)
		Higher borrowing rates		After tax borrowing rate		
Financing evaluation	Lessor might achieve a better acquisition and sale price	Positive effect on leasing	Schallheim, 1994)			
Financing evaluation	Deposits / advances	Positive impact on leasing	(Engelhardt, 1996)			
Financing evaluation	Repair costs and drop off charges, pick up time extensions must be negotiated	Negative impact on leasing	(Baker & Hubbard, 2003)			
Financing evaluation	Valuable options	Options to purchase, to renew or cancel the lease provide flexibility	(Copeland & Weston, 1982; Grenadier, 1995; Schallheim, 1994)		+	(Eades & Marston, 2002)
Operational	Additional ship (slot) capacity	positive effect	(Temple, 1987)			

Criteria category	Variable	Theoretical impact	Author	Indicator	Empirical test result	Author
Operational	Avoid loan restrictions	Positive effect on leasing	Schallheim, 1994)			
Operational	Avoid capital expenditure approvals					
Operational	Transaction and Information costs - Avoid purchase and disposal transaction - avoid capital expenditure approval - Reduce record keeping/administration - faster than purchasing and negotiating loans (standardized) - right equipment at right condition at right location - flexible and convenient - no ownership dilution - might include maintenance	Positive effect on leasing; Some "not sensible" reasons of leasing as avoiding capital expenditure approvals should have no effect according to Brealey (2008)	(Schallheim, 1994; Tan, 1983; Temple, 1987)			
Risk reducing	Risk sharing - avoid sale and residual risk - short term usage - protect against obsolescence - hedge of business risk if lease rate is tied to usage - reduced responsibility - hedge against a loss of tax shields in the case of declining profits	Positive effect on leasing	(Schallheim, 1994; Temple, 1987)			
Risk reducing	Degree of lessor competition	A limited number of powerful lessors (through mergers) leads to less leasing	(Temple, 1987)			
Industry and macro-economic	Industry condition / costs and demand	If the shipping line industry is in a good condition, more buying is expected		Oil price (fuel costs to drive the ships) / charter rates	- (no regression)	(B. Lemper, 2008; Temple, 1987)
				World trade growth / World GDP growth	+ (no regression)	

Criteria category	Variable	Theoretical impact	Author	Indicator	Empirical test result	Author
Industry and macro-economic	Inflation	Long-term leasing provides a hedge against Inflation; positive effect	Robichek (1965)			

Many variables in Table 2-2 do not affect the NPV analysis that is suggested in most corporate finance textbooks and theoretical academic literature (see 2.1.1). Table 2-2 also shows that the effects of many variables on the buy or lease decision have not been tested empirically at all (blank author fields on the right hand side). This includes the NPV, which is the most dominant variable in the theoretical literature. In chapters 3 and 4 regression techniques are used to show that NPV analysis and other variables have a statistically significant impact in practice.

To get direct feedback from industry practitioners on the relevance of the listed variables regarding the container buy or lease decision, a shipping line survey is performed. The survey results are presented in chapter 5.

Because both the regression analyses as well as the survey provide evidence of the importance of additional variables, an extended theoretical model is developed in chapter 6.

2.4 Summary of literature gap and lessons learned

The general buy-or-lease decision has been discussed in many books and articles. Most corporate finance textbooks as well as academic literature reports (see section 2.1.1) suggest computing the NPV advantage of leasing. If the NPV advantage is greater than zero, leasing should be chosen. Many authors suggest using the after-cost borrowing rate for discounting. However, the proposed analysis does not reflect advances and deposits as well as further variables summarized in Table 2.2. In chapter 6 a general model that includes these variables is developed, because the analysis presented in chapters 3 to 5 provides evidence that they are relevant.

For some industries, such as the car or real estate industry, specialized literature can be found. Coverage of the buy or lease decision regarding shipping containers is very limited. The industry-specific models for containers from Tan (1983) as well as Temple (1987) can only partly describe the real world. The assumptions made by Tan (1983) do not reflect the current situation on the market (for example: no residual value versus a value of about 800 USD). Temple (1987) gives explanations of why master leases are beneficial (e.g. unbalanced trade, growing market with minimum purchase volume, local imbalances, demand fluctuations; see chapter 2.1.2). Both papers cannot explain why even large companies with high tax rates use long-term leasing. Other aspects that have been described in the general theory section (see 2.1.1) as maintenance, agency and transaction costs have not been taken into account. In chapter 6.2, a decision model for shipping containers will be developed that includes the applicable variables mentioned in the general literature as well as additional industry specific variables. This model is necessary to take optimal buy or lease decisions that take all aspects into account.

The existing general empirical studies analyze the effect of several variables on the lease share of companies. Surveys from O'Brien & Nunnally (1983) and Mukherjee (1991) show that large corporations widely use the NAL for decision preparation. None of the existing empirical studies examine the effect of NPV calculations with a regression model. The availability of a unique dataset of shipping line and market data allows this regression analysis for the first time. In addition to the previously mentioned NPV drivers, the regression will analyze the impact of other macroeconomic and microeconomic variables, such as world trade growth, crude oil price, ship capacity, rating and firm size.

Two different datasets will be used for regression analysis to find statistically significant variables for the buy or lease decision. First, 30-year time-series data with aggregated market as well as macroeconomic data will be used. Second, panel data over 10 years from the top 20 shipping lines will be used to analyze macroeconomic as well as microeconomic effects.

Only one survey (Temple, 1987) has been conducted regarding the buy or lease decision of containers. Temple's survey gives some insights into the reasons for container leasing. The importance of the NPV analysis and several other decision criteria was not questioned. Furthermore the survey is outdated because it is more than 20 years old and not representative (there were only 15 participants). A new survey will be performed using an extended questionnaire. The results will be interpreted and compared with the results of Temple as well as the general buy or lease survey of Mukherjee (1991).

The following chart provides an overview of the main literature gaps regarding the buy or lease decision:

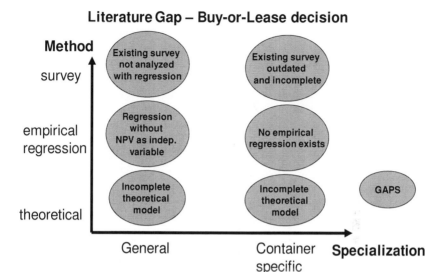

Figure 2-1 Buy or lease literature gap

As described above, all major literature gaps shown in Figure 2-1 will be addressed in this thesis: The first empirical regression analysis incl. NPV as an independent variable is presented in chapters 3 (macroeconomic model) and 4 (microeconomic model). Next, for the first time a more detailed buy or lease survey will be analyzed using regression analysis in chapter 5. Finally, an extended general as well as container-specific theoretical model will be developed in chapter 6 based on the knowledge gathered in the empirical analysis (chapters 3 to 5).

3 Macroeconomic time series evaluation

The focus of this chapter is an empirical analysis of the buy or lease decision made by shipping lines regarding containers. Aggregated time series industry data are used for regression analysis. The impact of several variables on the aggregated share of leased containers and the absolute volume of additionally leased containers per year are analyzed.

Theory suggests that shipping lines should calculate the NAL and lease if it is positive or purchase (and finance with debt) if not (Brealey, et al., 2008). Other macroeconomic variables such as interest rate spread, oil prices and freight costs have an impact on the availability of funds and the profitability of shipping lines. This might have an influence on the leasing decision. The existing general empirical literature does not analyze the effect of the NAL calculation on the leasing share using regression methods. Only surveys (Mukherjee, 1991; O'Brien & Nunnally, 1983) have found that NAL calculations are used in praxis. The existing industry-specific literature on container leasing does not contain any regression analysis. Using a regression analysis, this chapter provides the first evidence that the NAL calculation has an effect on the lease share. Furthermore, it discusses the impact of several macroeconomic variables on the aggregated lease share as well as additionally leased volume for the first time.

This chapter will summarize the concept, model, data and results of an empirical time series analysis using aggregated data for the shipping industry as well as macroeconomic data for the years 1977 to 2008. The target is to find indicators that show a statistically significant impact on the aggregated leasing share and added volume of shipping containers.

3.1 Impact on lease share

3.1.1 Hypotheses

Many authors analyze the impact of taxes (Adedeji & Stapleton, 1996; Graham, et al., 1998; Sharpe & Nguyen, 1995) or firm-specific financial figures (Deloof, et al., 2007; Eisfeldt, 2007; Graham, et al., 1998; Krishnan & Moyer, 1994; Sharpe & Nguyen, 1995) on the buy or lease decision using regression methods. None of them analyzed the impact of the theoretically most important variable that should influence the buy or lease decision, the NAL. This is the first empirical analysis estimating the importance of the NAL calculation for the buy or lease decision using regression techniques.

The impact of several other macroeconomic and industry variables are tested here. Lemper (2008) and Temple (1987) state the impact of the world gross domestic product (GDP) and world trade growth on the shipping industry. Lemper (2008) addresses the importance of the oil price (bunker/fuel costs for the operation of ships) and the charter rate of ships as well as freight rates for the profitability of shipping lines. Ang & Peterson (1984) found a negative relation between leasing and profits. As proposed by WCN (2000), easy availability of low cost debt can be a driver for more purchasing rather than leasing.

For the regression analysis, the null hypothesis of all above mentioned independent variables is that they have no impact. The research (alternative) hypothesis regarding a change in the NAL is that an increasing NAL is positively associated with a rising leasing share.

World GDP and world trade growth have a positive effect on the demand for containers, both leased and owned. Nevertheless, it is unclear whether the leasing share is affected by world GDP and world trade growth. Therefore the research hypothesis is two-sided.

Oil prices affect the operational costs (bunker/fuel) of shipping lines. If operational costs go up, the profitability of the shipping lines should be weaker, which leads to more leasing. The research hypothesis is a positive association of changes in oil prices with the change in lease share. The freight rates have a positive impact on the shipping lines' profitability. Higher freight rates should lower the share of leasing, as shippers can afford to buy more. The research hypothesis is a negative impact of changes in freight rates on the change of lease share.

Finally, easier availability of low cost debt should have a negative impact on the lease share as shippers can finance owned equipment easier and more cheaply with debt. The research hypothesis is a negative association of change in easy availability of low cost debt and change in lease share.

3.1.2 Data and measurement issues

Various data sources are used for the time series analysis. The data for the dependent variable (change in percent of leased containers / total shipping containers [%]) is calculated based on data obtained from Foxcroft (2008, 2009b). Containers on finance lease or lease purchase are defined as owned by the shipping lines. Therefore, the lease ratio is defined as operating leases to total containers. Because the analysis focuses on containers owned and leased by shipping lines, regional containers are not taken into account. For the years 1977 to 1989, the number of containers purchased by shipping lines was not published by *Containerization International*. To complete the dataset, the number of container purchased by shipping lines is estimated by multiplying the ocean carriers and other purchases by the average share of purchases by ocean carriers (89%) in the period from 1990 to 2007. This estimate should be a rather credible one because the standard deviation of the share of purchases by ocean carriers is only 1.3%.

For simplification, the analysis focuses on a 20 DV with the following container-specific variables. The NPV analysis that shipping lines should use according to theory (Brealey, et al., 2008) is not possible to perform based on aggregated industry data. Particularly, tax rates cannot be taken into account on this aggregation level. Therefore an industry-wide NPV variable is calculated as an approximation using the formula

$$NPV = A_0 - \sum_{t=1}^{10} \frac{L_t}{(1+i)^t} - \frac{S_{10}}{(1+i)^{10}}$$

Equation 3-1

Where:

NPV	= net present value advantage of leasing [currency]
A_0	= acquisition price of the equipment [currency]
L_t	= lease payment in period t [currency]
S_{10}	= salvage value in period 10 [currency]
i	= discount rate [%]

The rental per diem is reduced by 20% after year five (end of the first long-term lease), and the average bond interest rate (with rating BAA[7]) is used for discounting. For simplification, it is assumed that the container is used for 10 years for shipping and then sold at the terminal value for other usage. This assumption may slightly underestimate the life of a container, as containers are used up to 15 years for sea shipping.

The purchase price, rental per diem and terminal value are also obtained from Foxcroft (2008). As the terminal/residual value is only available from 1995, the residual value for the years 1980 to 1994 is estimated. The estimate is calculated by multiplying the average residual in percent of new container price in the period 1995 to 2008 (44%) by the new container price in the respective year.

The BAA bond interest rate used as discount factor in the NPV calculation is obtained from the U.S. Federal Reserve (FED, 2010b).

The Maritime Economics Freight index (variable name: freightindex [-]) data was extracted from the book *Maritime Economics* (Stopford, 2009). Because the value for 2008 was not given, it is estimated based on the change of the Baltic Dry Index (Bloomberg, 2010) from 2007 to 2008.

World GDP and world trade growth figures are obtained from the World Economic Outlook published by the International Monetary Fund (IMF, 2009).

---

7   For a definition of Moody's rating categories, see (Rehkugler & Glunz, 2007).

To avoid collinearity and to save degrees of freedom, an indicator (variable name: demand [%] is constructed:

demand = (world GDP growth + world trade growth)/2　　　　Equation 3-2

The crude oil price (variable name: oil [currency]) source is obtained from the Energy Information Administration (EIA, 2009).

The indicator used for easily obtainable and low cost debt (variable name: spread [%]) is the spread of BAA bonds (FED, 2010b) over five-year government bonds (FED, 2010a). Both are received from the U.S. Federal Reserve.

In a second analysis, a model with real data (inflation-corrected) is used. For the inflation (variable name: inflation [%]) correction, the U.S. GDP deflator published by the U.S. Bureau of Economic Analysis (BEA, 2009) is used. The U.S. Consumer Price Index deflator published by the U.S. Bureau of Labor statistics (BLS, 2009) leads to similar results.

To control for trends, the variable year [-] is introduced.

3.1.3 Sample statistics and simple correlations

The following table summarizes the variables, their means, standard deviations and minimum as well as maximum values. All variables are defined as change from previous period (with the exception of the variables inflation and demand, which are defined as percent change from previous period). Stata is used to analyze the data.

Table 3-1 Sample statistics

Description	Variable	Obs	Mean	Std. Dev.	Min	Max
Year	year	32	16.5	9.380832	1	32
Percent leased change	pl	31	-.1286645	1.620664	-2.2157	4.0416
Percent leased change t-1	plt0	30	-.09437	1.636889	-2.2157	4.0416
NPV change	npv	28	76.5182	166.8309	-305.8927	536.6369
Real NPV change	realnpv	28	423.335	827.7725	-901.0561	3161.09
Inflation	inflation	31	3.484758	2.204541	1.1271	9.4294
Spread ov.gov change	spread	31	.0858064	.7607442	-.95	2.59
World GDP and trade growth	demand	32	5.555353	3.092188	.195	14.8133
Freight index change	freightindex	31	34.95116	123.5248	-72	567.4861
Real Freightindexch	realfreighindex	31	28.26514	122.3352	-129.5316	511.6074
Crude oil price	oil	31	2.610645	9.263572	-11.85	37.08
Real crude oil price	realoil	31	1.733336	10.56636	-19.5052	33.0839

The change in share of leased containers varies between -2.2 and 4 percentage points in the years from 1977 to 2008. The nominal change in NPV ranges from -305 to 537.

58

As the time series data are on an aggregated level, only one observation per year is available. This leads to a total number of observations of 28, which is rather low.

The correlation matrix is provided in the next table. It shows the correlation between two variables without taking into account the simultaneous effect of other variables.

Table 3-2 Correlation matrix

```
. corr
(obs=28)
```

	year	pl	plt0	npv	inflat~n	spread	demand	freigh~x	oil
year	1.0000								
pl	-0.0224	1.0000							
plt0	-0.1269	0.4041	1.0000						
npv	0.0536	0.2262	0.1943	1.0000					
inflation	-0.5558	-0.0490	0.2632	0.2848	1.0000				
spread	0.1589	-0.1417	-0.0314	0.2408	-0.1307	1.0000			
demand	0.3505	0.0085	-0.1812	-0.1135	-0.2875	-0.6259	1.0000		
freightindex	0.4562	-0.1285	-0.1889	0.0580	-0.1659	0.4626	0.0607	1.0000	
oil	0.4464	-0.2166	-0.0703	0.3144	0.0702	0.4189	0.0961	0.5971	1.0000

The change in share of leasing is positively correlated with increasing NPV advantage, as hypothesized. The change in NPV shows the highest correlation to change in lease share. Inflation has a small negative correlation. The negative correlation with the change in spread is contrary to expectation. The correlation with demand (world GDP and trade growth) is very low. The correlation of the freight index is low, but in the expected direction. The oil price correlation is not in the expected direction. The correlations have to be confirmed by the regression analysis, which shows the joint impact of the variables.

Multi-collinearity reduces the significance of regression results. The result of a multi-collinearity test run in Stata is shown in the next table.

Table 3-3 VIF test results

```
vif
```

Variable	VIF	1/VIF
spread	3.66	0.273369
demand	3.17	0.315570
freightindex	2.05	0.486847
oil	2.05	0.487080
year	1.66	0.603881
npv	1.24	0.809400
plt0	1.14	0.876916
Mean VIF	2.14	

As the variance inflation factor (VIF) is below 10 with all variables, low multi-collinearity can be concluded.

To check the functional form which can be used for the regression, scatter plots (generated in Stata) for the relations between the change in lease share and each independent variable are provided below.

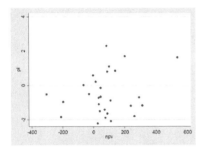

Figure 3-1 Scatter plot: Change in lease share and change in NPV

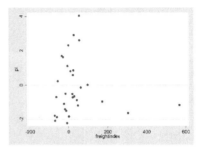

Figure 3-3 Scatter plot: Change in lease share and change in freight index

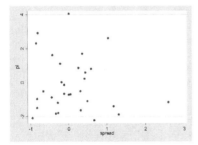

Figure 3-2 Scatter plot: Change in lease share and change in spread

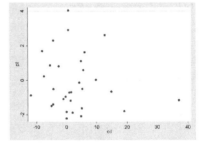

Figure 3-4 Scatter plot: Change in lease share and change in oil price

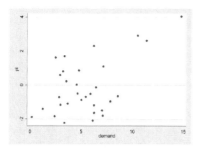

Figure 3-5 Scatter plot: Change in lease share and change in demand

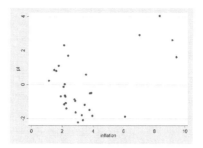

Figure 3-6 Scatter plot: Change in lease share and inflation

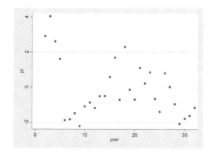

Figure 3-7 Scatter plot: Change in lease share over time

Figures 3-1 to 3-7 either show a linear relation to the change in lease share or no clear functional form. Therefore a linear model is appropriate. The trend (variable year) shown in Figure 3-7 could be linear or polynomial. Since the graph might show two minima and one maxima, the polynomial form could be year, year^2 and year^3.

Therefore, the first approach is a linear ordinary least square model (OLS) regression model. A second approach with a polynomial trend variable will be used to check if this improves the fit of the model.

3.1.4 Regression model

A regression analysis is used to find the variables that have a statistical signifi-cant impact on the dependent variable. To minimize autocorrelation, all variables are defined as differences between the current year and previous year.

The dependent variable

$$pl = \frac{leased_t}{total_t} - \frac{leased_{t-1}}{total_{t-1}}$$ **Equation 3-3**

Where:

pl   = change of percent leased containers from the previous period [%]

$leased_t$ = number of leased containers in period t [TEU]

$total_t$ = total number of shipping containers in period t [TEU]

pl varied only between minus 2.2 and plus 4 percent in the years 1977 to 2008.

Sharpe and Nguyen (1995) and many other authors use a Tobit regression model to analyze the buy or lease decision because their data includes many zeros (i.e., firms that do not lease). This is not the case here because aggregated industry data is analyzed. As the change in share of leased containers is rather normally distributed (see Figure 3-8), an OLS regression can be used (Bamberg & Baur, 1991, pp. 42 - 51).

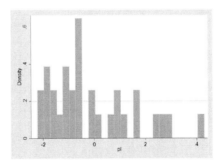

Figure 3-8 Histogram of percent of leased containers

All variables are defined as differences to the previous period or percentage changes. This reduces the omitted variable bias and corrects for autocorrelation and underlying trends. The regression equation is

$$pl_{t2-t1} = \alpha + \beta_1 npv_{t2-t1} + \beta_2 spread_{t2-t1} + \beta_3 freightindex_{t2-t1}$$

$$+ \beta_4 oil_{t2-t1} + \beta_5 demand_{t2} + \beta_6 year_{t2} + pl_{t1-t0} + \varepsilon_{t2} \qquad \textbf{Equation 3-4}$$

where the variables have the above defined meaning, β_i [-] are the coefficients of those variables, α [-] is a constant and ε_{t2} [-] the error term.

3.1.5 Model estimates

The first table shows the Stata OLS regression results using nominal values.

Table 3-4 OLS regression result (change in change)

```
. reg  pl npv spread demand freightindex oil year plt0
```

Source	SS	df	MS		Number of obs =	28
					F(7, 20) =	1.16
Model	11.8747751	7	1.69639644		Prob > F =	0.3664
Residual	29.1793306	20	1.45896653		R-squared =	0.2892
					Adj R-squared =	0.0405
Total	41.0541057	27	1.52052243		Root MSE =	1.2079

pl	Coef.	Std. Err.	t	P>|t|	[95% Conf. Interval]	
npv	.0021357	.0015488	1.38	0.183	-.001095	.0053663
spread	-.1913219	.5840964	-0.33	0.747	-1.409726	1.027082
demand	.0106314	.1995714	0.05	0.958	-.4056673	.4269302
freightindex	.0013806	.0025611	0.54	0.596	-.0039617	.0067229
oil	-.048463	.0348645	-1.39	0.180	-.121189	.024263
year	.0182823	.0363645	0.50	0.621	-.0575727	.0941374
plt0	.3308692	.182945	1.81	0.086	-.0507474	.7124858
_cons	-.8345076	.8988785	-0.93	0.364	-2.709535	1.04052

The NPV coefficient is significant at the 10% level (p value needs to be divided by two since the hypothesis is one-sided). No other variable shows statistical significance. The F test shows no significance (p = 37%) that all coefficients are different from zero. Furthermore, the adjusted R square is very low (4%), signalling a rather low fit of the model. One reason for this might be heteroscedaticity.

Next, a robust regression with heteroscedastically consistent robust standard errors is performed to improve the fit of the model.

Table 3-5 OLS regression result (change in change, robust standard errors)

```
. reg  pl npv spread demand freightindex oil year plt0, robust
```

Linear regression

					Number of obs =	28
					F(7, 20) =	2.69
					Prob > F =	0.0389
					R-squared =	0.2892
					Root MSE =	1.2079

pl	Coef.	Robust Std. Err.	t	P>|t|	[95% Conf. Interval]	
npv	.0021357	.00121	1.77	0.093	-.0003883	.0046597
spread	-.1913219	.5543034	-0.35	0.734	-1.347578	.9649347
demand	.0106314	.1621758	0.07	0.948	-.3276613	.3489241
freightindex	.0013806	.002148	0.64	0.528	-.0031001	.0058612
oil	-.048463	.0298879	-1.62	0.121	-.110808	.013882
year	.0182823	.036349	0.50	0.620	-.0575404	.0941051
plt0	.3308692	.1332032	2.48	0.022	.0530121	.6087263
_cons	-.8345076	.6631548	-1.26	0.223	-2.217824	.548809

The F test is significant (p = 4%) using robust standard errors. This means that the null hypothesis (all coefficients are zero) can be rejected. Furthermore, the p value of the NPV change variable has improved. The change in NPV is now significant on the 5% level. Other variables still do not show statistical significance.

To check for autocorrelation, a Durbin Watson test is performed using Stata.

```
estat dwatson
Durbin-Watson d-statistic(  8,    28) =   2.025967
```

Because the d-statistic is close to 2, minimal autocorrelation can be concluded.

Next, it is checked whether it is possible to improve the fit of the model by implementing a polynomial functional form regarding the trend variable (year, year^2, year^3). Since the NPV/year graph above might show two minima and one maxima, this polynomial is chosen.

Table 3-6 OLS regression result (change in change, nonlinear trend, robust)

```
. reg pl npv spread demand freightindex oil year  yearq yearqq plt0, robust

Linear regression                               Number of obs =        28
                                                F(  9,     18) =      3.83
                                                Prob > F      =    0.0074
                                                R-squared     =    0.5793
                                                Root MSE      =    .97961
```

pl	Coef.	Robust Std. Err.	t	P>|t|	[95% Conf. Interval]
npv	.0034434	.0014171	2.43	0.026	.0004662	.0064205
spread	-.9924532	.4980468	-1.99	0.062	-2.038811	.0539044
demand	-.2776478	.1682051	-1.65	0.116	-.6310337	.075738
freightindex	.0067278	.0021034	3.20	0.005	.0023087	.011147
oil	.0102197	.0267587	0.38	0.707	-.0459982	.0664376
year	-.5545265	.7000485	-0.79	0.439	-2.025274	.9162209
yearq	.055702	.0433399	1.29	0.215	-.0353518	.1467557
yearqq	-.0013379	.0008113	-1.65	0.117	-.0030424	.0003667
plt0	-.1069129	.216567	-0.49	0.628	-.5619034	.3480775
_cons	1.228976	3.088297	0.40	0.695	-5.259295	7.717246

The Stata output shows a drastic improvement of the r square from 29% to 58%. Furthermore, the NPV advantage change is now significant on the 2% level. The probability is only 1.3% to achieve the estimated coefficient if the null hypothesis (no impact of NPV changes on lease share changes) were true. The impact of NPV advantage change is positive, as hypothesized. The NPV coefficient of 0.003 means that a NPV change increase of 1 USD is associated with a 0.003 percentage-point increase of lease share change if all other independent variables are held constant. In other words, an increase in NPV change of 500 USD (which is within the range shown above) is associated with a 1.5 percentage-point increase of lease share change. As the lease share varies only between -2.2 and 4.0 percentage points, an increase of 1.5 percentage points can explain much.

In addition, the change of the freight index shows significance at the 1% level. The direction is opposite to what was expected. Higher freight index changes are associated with higher lease share changes. One explanation could be that the freight index has a negative impact on profitability of shipping lines. An increase of one unit in freight index change has an impact of 0.007 percentage points on the change in lease share.

The t values of the other independent variables do not allow rejection of the null hypothesis that they do not have an impact on the lease share change.

To check the robustness of the results against inflation, the regression is performed using real variables (all relevant variables corrected with GDP deflator). The regression without the polynomial trend variables (year^2, year^3) does not provide any statistical significant results. Therefore, only the results including the polynomial trend variables are shown.

Table 3-7 OLS regression results (change in change, real, nonlinear, robust)

```
reg pl realnpv spread demand  realfreightindex realoil year  yearq yearqq plt0,
robust
```

```
Linear regression                                  Number of obs =        28
                                                   F( 9,     18) =      6.38
                                                   Prob > F      =    0.0004
                                                   R-squared     =    0.6547
                                                   Root MSE      =    .88747
```

pl	Coef.	Robust Std. Err.	t	P>|t|	[95% Conf. Interval]	
realnpv	.0019759	.0006564	3.01	0.008	.0005969	.0033548
spread	-1.172245	.5234074	-2.24	0.038	-2.271883	-.0726068
demand	-.1945237	.169229	-1.15	0.265	-.5500607	.1610134
realfreigh~x	.0080456	.0021604	3.72	0.002	.0035068	.0125844
realoil	.0100236	.020759	0.48	0.635	-.0335895	.0536367
year	.6134633	.6384917	0.96	0.349	-.727958	1.954885
yearq	.0031125	.0359967	0.09	0.932	-.0725138	.0787389
yearqq	-.0005828	.0006475	-0.90	0.380	-.0019432	.0007777
plt0	-.333776	.2434359	-1.37	0.187	-.8452159	.1776639
_cons	-7.431905	3.79389	-1.96	0.066	-15.40257	.5387619

The r square further increased to 65%, signaling an improved fit of the model. The F test also shows an increased probability (99%) for rejecting the null hypothesis that all coefficients are zero.

The real NPV advantage change once again has a positive impact on the lease share change. Its significance improved to the 1% level. The NPV coefficient reduced slightly to 0.002. The significance (1% level) and effect (0.008) of the real freight index change also improved compared to the nominal model. The change in interest spread between 5-year treasury and corporate bonds shows significance on the 5% level. The impact is negative, which is opposite of what was expected. A real freight index change increase of 100 points (which is within the observed range) is associated with an increase of lease share of 0.8 percentage points.

Changes in real oil price and demand (GDP and trade growth) do not show a significant influence on the lease share.

3.2 Impact on lease volume

In this section, a different approach that uses the same data as described previously is demonstrated. The major difference is not the change in the difference of lease share, which is regressed, but the change of TEU volume of leased containers in one year.

3.2.1 Hypotheses

The hypotheses are similar to the ones stated previously. For the regression analysis, the null hypothesis of all above mentioned independent variables is that they have no impact. The research (alternative) hypothesis regarding a NPV advantage of leasing is that an increasing NPV advantage is positively associated with more leasing in one year.

World GDP and world trade growth have a positive effect on the demand for containers (leased and owned). Therefore, the research hypothesis is a positive association between increased world GDP / world trade growth (variable demand) and more leased containers in one year.

The oil price affects the operational costs (bunker/fuel) of shipping lines. If operational costs go up, the profitability of the shipping lines should be weaker, which leads to more leasing. The research hypothesis is a positive association of oil price changes with more leased containers in one year. The freight rates have a positive impact on the shipping lines' profitability, which decreases their leasing demand. The research hypothesis is a negative impact of freight rate changes (variable: freightindex) on lease volume changes.

Finally, an easier availability of low cost debt should have a negative impact on the leasing volume because shippers can finance owned equipment easier and more cheaply with debt. The research hypothesis is a negative association of easy availability of low cost debt change (variable spread) with volume of leasing change.

3.2.2 Data and measurement issues

The data basis for the lease volume approach is the same as in the lease share approach. In this section, the dependent variable (change in number of leased containers in 1000 TEU in one year) is calculated as follows:

$$leased_t = vl_t - vl_{t-1}$$

Equation 3-5

Where:

leased$_t$ = change in number of leased containers [1000 TEU]
vl$_t$ = volume of leased containers in period t [1000 TEU]

The change in total volume of containers added (bought and leased) is used as an exposure variable (total) and measured in 1000 TEU.

The independent variables' NPV advantage [USD], spread between government and corporate (BAA) bonds [%], freightindex [-] and crude oil price [USD] are defined as changes to previous year as above. The demand variable (GDP and trade growth) is calculated as in the lease share model [% change to previous year].

The variable year [-] may be used to control for an underlying trend.

3.2.3 Sample statistics and simple correlations

The following table shows sample statistics.

Table 3-8 Sample statistics (leased volume)

```
. sum

    Variable |    Obs        Mean    Std. Dev.        Min        Max
-------------+--------------------------------------------------------
      leased |     28    324.3929     230.6269         29        815
         npv |     28     76.5182     166.8309  -305.8927   536.6369
      spread |     28    .0864286     .7611697       -.95       2.59
      demand |     28    4.699321     2.073456       .195     8.5615
 freightindex|     28    33.83879     130.0838        -72   567.4861
         oil |     28    2.393571     9.553394     -11.85      37.08
     leasedt0|     28    323.8929     230.6452         29        815
       total |     28    818.8929     612.6778        158       2745
        year |     28        14.5     8.225975          1         28
```

The volume of additionally leased containers in one year was between 29,000 and 815,000 TEU in the period from 1978 to 2008. The total volume of added container equipment ranged from 158,000 to 2,745,000 TEU. The change in NPV advantage of leasing ranges from minus 306 to plus 537.

The Stata correlation matrix (next table) shows the correlation between two variables without taking into account the joint effect of other variables.

Table 3-9 Correlation matrix (leased volume)

```
. corr leased total npv  spread demand freightindex oil
(obs=29)
```

	leased	total	npv	spread	demand	freight~x	oil
leased	1.0000						
total	0.8045	1.0000					
npv	0.6280	0.8003	1.0000				
spread	0.0196	0.0698	0.3343	1.0000			
demand	0.3624	0.3083	0.0016	-0.4790	1.0000		
freightindex	0.3149	0.6140	0.5929	0.4145	0.0546	1.0000	
oil	0.1144	0.5074	0.4525	0.3875	-0.0726	0.8476	1.0000

The volume of added leased equipment is strongly and positively correlated with the total equipment added and the NPV advantage, as hypothesized. The spread has a low positive correlation with leased volume, as expected. The correlation with demand (defined as index combining world GDP and trade growth as above) is positive, as expected. The correlation of the freight index is positive, which is contrary to expectation. The oil price correlation (positive) is in the expected direction. The correlations have to be confirmed by the regression analysis, which shows the joint impact of the variables.

The result of a Stata multi-collinearity test is shown in the next table.

Table 3-10 VIF test results (leased volume)

```
vif
```

Variable	VIF	1/VIF
spread	3.33	0.300525
demand	2.86	0.349588
freightindex	2.20	0.453921
oil	2.08	0.479830
total	1.85	0.541864
npv	1.19	0.843746
Mean VIF	2.25	

As the VIF is below 10 for all variables, low collinearity can be concluded.

To check the functional form, Stata scatter plots for the relations between the lease volume change and each independent variable are provided as follows.

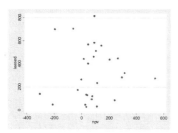

Figure 3-9 Scatter plot: Additionally leased containers and change in NPV

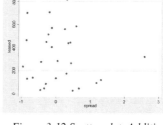

Figure 3-12 Scatter plot: Additionally leased containers and change in spread

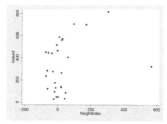

Figure 3-10 Scatter plot: Additionally leased containers and change in freightindex

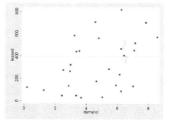

Figure 3-13 Scatter plot: Additionally leased containers and change in demand

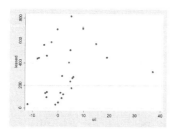

Figure 3-11 Scatter plot: Additionally leased containers and change in oil price

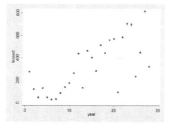

Figure 3-14 Scatter plot: Additionally leased containers over time

Because a linear relation between the additional leased containers and all other variables could be concluded in all Stata scatter plots, a linear model will be used for regression analysis.

3.2.4   Regression model

A regression analysis is used to find the variables that have a statistically significant impact on the dependent variable. The research design is non-experimental because available time series data and statistical controls are used. No random selection or usage of random effects can be used to construct a randomized field experiment or a quasi experiment.

The dependent variable is the volume of added leased containers in one year (measured in 1000 TEU). Since this variable is a count variable (positive in all years), a negative binominal regression is appropriate (Leiner, 1995, p. 15). The following chart shows the histogram of the volume of leased containers per year, which confirms the negative binominal distribution.

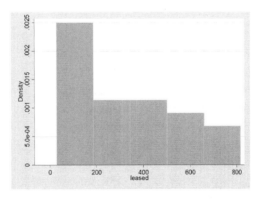

Figure 3-15 Histogram: Additionally leased equipment per year

The regression equation is

$$leased_t = \alpha + \beta_1 npv_t + \beta_2 spread_t + \beta_3 freightindex_t$$

$$+ \beta_4 oil_t + \beta_5 demand_t + \beta_6 leased_{t-1} + \varepsilon_t \qquad \text{Equation 3-6}$$

where the variables have the above defined meaning, β_i are the coefficients of those variables, α is a constant and ε_t the error term. The variable total is used as exposure variable.

3.2.5 Model estimates

The first table shows the negative binominal regression results using nominal values and robust standard errors.

Table 3-11 Negative binominal regression results (nominal, robust)

```
. nbreg leased npv spread demand freightindex oil leasedt0 year, vce(robust) expo-
sure(total)

Negative binomial regression              Number of obs   =        28
Dispersion          = mean                Wald chi2(7)    =     10.97
Log pseudolikelihood = -167.57117         Prob > chi2     =    0.1399

-----------------------------------------------------------------------------
             |             Robust
      leased |    Coef.   Std. Err.     z    P>|z|    [95% Conf. Interval]
-------------+---------------------------------------------------------------
         npv |  .0006705   .0003904    1.72   0.086   -.0000946    .0014357
      spread | -.1327107    .206797   -0.64   0.521   -.5380254     .272604
      demand | -.0025153   .0617071   -0.04   0.967    -.123459    .1184285
 freightindex | -.0001835   .0009889   -0.19   0.853   -.0021217    .0017547
         oil | -.0108254   .0140879   -0.77   0.442   -.0384372    .0167865
     leasedt0 |   -.00002   .0005317   -0.04   0.970   -.0010622    .0010221
        year |  .0087858   .0177194    0.50   0.620   -.0259436    .0435152
        _cons | -1.048454   .2412355   -4.35   0.000   -1.521267   -.5756409
       total | (exposure)
-------------+---------------------------------------------------------------
     /lnalpha | -1.823398   .2242595                   -2.262938   -1.383857
-------------+---------------------------------------------------------------
        alpha |  .1614761   .0362126                    .1040443     .25061
-----------------------------------------------------------------------------
```

The change in the NPV advantage of leasing is significant at the 5% level, and the effect is positive as hypothesized (the p value has to be divided by two because of the one-sided research hypothesis). An increase of 1 USD in NPV advantage is associated with 0.7 additional TEU leased equipment. In other words, an increase of 500 USD in NPV advantage is associated with 350 additional TEU leased if all other variables are held constant. The absolute significance is rather low, as the TEU volume leased goes up to 800,000 in one year. All other independent variables do not show a statistically significant effect.

The chi-square test result allows rejection of the null hypothesis that all independent variables have no impact on the leased volume at the 14% level. The model seems to have room for improvement.

Next, a non linear trend (year^2) is introduced to improve the functional fit. The scatterplot between leased and year showed a quadratic trend.

Table 3-12 Negative binominal regression results (nominal, nonlinear, robust)

```
. nbreg leased npv spread demand freightindex oil leasedt0 year yearq, vce(robust)
exposure(total)

Negative binomial regression                    Number of obs   =          28
Dispersion              = mean                   Wald chi2(8)    =       25.24
Log pseudolikelihood = -164.6927                 Prob > chi2     =      0.0014

-----------------------------------------------------------------------------
             |               Robust
      leased |      Coef.   Std. Err.      z    P>|z|     [95% Conf. Interval]
-------------+---------------------------------------------------------------
         npv |   .0009177   .0004102     2.24   0.025     .0001138    .0017217
      spread |  -.2971529   .1992282    -1.49   0.136    -.6876329    .0933272
      demand |  -.0692761   .0583225    -1.19   0.235    -.1835861    .0450338
 freightindex|   .0007718   .0009526     0.81   0.418    -.0010953     .002639
         oil |   .0002036   .0096364     0.02   0.983    -.0186834    .0190906
     leasedt0 |   2.60e-06   .0004835     0.01   0.996    -.0009451    .0009503
        year |   .1203505   .0418491     2.88   0.004     .0383278    .2023732
       yearq |  -.0040729   .0014358    -2.84   0.005     -.006887   -.0012589
       _cons |  -1.316244   .2519177    -5.22   0.000    -1.809993   -.8224942
       total | (exposure)
-------------+---------------------------------------------------------------
    /lnalpha |  -2.035127   .2266683                     -2.479389   -1.590865
-------------+---------------------------------------------------------------
       alpha |   .1306639   .0296174                      .0837944    .2037492
-----------------------------------------------------------------------------
```

The model / chi square improved significantly. The chi square test result allows rejection of the null hypothesis that all independent variables have no impact on the leased volume on the 1% level.

The NPV advantage has a positive impact as hypothesized and is now significant at the 1% level. A 500 USD increase in NPV is associated with 500 additional TEU leased. Therefore, the absolute significance is still very low.

The trend variables year and year^2 are statistically significant, which confirms their importance for the model fit. All other independent variables still do not show significant results. One reason might be the low number of observations, which biases the results towards non-significance. At the same time, this effect stresses the importance of the NPV advantage for the additional containers leased in one year.

In another regression, the logarithm of both freightindex and oil is applied to get a more linear functional form. The functional form shows an improvement, but the regression result is more or less unchanged.

Last, a model with inflation-corrected variables is used to check the results obtained in the nominal model. All relevant variables are inflation corrected using the GDP deflator.

Table 3-13 Negative binominal regression results (inflation corrected, robust)

```
. nbreg leased  realnpv spread demand  realfreightindex realoil leasedt0 year
yearq, vce(robust) exposure(total)
```

```
Negative binomial regression                    Number of obs   =         28
Dispersion            = mean                    Wald chi2(8)    =     126.16
Log pseudolikelihood = -155.37722               Prob > chi2     =     0.0000
```

leased	Coef.	Robust Std. Err.	z	P>|z|	[95% Conf. Interval]	
realnpv	.0006991	.0001322	5.29	0.000	.00044	.0009582
spread	-.3742451	.1220347	-3.07	0.002	-.6134287	-.1350615
demand	-.0241035	.0456912	-0.53	0.598	-.1136567	.0654496
realfreigh~x	.0022841	.0007179	3.18	0.001	.000877	.0036911
realoil	.0013685	.0072353	0.19	0.850	-.0128124	.0155494
leasedt0	-.0006587	.0003747	-1.76	0.079	-.001393	.0000757
year	.283667	.0416837	6.81	0.000	.2019685	.3653656
yearq	-.0084593	.0012969	-6.52	0.000	-.0110012	-.0059173
_cons	-2.752313	.3686127	-7.47	0.000	-3.474781	-2.029845
total	(exposure)					
/lnalpha	-2.735015	.2169842			-3.160296	-2.309733
alpha	.064893	.0140808			.0424132	.0992877

The chi square improved even further compared to the nominal model. This means that the significance of the model is high.

The real NPV advantage of leasing shows a statistically significant impact at the 1% level. The impact of the real NAL shows a positive impact on the additional volume leased, which is as expected and as theory suggests. The absolute impact is low, as a NPV increase of 500 USD is only associated with 350 additional TEU leased.

The spread (interest on BAA bonds minus government bonds) is significant at the 1% level. The effect on the additional volume leased is negative, which is opposite to what was hypothesized. The effect is not very significant because a spread increase of 1% is only associated with 374 less containers leased.

The realfreightindex shows significance at the 1% level as well. The direction is positive, which is opposite to what was expected. A freightindex increase of 500 points is associated with 1000 additional TEU leased. This absolute value is again rather insignificant compared to the maximal addition of 800,000 TEUs in one year.

3.3 Summary of macroeconomic analysis and lessons learned

The empirical analysis using the change in change lease share model shows a statistical and absolute significant positive impact of the change in NPV advantage and the change in freight index on the lease ratio change. This result is robust against inflation correction. The effect of the freight index is positive, which is opposite of what was hypothesized. The result regarding NPV advantage is consistent with theory and the hypothesis. It confirms the relevance of the NPV calculation regarding the buy or lease decision for the first time using regression techniques.

In a second approach, a negative binominal model is used to find the impact of several variables on the additional volume of leased containers in one year. The NPV advantage variable is again statistically significant using nominal and real values, but the absolute significance is rather low.

As the data used are on an aggregated level (total containers bought by lessors and shipping lines per year), the external validity of this study is limited to the shipping industry. To verify the effect of the NPV analysis in other industries, more research with other industry data is necessary. The aggregation level used and the simplified method of NPV advantage calculation do not allow generalization of the results to the shipping line level. Further research at the firm level is needed to confirm the results.

The other variables either did not show statistical significance, or the result is not the same in the nominal and the real model. One reason for the insignificance of the other independent variables can be the low number of observations (n = 28). A low number of observations biases the result towards non-significance, and therefore non-rejection of the null hypothesis (no impact). More research with a higher number of observations is needed to confirm the results regarding NPV and to improve the significance of the impact of the other variables.

The macroeconomic empirical analysis shows that besides the NPV analysis the freight index has a statistically significant impact on the buy or lease decision. Therefore the variable freightindex shall be integrated in the extended container buy or lease evaluation model which will be developed in chapter 6.2.

The next chapter will provide further insights by analyzing panel data from the top 25 shipping lines.

4 Microeconomic panel analysis

The focus of this chapter is an empirical analysis of the buy or lease decision shipping lines make regarding containers. Data from individual shipping lines as well as macroeconomic data are used in this chapter for regression analysis. This chapter also evaluates the impact of several variables on the share of leased containers.

The analysis presented in the last chapter showed the empirical relevance of the NAL calculation for the first time on an aggregated level. This chapter will investigate if this result also can be found on the microeconomic level (e.g., the firm level). The effect of several firm-specific financial variables as well as the effect of macroeconomic variables on the buy or lease decision are shown in this chapter.

This chapter shall summarize the concept, model, data and results of an empirical panel analysis using data from individual shipping lines as well as macroeconomic data for the years 1994 to 2008. The goal is to find indicators that show a statistically significant impact on the container leasing share of shipping lines.

4.1 Impact on lease share

4.1.1 Hypotheses

In this section, the theoretically expected direction of the impact of all independent variables on the lease share of containers is described. For the regression analysis, the null hypothesis of all independent variables is that they have no impact. The alternative hypothesis is the expected impact.

4.1.1.1 NPV, interest rates and inflation

The theoretically most important variable that should influence the buy or lease decision is the NAL (Brealey, et al., 2008). The research presented in this chapter is the first empirical analysis estimating the importance of the NAL calculation for the buy or lease decision using regression techniques at the firm level. The research (alternative) hypothesis regarding NAL is that an increasing NAL is positively associated with a rising leasing share.

As proposed by WCN (2000), easy availability of low cost debt can be a driver for purchasing over leasing. The easy availability of low cost debt should have a negative impact on the lease share because shippers can finance owned equipment more easily and more cheaply with debt. The spread between government and corporate bonds can be used as a measure for the easy availability of loans. The higher the spread, the more difficult and expensive loans can be obtained. The research hypothesis is a positive association between spread and lease share.

The effect of inflation was discussed by Robichek (1965). Because the direction of the impact is unclear, the research hypothesis is two-sided.

4.1.1.2 Container demand

Lemper (2008) and Temple (1987) discuss the impact of world GDP and world trade growth on the shipping industry. World GDP and world trade growth have a positive effect on the demand for containers (leased and owned). Nevertheless, it is unclear whether the leasing share is affected by world GDP and world trade growth. Therefore, the research hypothesis is two-sided. The same research hypothesis is applies for sea trade volume, container handling volume and total number of container slots (ship capacity). Ship capacity (number of container slots) and the volume of containers developed are very similar in most years. Figure 4-1 shows the development of the container ship slot ratio (containers divided by ship capacity).

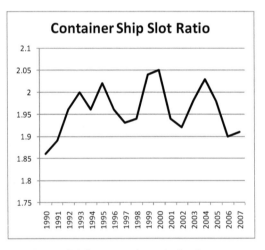

Figure 4-1 Container slot ratio development

For each TEU container slot added between 1990 and 2007, on average 1.95 TEU containers were added (see Figure 4-1). The standard deviation of the ship slot ratio was only 5% (Foxcroft, 2008, p. 39).

4.1.1.3 Industry prices

Lemper (2008) describes the importance of oil prices (bunker/fuel costs for the operation of ships) and the charter rate of ships as well as freight rates for the profitability of shipping lines.

Oil prices affect the operational costs (bunker/fuel) of shipping lines. If operational costs go up, the profitability/cash position of the shipping lines should be weaker, which should lead to more leasing. The research hypothesis is a positive association of bunker prices andwith lease share.

Ship charter rates as measured by the Harpex index have a negative effect on the cash situation and profitability of shipping lines. This should increase the demand for leasing. Therefore, the alternative hypothesis is that the lease share rises with rising ship charter rates.

If freight rates go up, this might indicate a freight demand surplus, which also could indicate an increased demand for container leasing. The research hypothesis is a positive relationship between freight rates and lease share.

There are two consequences of rising ship prices. On one hand, shipping lines have to pay more for additional ships, which weakens their cash position and debt capacity. One the other hand, these rising prices increase the value of the existing fleet. The total effect on lease share is unclear. Therefore, the research alternative is two-sided.

Higher stock prices for shipping lines could signal an increased profitability, which allows them to buy more. Furthermore, higher stock prices allow firms to obtain fresh equity more easily and at more attractive prices. Therefore, the research hypothesis is a negative association between stock prices and lease share.

4.1.1.4 Firm-specific data

The impact of firm-specific financial figures on the buy or lease decision using regression methods has been analyzed by many authors (Deloof, et al., 2007; Eisfeldt, 2007; Graham, et al., 1998; Krishnan & Moyer, 1994; Sharpe & Nguyen, 1995). The establishment year of a firm might affect the decision. Young firms might lease more because of missing alternatives. The research hypothesis is a rising lease share with increasing establishment year of the firm.

The rating of a firm has an impact on the availability of debt and the level of interest rates. Several authors found a negative relationship between lease share and creditability (e.g., Deloof et al., (2007); Eisfeldt, (2007)). The research hypothesis is a positive association between lease share and rating (worsening creditability).

Several authors, including Graham et al. (1998) and Krishnan & Moyer (1994) found a negative relationship between firm size and lease share. Therefore, the research alternative is a negative relationship between firm size and lease share.

Ang & Peterson (1984) found a negative relationship between leasing and profits. A higher net income leads to more cash/internal funds that are available for investments (e.g., in containers). Consequently, the alternative hypothesis is declining lease share with increasing net income.

Many authors analyze the impact of taxes (Adedeji & Stapleton, 1996; Graham, et al., 1998; Sharpe & Nguyen, 1995). They found a negative relationship between tax rate and lease share, which is used as research hypothesis here.

Several authors discuss whether leasing and debt are substitutes (Yan, 2006) or complements (the so called "leasing puzzle" described by Ang & Peterson (1984)). Theory suggests that leasing and debt are substitutes (Brealey, et al., 2008). In turn, the alternative hypothesis is that a higher debt to assets ratio is associated with a lower lease share.

Finally, the share of ships chartered could be an indicator for the share of containers leased if shipping lines follow a general strategy. The research hypothesis is that a rising ship charter share is associated with a higher container lease share.

4.1.2 Data and measurement issues

Various data sources are used for the panel analysis. The definition of the variables and the data sources are described in detail below.

4.1.2.1 Dependent variable

The data for the dependent variable (percent of leased containers; variable name: leasedshare) is obtained from Andrew Foxcroft (2009c). Containers on finance lease or lease purchase are defined as owned by the shipping lines. Therefore, the lease ratio is defined as operating leases to total containers. The share of leased containers was obtained for the top 23 shipping lines (APL, China Shipping, CMA, Cosco, CSAV, Evergreen, Hamburg Sued, Hanjin, Hapag Lloyd, Hyundai, IRISL, K-Line, Maersk, MISC, Mitsui, MSC, NYK, OOCL, PIL, United Arab Shipping, Wan Hai, Yangming and ZIM) in the years 1994 to 2008.

Because of insufficient financial data, the following shipping lines are eliminated from the dataset: CMA, Hamburg Sued, IRISL, MISC, MSC, PIL, United Arab Shipping and ZIM. Fifteen shipping lines remain in the dataset.

4.1.2.2 NAL, interest rates and inflation

According to theory (Brealey, et al., 2008), shipping lines should perform the following NAL calculation:

$$\textbf{naldebt} \ = \ \textbf{D}_0 + \sum_{t=1}^{N} \frac{-L_t(1-T)-D_tT+O_t(1-T)}{[1+r_d(1-T)]^t} - \frac{S_N}{[1+r_d(1-T)]^N} \qquad \textbf{Equation 4-1}$$

Where:

naldebt	= net advantage of leasing discounted at after tax debt rate [currency]
D_0	= initial financing provided (debt amount received) in t_0 [currency]
N	= length of the lease in years [-]
L_t	= lease payment in period t [currency]
T	= marginal corporate tax rate [%]
D_t	= depreciation in period t [currency]
O_t	= operative costs incl. in lease (e.g. maintenance, insurance) [currency]
S_N	= after tax salvage value (terminal value) of the asset at time N [currency]
$r_d(1-T)$	= discount rate (risk equivalent opportunity costs/after tax cost of debt) [%]

To calculate the NAL, several assumptions have to be made. To simplify the analysis, one 20-foot standard container is considered.

Assumptions:

D_0	= market average asset costs (Foxcroft, 2009b); no immediate lease payment
N	= 12 years
L_t	= assumed lease payment (see below) reduced by 20% after year five (end of the first long-term lease)
T	= gliding four-year tax rate average (Reuters, 2009b)
D_t	$= \frac{A_n}{10}$ (linear depreciation over 10 years to zero)
O_t	= 0 (maintenance, insurance etc. are paid by shipping line)
S_N	= market average salvage value (Foxcroft, 2008) * (1-T)
r_d	= firms interest on debt (Reuters, 2009a) divided by debt (Reuters, 2009b)

For simplification, it is assumed that the container is used for 10 years and sold at the terminal value for other usage. This assumption may slightly underestimate the life of a container because containers are used up to 15 years for sea shipping.

Because rental per diem data (L_t) for each year and firm is not available, an approximation is used. The following data regarding 287 long-term leasing contracts from 1997 to 2008 was received from three different lessors and analyzed with Stata:

Table 4-1 Sample statistics (year, per diem, rating)

. sum

```
    Variable |       Obs        Mean    Std. Dev.       Min        Max
-------------+--------------------------------------------------------
        year |       287    2004.178    2.430817       1997       2008
     perdiem |       287    .7501045    .1562061        .37       1.88
      rating |       287    4.370732    1.377858          1          6
-------------+--------------------------------------------------------
```

A robust linear regression with time-fixed as well as firm-fixed (top 25 firms only) effects will lead to an estimation equation for the per diem rate. The hypothesis regarding rating is that a higher rating is associated with a higher per diem rate. The Stata output is presented as follows.

Table 4-2 OLS regression results (per diem, rating, year)

. reg perdiem rating year2008 year2007 year2006 year2005 year2004 year2003
year2002 year2001 year2000 year1999 year1998 apl chinaship cma cosco csav evergreen
hamburgsued hanjin hapag hyundai maersk msc mitsui kline wanhai yangming, robust

```
Linear regression                              Number of obs =      287
                                               F( 25,    258) =       .
                                               Prob > F       =       .
                                               R-squared      =  0.3350
                                               Root MSE       =  .13412
```

```
----------------------------------------------------------------------------
             |              Robust
     perdiem |     Coef.   Std. Err.      t    P>|t|    [95% Conf. Interval]
-------------+--------------------------------------------------------------
      rating |    .014293   .0083416    1.71   0.088   -.0021333    .0307194
    year2008 |  -.0373218   .0455169   -0.82   0.413   -.1269538    .0523102
    year2007 |  -.0970405   .0570757   -1.70   0.090   -.2094341     .015353
    year2006 |   -.154259   .0352107   -4.38   0.000   -.2235959    -.084922
    year2005 |   -.037784   .0303952   -1.24   0.215   -.0976382    .0220702
    year2004 |  -.0245798   .0322717   -0.76   0.447   -.0881294    .0389697
    year2003 |  -.2079633   .0331596   -6.27   0.000   -.2732614   -.1426653
    year2002 |  -.1950124   .0308381   -6.32   0.000   -.2557389   -.1342859
    year2001 |  -.1966873   .0600119   -3.28   0.001   -.3148628   -.0785117
    year2000 |     -.1556   .0400972   -3.88   0.000   -.2345594   -.0766407
    year1999 |  -.0706137   .1023046   -0.69   0.491    -.272072    .1308446
    year1998 |  -.0431851   .0498273   -0.87   0.387    -.141305    .0549349
         apl |  -.0350109   .0813256   -0.43   0.667   -.1951573    .1251355
   chinaship |   .0003358   .0389217    0.01   0.993   -.0763088    .0769804
         cma |   .0141427   .0294341    0.48   0.631    -.043819    .0721044
       cosco |   .0310418    .031373    0.99   0.323    -.030738    .0928216
        csav |   .0027572   .0494437    0.06   0.956   -.0946073    .1001217
   evergreen |   .1572536    .072206    2.18   0.030    .0150654    .2994418
 hamburgsued |   .0461412   .0291357    1.58   0.114   -.0112327    .1035152
      hanjin |   .0104809   .0373526    0.28   0.779   -.0630738    .0840356
       hapag |  -.0355826   .0481651   -0.74   0.461   -.1304295    .0592643
     hyundai |   .0012595   .0213891    0.06   0.953   -.0408599    .0433789
      maersk |  -.0072323   .0384927   -0.19   0.851   -.0830322    .0685676
         msc |  -.1822408   .0603848   -3.02   0.003   -.3011505    -.063331
      mitsui |    -.11536   .0254198   -4.54   0.000   -.1654167   -.0653033
       kline |  -.1212952   .0245088   -4.95   0.000   -.1695579   -.0730325
      wanhai |  -.1638587   .0291357   -5.62   0.000   -.2212327   -.1064847
    yangming |   .1202095   .0296833    4.05   0.000    .0617571    .1786619
       _cons |   .7752386   .0500582   15.49   0.000     .676664    .8738133
----------------------------------------------------------------------------
```

As hypothesized, the effect of rating is positive. Since the rating hypothesis is one sided, the p value has to be divided by two. Therefore, the positive effect of rating on the per diem rate is statistically significant at the 5% level. The rating data was collected from several sources, but Bloomberg, Reuters, and MCR data were the main sources. The rating data is converted to the scale of MRC and Dynamar: 1 (best rating) to 10 (worst rating). For the regression analysis, only leasing contract data with a rating between 1 and 6 is selected because the top 25 shipping lines (with rating 1 to 6) analyzed in this chapter are in this category. A rating increase of one point is associated with a 1.4 cent higher per diem rate. Taking into account that the average per diem rate is 75 cents, this would be a rating increase of one point, which would increase the per diem rate by 1.9%. This also signals an absolute but not very high significance, because a 5-point higher rating is associated with about 10% higher leasing costs.

The formula used to estimate the per diem rate (L_t) is as follows:

perdiem = 0.775 + 0.014*rating + year coefficient + firm coefficient   Equation 4-2

The market per diem, purchase price and terminal value are obtained from Foxcroft (2008). Since the terminal/residual value is only available from 1995, the value for 1994 is estimated. The estimate is calculated by multiplying the average residual in percent of new container price in the period 1995 to 2008 (44%) by the new container price in 1994.

The after-tax costs of debt are calculated using the published interest expenses (Reuters, 2009a) divided by the debt amount (Reuters, 2009b) and multiplied with one minus the calculated tax rate in each year. The tax rate is calculated as a gliding four-year average (Reuters, 2009b). If the calculated four-year average tax rate is negative, a zero tax rate is assumed. This tax rate is also used to calculate the after tax-leasing payments, the tax shield of depreciation and the after-tax residual value.

In an alternative NAL calculation scenario, the WACC is used as a discount rate (variable name: nalwacc). The WACC is calculated as follows (R. A. Brealey & Myers, 1991, p. 408):

$$\text{WACC} = \frac{D}{D+E} * r_d(1-T) + \frac{E}{D+E} * r_e \qquad\qquad \textbf{Equation 4-3}$$

with $r_e = r_f + \beta * r_m$ \qquad\qquad **Equation 4-4**

Where:

WACC	= weighted average cost of capital
D	= debt amount [currency]
E	= equity amount (share price * number of shares) [currency]
r_d	= cost of corporate debt before taxes [%]
T	= corporate tax rate [%]
r_e	= required or expected rate of return on equity [%]
r_f	= risk free rate (government bond rate) [%]
β	= Beta coefficient [-]
r_m	= market return rate (marketwide stock index) [%]

A risk-free rate of 3% and a market rate of 15% is assumed. Since not all analyzed companies are listed, the beta coefficient is not completely known. To simplify the analysis, a beta of one is assumed for all shipping lines to calculate the WACC.

The indicator used for easily obtainable and low cost debt (variable name: spread) is the spread of BAA bonds (FED, 2010b) over five-year government bonds (FED, 2010a). Both are taken from the U.S. Federal Reserve webpage (http://www.federalreserve.gov/releases/h15/data.htm).

For inflation, the U.S. GDP deflator (BEA, 2009) published by the U.S. Bureau of Economic Analysis (variable name: inflation) is used. The U.S. CPI deflator (BLS, 2009) leads to similar results. The U.S. inflation is preferred because most international shipping business is denominated in USD.

4.1.2.3 Container demand

World GDP and world trade growth figures are obtained from the World Economic Outlook (IMF, 2009). The seatrade volume as well as the container handling volume was obtained from the Institute of Shipping Economics and Logistics in Bremen (ISL, 2008) based on Farnley Review 2008 and ISL expectations. The container slot development source was provided by the ISL (2009).

To improve measurement, avoid collinearity and to save degrees of freedom, one indicator (variable name: demand) is constructed:

demand = (gdp + trade + seatrade + handling + slots)/5   **Equation 4-5**

Where:

demand	= indicator for container demand as calculated above [%]
gdp	= world GDP growth [%]
trade	= world trade growth [%]
seatrade	= world sea trade growth [%]
handling	= container handling growth [%]
slots	= container slot growth [%]

4.1.2.4 Industry prices

The bunker price (variable name: bunkerprice) source is the ISL (2009). The yearly average bunker prices in Hamburg - Le Havre are used.

As an indicator for the ship charter rate, the HARPEX (variable name: harpex) is used (Harper, 2009). A HARPEX value of 1000 signals that all financing and operating costs can be paid by the charter.

Two indicators are used for freight rates. First, the Baltic Dry Index (variable name: balticdry) data were found on Bloomberg (2010). The Baltic Dry Index measures shipping costs for raw materials. Second, the U.S. Transportation Index (TSI) is published on the website of the U.S. Department of Transportation (DoT, 2009). The TSI (variable name: ustransport) is the broadest monthly measure of U.S. domestic transportation services. As this analysis focuses on freight, the passenger transportation part of the index is not taken into account. The two indicators are not combined in one index because of the differences regarding region and measured service scope. Their correlation is only 31%.

Ship prices (variable name: shipprice) are obtained from the ISL (2008, p. 98). The Containershipsize Panamax (3500 TEU) measured in Mio USD at the end of each calendar year is used as a reference price.

A container shipping stock index is developed as an indicator for stock prices (variable name: stockindex). All available stock prices of container shipping firms were used (Reuters, 2009c). The index starts in 1993 with a value of 100. The average stock price change in percentages in each year is calculated and deployed on the previous index figure to generate the following index value.

4.1.2.5 Firm-specific data

The establishment year (variable name: established) of each shipping line is obtained from Dynamar (2007).

The source of the rating information (variable name: rating) is described previously in the NAL section.

83

Firm size is measured by revenues, assets and ship capacity. Revenues and assets are obtained from Thomson Reuters (2009a, 2009b). The ship capacity is provided by ISL (2009). One index is created to improve measurement: For each revenue, total assets and ship capacity (the percentage of the highest value in the respective year) are calculated. The index is the simple average of the three percentages. The largest firm has an index value (variable name: size) of 100 in the year 2008 (Maersk) whereas the smallest company has an index value of 3.75 (Wan Hai).

The net income (variable name: netincome) is received from Thomson Reuters (2009a) as well.

The tax rate (variable name: taxrate or taxmean, using a four-year gliding average) is calculated based on pretax and net income figures provided by Thomson Reuters (2009a).

The debt to assets ratio (variable name: debtshare) is calculated based on Thomson Reuters (2009b) data.

The percent of ships chartered (variable name: chartershare) is provided by ISL (2009) based on the MDS Transmodal Containerdatabase.

To limit autocorrelation, the share of leased containers in the previous year (variable name: leasedprev) is used as a control variable. In a second approach, a change in change model is used to prevent autocorrelation.

A dummy variable called merger is used to signal the year after a merger when the container capacities are combined and therefore the share of leased equipment is changed.

Fixed effect dummy variables for every year except one (variable names: dy1994 to dy2007) and every firm except one (variable names: df1 to df14) are introduced.

4.1.3 Sample statistics and simple correlations

The following Stata table summarizes the variables, their means, standard deviations and minimum as well as maximum values. All variables are defined as nominal values (with the exception of the variables inflation and demand, which are defined as percent change from previous period).

Table 4-3 Sample statistics of panel data (share of leased containers)

. sum

Variable	Obs	Mean	Std. Dev.	Min	Max
firmnumber	225	8	4.330127	1	15
year	225	2001	4.330127	1994	2008
leasedshare	220	35.75273	20.63453	0	97.4
naldebt	197	-333.844	423.2227	-1371.34	868.49
nalwacc	197	150.745	352.5603	-827.74	1202.31
spread	225	2.562667	.918839	1.65	4.64
inflation	225	2.696	.6219296	1.56	3.84
demand	225	7.507333	1.489564	3.43	9.22
bunkerprice	225	188.8653	121.3407	76.38	509.5
harpex	225	1016.627	344.6518	515.13	1928.97
balticdry	225	2581.667	2101.886	709	8756
ustransport	225	101.54	7.487204	86.5	111.2
shipprice	225	48.09267	8.171744	34.5	63
stockindex	225	130.2053	80.7652	42.51	297.42
established	225	1925.467	49.09748	1847	1997
rating	225	3.269778	.8331162	1	6
size	217	28.04627	23.18364	1.4	100
netincome	203	279.9749	638.8654	-1233.73	4690
taxrate	197	20.33437	33.64007	-190.62	108.46
taxmean	201	23.04075	18.74687	0	67.13
debtshare	197	54.02015	19.18453	18.18	100
chartershare	217	38.08682	23.7834	0	99.41
leasedprev	210	35.12952	20.55496	0	97.3
merger	225	.0311111	.1740051	0	1
df1	225	.0666667	.25	0	1
df2	225	.0666667	.25	0	1
df3	225	.0666667	.25	0	1
df4	225	.0666667	.25	0	1
df5	225	.0666667	.25	0	1
df6	225	.0666667	.25	0	1
df7	225	.0666667	.25	0	1
df8	225	.0666667	.25	0	1
df9	225	.0666667	.25	0	1
df10	225	.0666667	.25	0	1
df11	225	.0666667	.25	0	1
df12	225	.0666667	.25	0	1
df13	225	.0666667	.25	0	1
df14	225	.0666667	.25	0	1
dy1994	225	.0666667	.25	0	1
dy1995	225	.0666667	.25	0	1
dy1996	225	.0666667	.25	0	1
dy1997	225	.0666667	.25	0	1
dy1998	225	.0666667	.25	0	1
dy1999	225	.0666667	.25	0	1
dy2000	225	.0666667	.25	0	1
dy2001	225	.0666667	.25	0	1
dy2002	225	.0666667	.25	0	1
dy2003	225	.0666667	.25	0	1
dy2004	225	.0666667	.25	0	1
dy2005	225	.0666667	.25	0	1
dy2006	225	.0666667	.25	0	1
dy2007	225	.0666667	.25	0	1

The share of lease containers varies between zero and 97.4%. There are only a few instances with zero percent leased. The mean is 36%, and the standard deviation 21%, which signals that the leasing strategy varies significantly between the top 25 shipping lines.

The NALdebt is on average -334 and varies between -371 and 868. The NALwacc is higher (average 151, varies between -828 and 1202). Using the NALwacc leads to more leasing compared with NALdebt.

The Stata correlation matrix regarding the main variables is provided in the next table. It shows the correlation between two variables without taking into account the simultaneous effect of other variables.

Table 4-4 Correlation matrix (share of leased containers)

```
. corr  leasedshare naldebt nalwacc spread inflation demand bunkerprice harpex balticdry ustransport ship-
price s
> tockindex established rating size netincome taxrate debtshare chartershare
(obs=197)

             | leased~e  naldebt  nalwacc   spread inflat~n   demand bunker~e   harpex baltic~y ustran~t
-------------+--------------------------------------------------------------------------------------------
 leasedshare |  1.0000
     naldebt | -0.1436   1.0000
     nalwacc | -0.0845   0.7694   1.0000
      spread |  0.0912  -0.0256  -0.0295   1.0000
   inflation |  0.0869   0.1269   0.4252   0.0075   1.0000
      demand |  0.0456  -0.0826   0.0025  -0.5486  -0.0342   1.0000
 bunkerprice |  0.1719   0.0513   0.3865   0.3323   0.6781  -0.0030   1.0000
      harpex |  0.1003  -0.0990   0.0450  -0.3452   0.0860   0.7102  -0.0228   1.0000
   balticdry |  0.1669   0.0453   0.3955   0.4128   0.6587  -0.0701   0.8591   0.1782   1.0000
 ustransport |  0.2029  -0.2052  -0.1049   0.1589   0.0001   0.2313   0.3995   0.3762   0.2982   1.0000
   shipprice |  0.0936   0.1051   0.4743  -0.2503   0.4388   0.5030   0.4388   0.4116   0.6586   0.0649
  stockindex |  0.1957  -0.0461   0.2597  -0.1304   0.3925   0.5030   0.6316   0.6336   0.5252   0.6610
 established | -0.2324  -0.4023  -0.2789   0.0381   0.0299   0.0139   0.0727   0.0240   0.0629   0.0902
      rating | -0.0019   0.1510   0.0701   0.0460   0.0460   0.0099   0.0287  -0.0150   0.0735  -0.1651
        size | -0.1177   0.3511   0.2386  -0.0082  -0.0707  -0.0406  -0.1117  -0.0195  -0.0769  -0.0844
   netincome |  0.0586  -0.0352   0.1802   0.0447   0.2050   0.1323   0.3082   0.2811   0.3469   0.3068
     taxrate | -0.2000   0.0428   0.1056  -0.1246  -0.0130   0.0610  -0.0622   0.0206  -0.0629  -0.1015
   debtshare | -0.3233   0.0490  -0.4222   0.0377  -0.2168  -0.1142  -0.2772  -0.1750  -0.2761  -0.1669
chartershare |  0.5193   0.0871   0.1840   0.2527   0.1923  -0.0196   0.3880   0.0840   0.3295   0.4306

             | shippr~e stocki~x establ~d   rating     size netinc~e  taxrate debtsh~e charte~e
-------------+---------------------------------------------------------------------------------
   shipprice |  1.0000
  stockindex |  0.7188   1.0000
 established |  0.0274   0.0693   1.0000
      rating |  0.1089  -0.0525   0.0660   1.0000
        size | -0.0730  -0.1002  -0.5005  -0.2227   1.0000
   netincome |  0.2847   0.3835  -0.0630  -0.2351   0.4665   1.0000
     taxrate |  0.0305  -0.0337  -0.1078  -0.0547   0.3073   0.1515   1.0000
   debtshare | -0.3047  -0.3144  -0.1212   0.1621   0.2054  -0.2384   0.1283   1.0000
chartershare |  0.1153   0.3448  -0.1412   0.1689  -0.0919   0.1391  -0.1007  -0.3285   1.0000
```

The share of leasing is negatively correlated with nalwacc and naldebt, which is opposite expectations. In addition, the following variables have a correlation with lease share opposite to the hypothesis: spread, bunkerprice, stockindex, rating, netincome and chartershare.

The following variables show the expected correlation with lease share: harpex, baltidry, ustransport, established, size, taxrate and debtshare. Demand and shipprice show a positive correlation, whereas the hypothesis is two- sided. The correlations have to be confirmed by the regression analysis, which shows the joint impact of the variables.

The result of a Stata multi-collinearity test is shown in the next table.

Table 4-5 VIF test (share of leased containers)

```
. vif

    Variable |       VIF       1/VIF
-------------+----------------------
 bunkerprice |    231.72    0.004316
   shipprice |    105.47    0.009482
      harpex |     88.32    0.011323
  stockindex |     84.52    0.011832
   balticdry |     78.38    0.012759
 ustransport |     38.07    0.026271
      spread |     35.38    0.028262
      demand |     20.02    0.049951
 established |     19.45    0.051421
        size |     17.96    0.055677
   inflation |     16.61    0.060208
        df10 |     10.07    0.099339
         df4 |      8.14    0.122877
 chartershare |      7.39    0.135260
  leasedprev |      6.90    0.144948
      dy2003 |      5.57    0.179620
         df1 |      5.24    0.190967
        df12 |      5.08    0.197026
     naldebt |      4.99    0.200269
         df8 |      4.91    0.203690
         df6 |      3.93    0.254283
   debtshare |      3.79    0.264183
         df9 |      3.68    0.272018
   netincome |      3.36    0.297717
        df14 |      2.96    0.337359
         df2 |      2.69    0.372060
      dy2005 |      2.57    0.389673
        df11 |      2.54    0.394169
        df13 |      2.13    0.469644
         df5 |      2.04    0.490204
      rating |      1.98    0.505328
         df3 |      1.93    0.518501
      dy1996 |      1.71    0.584289
      dy1999 |      1.68    0.595543
     taxrate |      1.59    0.629432
      merger |      1.39    0.720299
-------------+----------------------
    Mean VIF |     23.17
```

The VIF is above 10 for several variables. This indicates multi-collinearity, which can lead to statistical insignificance. If important variables nevertheless show statistical significance, this is not problematic. To improve the significance of some variables, further indices could be constructed.

To check the functional form, Stata scatter plots for the relationship between the lease share and each independent variable are provided below.

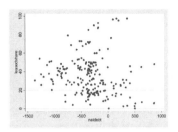

Figure 4-2 Scatter plot: leasedshare and naldebt

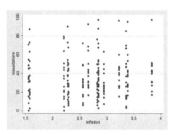

Figure 4-5 Scatter plot: leasedshare and inflation

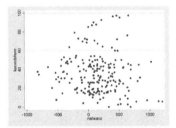

Figure 4-3 Scatter plot: leasedshare and nalwacc

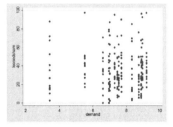

Figure 4-6 Scatter plot: leasedshare and demand

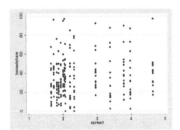

Figure 4-4 Scatter plot: leasedshare and spread

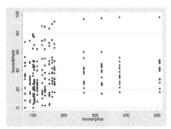

Figure 4-7 Scatter plot: leasedshare and bunkerprice

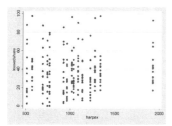

Figure 4-8 Scatter plot: leasedshare and harpex

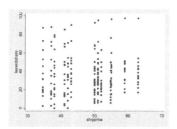

Figure 4-11 Scatter plot: leasedshare and shipprice

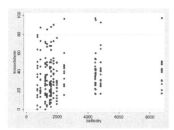

Figure 4-9 Scatter plot: leasedshare and balticdry

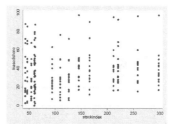

Figure 4-12 Scatter plot: leasedshare and stockindex

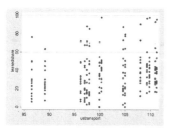

Figure 4-10 Scatter plot: leasedshare and ustransport

Figure 4-13 Scatter plot: leasedshare and establishment year

89

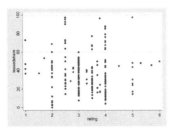

Figure 4-14 Scatter plot: leasedshare and rating

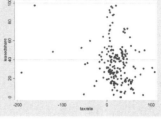

Figure 4-17 Scatter plot: leasedshare and taxrate

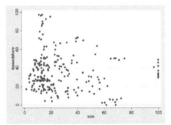

Figure 4-15 Scatter plot: leasedshare and size

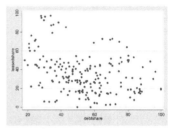

Figure 4-18 Scatter plot: leasedshare and debtshare

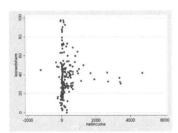

Figure 4-16 Scatter plot: leasedshare and netincome

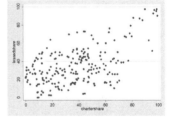

Figure 4-19 Scatter plot: leasedshare and chartershare

Because Figures 4-2 to 4-19 either show a linear or unclear relationship between leasedshare and the other independent variables, a linear model seems appropriate. Therefore a linear OLS regression model will be used for parameter estimation.

4.1.4 Regression model

A panel regression analysis is used to find the variables that have a statistical significant impact on the dependent variable. The dependent variable (share of leased containers) varied between 0 and 97% from 1994 to 2008. Only a few values of zero are included in the dataset.

Sharpe and Nguyen (1995) and many other authors use a Tobit regression model to analyze the buy or lease decision because their data include many zeros (i.e., firms that do not lease). This is not the case here. Because the share of leased containers is rather normally distributed (see Figure 4-20 below), an ordinary least square model (OLS) is applied for the panel regression.

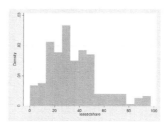

Figure 4-20 Histogram: Panel, share of lease containers

The regression equation is

leasedshare $= \alpha + \beta_1$naldebt $+ \beta_2$spread $+ \beta_3$inflation $+ \beta_4$demand $+$
$\beta_5$bunkerprice $+ \beta_6$harpex $+ \beta_7$balticdry $+ \beta_8$ustransport $+ \beta_9$shipprice $+$
β_{10}stockindex $+ \beta_{11}$established $+ \beta_{12}$rating $+ \beta_{13}$size $+ \beta_{14}$netincome $+$
β_{15}taxrate $+ \beta_{16}$debtshare $+ \beta_{17}$chartershare $+ \beta_{18}$leasedprev $+ \beta_{19}$merger $+$
$\sum_{i=1994}^{2007} \gamma_i$ dyi $+ \sum_{j=1}^{14} \delta_j$ dfj $+ \varepsilon$

Equation 4-6

Where:

leasedshare	= share of leased containers [%]
α	= constant [-]
β_i	= coefficients of independent variables [-]
naldebt	= NPV advantage of leasing [USD]
spread	= spread of Baa bonds over treasuries [%]
inflation	= inflation rate [%]
demand	= index of several container demand variables [%]
bunkerprice	= average bunker price [USD]
harpex	= harpex index [-]
balticdry	= Baltic Dry Index [-]

ustransport	= U.S. Transportation Index [-]
shipprice	= average ship price [USD millions]
stockindex	= shipping lines stock index [-]
established	= establishment year [-]
rating	= rating of the shipping lines [-]
size	= index of several variables for the size of the shipping line [-]
netincome	= net income of the shipping lines [USD millions]
taxrate	= tax rate of the shipping line [%]
debtshare	= share of debt on total assets [%]
chartershare	= share of chartered ships based on TEU capacity [%]
leasedprev	= share of leased equipment in previ
merger	= dummy variable – equals one in year after merger [-]
γ_i	= coefficients of year fixed dummy variables [-]
dyi	= year fixed dummy variables [-]
δ_j	= coefficients of firm fixed dummy variables [-]
dfj	= fixed dummy variables [-]
ε	= error term [-]

4.1.5 Model estimates

The first table shows the Stata OLS regression results using naldebt as an independent variable and no correction for heteroskedasticity. Several year dummies were omitted by Stata because of collinearity. This might be the case because several macroeconomic and industry figures are the same for all companies.

Table 4-6 OLS regression result (panel, share of leased container, non robust)

```
. reg leasedshare naldebt spread inflation demand bunkerprice harpex balticdry us-
transport shipprice stockindex established rating size netincome  taxrate debtshare
chartershare leasedprev merger df1 df2 df3 df4 df5 df6 df7 df8 df9 df10 df11 df12
df13 df14 dy1994 dy1995 dy1996 dy1997 dy1998 dy1999 dy2000 dy2001 dy2002 dy2003
dy2004 dy2005 dy2006 dy2007
note: df7 omitted because of collinearity
note: dy1994 omitted because of collinearity
note: dy1995 omitted because of collinearity
note: dy1997 omitted because of collinearity
note: dy1998 omitted because of collinearity
note: dy2000 omitted because of collinearity
note: dy2001 omitted because of collinearity
note: dy2002 omitted because of collinearity
note: dy2004 omitted because of collinearity
note: dy2006 omitted because of collinearity
note: dy2007 omitted because of collinearity
```

```
      Source |       SS           df       MS              Number of obs =     187
-------------+------------------------------              F( 36,   150) =   54.62
       Model |  76267.1804        36   2118.53279         Prob > F      =  0.0000
    Residual |  5818.04552       150   38.7869701         R-squared     =  0.9291
-------------+------------------------------              Adj R-squared =  0.9121
       Total |  82085.2259       186   441.318419         Root MSE      =  6.2279


  leasedshare |      Coef.   Std. Err.      t    P>|t|     [95% Conf. Interval]
-------------+----------------------------------------------------------------
      naldebt |   .0026867   .0024131     1.11   0.267    -.0020814    .0074548
       spread |  -2.802495   2.839451    -0.99   0.325    -8.412982    2.807992
    inflation |  -3.896296   2.869676    -1.36   0.177    -9.566503    1.773912
       demand |   1.949464   1.321131     1.48   0.142    -.6609652    4.559894
  bunkerprice |  -.0074304   .0551336    -0.13   0.893    -.1163692    .1015084
       harpex |   -.007546   .0116809    -0.65   0.519    -.0306262    .0155343
     balticdry |   .0042021   .0018218     2.31   0.022     .0006025    .0078018
   ustransport |  -.5383936   .3824671    -1.41   0.161    -1.294112    .2173252
     shipprice |  -1.085003   .5495849    -1.97   0.050    -2.170931    .0009249
    stockindex |   .0817895   .0491675     1.66   0.098    -.0153608    .1789398
   established |   .0625564   .0412688     1.52   0.132    -.0189868    .1440997
       rating |   .8644919   .7476986     1.16   0.249    -.6128899    2.341874
         size |   -.007388   .0872369    -0.08   0.933    -.1797599    .1649839
    netincome |  -.0017767   .0012639    -1.41   0.162    -.0042741    .0007206
      taxrate |  -.0081431   .0169487    -0.48   0.632     -.041632    .0253459
    debtshare |    .000512    .047196     0.01   0.991    -.0927429    .0937669
 chartershare |   .0378094   .0536943     0.70   0.482    -.0682854    .1439042
   leasedprev |   .7774074   .0569453    13.65   0.000     .6648889     .889926
       merger |   10.48465   3.045037     3.44   0.001     4.467942    16.50135
          df1 |   6.594608   3.960019     1.67   0.098    -1.230014    14.41923
          df2 |  -13.35397   4.236841    -3.15   0.002    -21.72556   -4.982372
          df3 |     .78852   3.331991     0.24   0.813    -5.795178    7.372218
          df4 |   11.65895   4.936756     2.36   0.019     1.904388    21.41351
          df5 |  -.4965393   2.471658    -0.20   0.841    -5.380301    4.387223
          df6 |  -5.381979   3.431767    -1.57   0.119    -12.16283    1.398868
          df7 |  (omitted)
          df8 |  -6.999307   3.967643    -1.76   0.080    -14.83899    .8403809
          df9 |  -6.053828   3.318012    -1.82   0.070    -12.60991    .5022502
         df10 |   .7439215   7.140575     0.10   0.917    -13.36518    14.85302
         df11 |   2.698078   2.730358     0.99   0.322    -2.718228    8.144379
         df12 |   7.974469   3.898653     2.05   0.043     .2710997    15.67784
         df13 |  -4.388491   2.525179    -1.74   0.084    -9.378005    .6010228
         df14 |  -6.037948   3.082984    -1.96   0.052    -12.12963     .053737
      dy1994 |  (omitted)
      dy1995 |  (omitted)
      dy1996 |   2.894019   2.431309     1.19   0.236    -1.910016    7.698055
      dy1997 |  (omitted)
      dy1998 |  (omitted)
      dy1999 |   1.307934   2.408227     0.54   0.588    -3.450495    6.066362
      dy2000 |  (omitted)
      dy2001 |  (omitted)
      dy2002 |  (omitted)
      dy2003 |    6.26977   3.956186     1.58   0.115    -1.547279    14.08682
      dy2004 |  (omitted)
      dy2005 |  -.8965278   2.685987    -0.33   0.739    -6.203783    4.410728
      dy2006 |  (omitted)
      dy2007 |  (omitted)
        _cons |   -17.8251    106.211    -0.17   0.867    -227.6879    192.0377
-------------+----------------------------------------------------------------
```

Using the Stata function XTREG (with the option fe [firm dummies] and year dummies) delivers the same result with exception of the constant term. The constant might be different because a different firm is chosen as a reference.

Besides year and firm dummies, only the variables balticdry, shipprice, leasedprev and merger show statistical significance at the 5% level. The impact of balticdry is in the expected direction. A one point higher Baltic Dry index is associated with a 0.004 percentage point higher lease share. In other words, a 1000 index points higher Baltic Dry index (which is in the data range) is associated with a 4 percentage point higher lease share. A 1 million USD higher ship price of is associated with a 1.1 percentage point lower lease share. The lease share in the previous year as well as a merger in the previous year shows a statistically significant positive effect on the lease share. A 1 percentage point higher lease share in the previous period explains a 0.8 percentage point higher lease share. A merger has a positive impact of 10.5 percentage points on the lease share. Both effects are of absolute importance. The positive impact of a merger on the lease share can be explained by reducing the lease share with the size of a shipping line. The purchasing firm has on average a lower lease share than the buying entity. The merged equipment therefore has a higher lease share than the buying firm before the merger.

All other variables do not show statistical significance. The F-test shows high significance (p=0%) that not all coefficients equal zero. Furthermore, the adjusted R square is very high (91%), signaling a very good fit of the model. One reason for the statistical insignificance of many variables might be heteroscedasticity.

Next, a robust regression with heteroscedastically consistent robust standard errors is performed.

Table 4-7 OLS regression result (panel, share of leased container, robust)

```
. reg leasedshare naldebt spread inflation demand bunkerprice harpex balticdry us-
transport shipprice stockindex established rating size netincome  taxrate debtshare
chartershare leasedprev merger df1 df2 df3 df4 df5 df6 df7 df8 df9 df10 df11 df12
df13 df14 dy1994 dy1995 dy1996 dy1997 dy1998 dy1999 dy2000 dy2001 dy2002 dy2003
dy2004 dy2005 dy2006 dy2007, robust
note: df7 omitted because of collinearity
note: dy1994 omitted because of collinearity
note: dy1995 omitted because of collinearity
note: dy1997 omitted because of collinearity
note: dy1998 omitted because of collinearity
note: dy2000 omitted because of collinearity
note: dy2001 omitted because of collinearity
note: dy2002 omitted because of collinearity
note: dy2004 omitted because of collinearity
note: dy2006 omitted because of collinearity
note: dy2007 omitted because of collinearity

Linear regression                              Number of obs =      187
                                               F( 36,   150) =   101.93
                                               Prob > F      =   0.0000
                                               R-squared     =   0.9291
                                               Root MSE      =   6.2279

-----------------------------------------------------------------------------
```

leasedshare	Coef.	Robust Std. Err.	t	P>|t|	[95% Conf. Interval]	
naldebt	.0026867	.0020875	1.29	0.200	-.0014379	.0068113
spread	-2.802495	3.153401	-0.89	0.376	-9.033316	3.428326
inflation	-3.896296	3.141499	-1.24	0.217	-10.1036	2.311009
demand	1.949464	1.421814	1.37	0.172	-.8599054	4.758834
bunkerprice	-.0074304	.0520525	-0.14	0.887	-.1102811	.0954204
harpex	-.007546	.0109273	-0.69	0.491	-.0291372	.0140453
balticdry	.0042021	.0019873	2.11	0.036	.0002754	.0081288
ustransport	-.5383936	.396988	-1.36	0.177	-1.322804	.2460171
shipprice	-1.085003	.5993515	-1.81	0.072	-2.269265	.0992591
stockindex	.0817895	.046407	1.76	0.080	-.0099063	.1734853
established	.0625564	.0370407	1.69	0.093	-.0106325	.1357454
rating	.8644919	.5628338	1.54	0.127	-.2476145	1.976598
size	-.007388	.0834945	-0.09	0.930	-.1723652	.1575892
netincome	-.0017767	.0011738	-1.51	0.132	-.004096	.0005426
taxrate	-.0081431	.017079	-0.48	0.634	-.0418895	.0256034
debtshare	.000512	.0443637	0.01	0.991	-.0871464	.0881704
chartershare	.0378094	.0544161	0.69	0.488	-.0697116	.1453304
leasedprev	.7774074	.0629328	12.35	0.000	.6530583	.9017566
merger	10.48465	5.026729	2.09	0.039	.5523045	20.41699
df1	6.594608	3.846734	1.71	0.089	-1.006174	14.19539
df2	-13.35397	3.622194	-3.69	0.000	-20.51108	-6.196855
df3	.78852	2.407674	0.33	0.744	-3.968816	5.545856
df4	11.65895	4.25824	2.74	0.007	3.245072	20.07283
df5	-.4965393	2.354946	-0.21	0.833	-5.149689	4.156611
df6	-5.381979	3.224796	-1.67	0.097	-11.75387	.9899119
df7	(omitted)					
df8	-6.999307	3.707822	-1.89	0.061	-14.32561	.3269979
df9	-6.053828	3.162991	-1.91	0.058	-12.3036	.1959437
df10	.7439215	6.390511	0.12	0.907	-11.88312	13.37097
df11	2.698076	2.637416	1.02	0.308	-2.513208	7.909359
df12	7.974469	4.073765	1.96	0.052	-.074906	16.02384
df13	-4.388491	2.139558	-2.05	0.042	-8.616055	-.1609275
df14	-6.037948	3.033229	-1.99	0.048	-12.03132	-.0445741
dy1994	(omitted)					
dy1995	(omitted)					
dy1996	2.894019	2.82714	1.02	0.308	-2.692141	8.48018
dy1997	(omitted)					
dy1998	(omitted)					
dy1999	1.307934	2.217885	0.59	0.556	-3.074397	5.690264
dy2000	(omitted)					
dy2001	(omitted)					
dy2002	(omitted)					
dy2003	6.26977	3.758553	1.67	0.097	-1.156775	13.69632
dy2004	(omitted)					
dy2005	-.8965278	2.247672	-0.40	0.691	-5.337715	3.54466
dy2006	(omitted)					
dy2007	(omitted)					
_cons	-17.8251	99.79639	-0.18	0.858	-215.0133	179.3631

Naldebt is now significant on the 10% level. The direction of the effect is positive as expected. A one USD higher naldebt is associated with a 0.003 percentage point higher leaseshare. The absolute importance is limited because a realistic 1000 USD higher naldebt increases the leaseshare only by about 3 percentage points. Baltic Dry index, leasedprev and merger are significant on the 5% level as above.

In addition, the establishment year has a statistically significant positive impact on the 5% level. Each year a company is established later is associated with a 0.06 percentage point higher lease share. Furthermore, the rating has a statistically significant positive effect (6% level) on the leaseshare. The direction of the effect is as expected. A one-point increase in rating is associated with an increase of 0.9 percentage points on leaseshare. This effect has a low absolute significance because an increase of 5 rating points only leads to 4.5 percentage points more leasing. The shipprice is now only significant on the 7% level. The impact is negative and in the same range as described above. No other variables show statistical significance at the 5% level.

The F test is significant (p=0%) using robust standard errors. This means that the null hypothesis (all coefficients are zero) can be rejected at the 1% level. The adjusted R square improved to 93%.

Next, the same analysis is performed with the dependent variable nalwacc instead of naldebt.

Table 4-8 OLS regression result (panel, share of leased, NALWACC, robust)

```
. reg  leasedshare nalwacc spread inflation demand bunkerprice harpex balticdry us-
transport shipprice stockindex established rating size netincome taxrate debtshare
chartershare leasedprev merger df1 df2 df3 df4 df5 df6 df7 df8 df9 df10 df11 df12
df13 df14 dy1994 dy1995 dy1996 dy1997 dy1998 dy1999 dy2000 dy2001 dy2002 dy2003
dy2004 dy2005 dy2006 dy2007, robust
```

Linear regression

Number of obs =	187
F(36, 150) =	95.04
Prob > F =	0.0000
R-squared =	0.9295
Root MSE =	6.2126

leasedshare	Coef.	Robust Std. Err.	t	P>|t|	[95% Conf. Interval]	
nalwacc	.0064017	.0037669	1.70	0.091	-.0010413	.0138447
spread	-2.921754	3.128177	-0.93	0.352	-9.102735	3.259227
inflation	-4.198281	3.118831	-1.35	0.180	-10.3608	1.964234
demand	1.671557	1.39344	1.20	0.232	-1.081748	4.424861
bunkerprice	-.0004878	.0513205	-0.01	0.992	-.1018922	.1009166
harpex	-.0049046	.0109412	-0.45	0.655	-.0265233	.0167141
balticdry	.0037296	.0019657	1.90	0.060	-.0001544	.0076135
ustransport	-.4310897	.3959458	-1.09	0.278	-1.213441	.3512617
shipprice	-1.050721	.5902658	-1.78	0.077	-2.21703	.1155883
stockindex	.0651157	.0478816	1.36	0.176	-.0294939	.1597253
established	.0794265	.0403004	1.97	0.051	-.0002033	.1590563
rating	.9576025	.5708506	1.68	0.096	-.1703443	2.085549
size	-.0196437	.0824384	-0.24	0.812	-.1825341	.1432468
netincome	-.0018747	.0011597	-1.62	0.108	-.0041661	.0004167
taxrate	-.0104603	.017582	-0.59	0.553	-.0452007	.0242802
debtshare	.049315	.0532155	0.93	0.356	-.0558338	.1544638
chartershare	.0398652	.0537862	0.74	0.460	-.0664113	.1461417
leasedprev	.7732549	.0622432	12.42	0.000	.6502682	.8962417
merger	10.34916	5.023933	2.06	0.041	.4223437	20.27598
df1	8.390473	4.209234	1.99	0.048	.073426	16.70752
df2	-14.28131	3.730969	-3.83	0.000	-21.65335	-6.909266
df3	1.048509	2.414289	0.43	0.665	-3.721898	5.818916
df4	13.43008	4.338827	3.10	0.002	4.856971	22.00319
df5	-.0887775	2.354955	-0.04	0.970	-4.741947	4.564392
df6	-5.794829	3.170711	-1.83	0.070	-12.05985	.4701967

```
     df7  |   (omitted)
     df8  |  -8.019306    3.819002    -2.10    0.037    -15.56529    -.4733193
     df9  |  -7.093367    3.289386    -2.16    0.033    -13.59288    -.593852
    df10  |   2.134172    6.406487     0.33    0.740    -10.52444    14.79278
    df11  |   3.100322    2.621269     1.18    0.239    -2.079057    8.279701
    df12  |   9.319282    4.283469     2.18    0.031     .8555534    17.78301
    df13  |  -4.704103    2.111864    -2.23    0.027    -8.876945    -.5312596
    df14  |  -7.534669    3.333556    -2.26    0.025    -14.12146    -.9478767
  dy1994  |   (omitted)
  dy1995  |   (omitted)
  dy1996  |   3.246127    2.864073     1.13    0.259     -2.41301    8.905264
  dy1997  |   (omitted)
  dy1998  |   (omitted)
  dy1999  |   1.625355     2.26427     0.72    0.474    -2.848628    6.099338
  dy2000  |   (omitted)
  dy2001  |   (omitted)
  dy2002  |   (omitted)
  dy2003  |   6.655408    3.748221     1.78    0.078    -.7507225    14.06154
  dy2004  |   (omitted)
  dy2005  |  -1.594268    2.287115    -0.70    0.487    -6.113391    2.924855
  dy2006  |   (omitted)
  dy2007  |   (omitted)
   _cons  |  -64.63769    106.0406    -0.61    0.543    -274.1638    144.8884
```

The independent variable nalwacc is statistically significant at the 5% level. A nalwacc increase of 1 USD is associated with a 0.006 percentage point higher lease share. In other words, a 1000 USD higher nalwacc (which is in the range of the observed nalwaccs) is associated with a 6 percentage point higher lease share. This absolute effect is also significant.

Interestingly, both the statistical significance and the coefficient level of the analysis with nalwacc are higher than the analysis with naldebt. Therefore it can be concluded that in practice nalwacc is more important than naldebt for the buy or lease decision regarding shipping containers.

As in the naldebt case, the independent variables balticdry, rating, established, netincome, leasedprev and merger are statistically significant, and the effects are in the hypothesized direction. The level of the coefficients is comparable to the naldebt case.

As many variables do not show significance, a Stata collinearity test is performed.

Table 4-9 VIF test result (panel, share of leased containers)

```
. vif

    Variable |       VIF       1/VIF
-------------+----------------------
 bunkerprice |    229.27    0.004362
   shipprice |    105.96    0.009437
  stockindex |     92.12    0.010855
      harpex |     89.79    0.011137
   balticdry |     81.34    0.012294
 ustransport |     41.48    0.024110
      spread |     35.20    0.028412
 established |     23.78    0.042050
      demand |     20.18    0.049544
        size |     18.42    0.054290
   inflation |     16.53    0.060505
     nalwacc |     12.21    0.081927
        df10 |     10.58    0.094531
         df4 |      8.71    0.114812
chartershare |      7.28    0.137299
   leasedprev |     6.93    0.144334
    debtshare |     6.50    0.153899
         df1 |      6.45    0.154943
        df12 |      5.89    0.169847
      dy2003 |      5.55    0.180249
         df8 |      5.21    0.192077
         df9 |      4.10    0.243877
        df14 |      3.88    0.257910
         df6 |      3.85    0.259600
   netincome |      3.36    0.298045
         df2 |      2.83    0.353731
      dy2005 |      2.67    0.373890
        df11 |      2.60    0.384634
        df13 |      2.16    0.462861
         df5 |      2.10    0.476381
      rating |      2.00    0.498867
         df3 |      1.89    0.529328
      dy1996 |      1.75    0.571457
      dy1999 |      1.72    0.582016
     taxrate |      1.59    0.627304
      merger |      1.39    0.718374
-------------+----------------------
    Mean VIF |     24.09
```

It is obvious that several price variables are collinear. The correlation matrix below shows that it makes sense to build an index to combine the variables bunkerprice, shipprice, stockprice and balticdry.

Table 4-10 Correlation matrix (panel, share of leased, priceindex)

```
. corr   bunkerprice shipprice stockindex balticdry(obs=225)

             | bunker~e shippr~e stocki~x baltic~y
-------------+------------------------------------
 bunkerprice |   1.0000
   shipprice |   0.6352   1.0000
  stockindex |   0.6418   0.7067   1.0000
   balticdry |   0.8631   0.6390   0.5450   1.0000
```

The variable priceindex is generated as an average of bunkerprice, shipprice, stockindex and balticdry/10. The balticdryindex is divided by 10 to put all variables in a similar datarange (average between 50 and 250). Because the hypotheses of the included variables are not identical, the hypothesis for the priceindex is two-sided.

Using the priceindex as an independent variable and dropping the variables bunkerprice, shipprice, stockindex and balticdry leads to the following Stata regression result.

Table 4-11 OLS regression result (panel, leaseshare, priceindex, robust)

```
. reg  leasedshare nalwacc  spread inflation demand harpex ustransport  priceindex
established rating size netincome taxrate debtshare chartershare leasedprev merger
df1 df2 df3 df4 df5 df6 df7 df8 df9 df10 df11 df12 df13 df14 dy1994 dy1995 dy1996
dy1997 dy1998 dy1999 dy2000 dy2001 dy2002 dy2003 dy2004 dy2005 dy2006 dy2007, ro-
bust
note: df7 omitted because of collinearity
note: dy1994 omitted because of collinearity
note: dy1995 omitted because of collinearity
note: dy1998 omitted because of collinearity
note: dy2001 omitted because of collinearity
note: dy2002 omitted because of collinearity
note: dy2004 omitted because of collinearity
note: dy2006 omitted because of collinearity
```

```
Linear regression                              Number of obs =      187
                                               F( 36,   150) =    95.04
                                               Prob > F      =   0.0000
                                               R-squared     =   0.9295
                                               Root MSE      =   6.2126
```

leasedshare	Coef.	Robust Std. Err.	t	P>|t|	[95% Conf. Interval]	
nalwacc	.0064017	.0037669	1.70	0.091	-.0010413	.0138447
spread	-.0491025	1.191614	-0.04	0.967	-2.403619	2.305414
inflation	-5.550659	2.838165	-1.96	0.052	-11.1586	.0572857
demand	-.0901287	.8195969	-0.11	0.913	-1.709575	1.529317
harpex	.0021927	.0022792	0.96	0.338	-.0023108	.0066963
ustransport	.0256517	.1527805	0.17	0.867	-.2762281	.3275314
priceindex	.03216	.0220981	1.46	0.148	-.0115037	.0758237
established	.0794265	.0403004	1.97	0.051	-.0002033	.1590563
rating	.9576025	.5708506	1.68	0.096	-.1703443	2.085549
size	-.0196437	.0824384	-0.24	0.812	-.1825341	.1432468
netincome	-.0018747	.0011597	-1.62	0.108	-.0041661	.0004167
taxrate	-.0104603	.017582	-0.59	0.553	-.0452007	.0242802
debtshare	.049315	.0532155	0.93	0.356	-.0558338	.1544638
chartershare	.0398652	.0537862	0.74	0.460	-.0664113	.1461417
leasedprev	.7732549	.0622432	12.42	0.000	.6502682	.8962417
merger	10.34916	5.023933	2.06	0.041	.4223437	20.27598
df1	8.390473	4.209234	1.99	0.048	.073426	16.70752
df2	-14.28131	3.730969	-3.83	0.000	-21.65335	-6.909266
df3	1.048509	2.414289	0.43	0.665	-3.721898	5.818916
df4	13.43008	4.338827	3.10	0.002	4.856971	22.00319
df5	-.0887775	2.354955	-0.04	0.970	-4.741947	4.564392
df6	-5.794829	3.170711	-1.83	0.070	-12.05985	.4701967
df7	(omitted)					
df8	-8.019306	3.819002	-2.10	0.037	-15.56529	-.4733193
df9	-7.093367	3.289386	-2.16	0.033	-13.59288	-.593852

```
df10   |    2.134172   6.406487    0.33   0.740   -10.52444    14.79278
df11   |    3.100322   2.621269    1.18   0.239   -2.079057    8.279701
df12   |    9.319282   4.283469    2.18   0.031    .8555534    17.78301
df13   |   -4.704103   2.111864   -2.23   0.027   -8.876945   -.5312596
df14   |   -7.534669   3.333556   -2.26   0.025   -14.12146   -.9478767
dy1994 |   (omitted)
dy1995 |   (omitted)
dy1996 |    2.262962   2.914203    0.78   0.439   -3.495227    8.021151
dy1997 |   -2.28542    2.304326   -0.99   0.323   -6.838551    2.267711
dy1998 |   (omitted)
dy1999 |    2.375692   2.556142    0.93   0.354   -2.675003    7.426388
dy2000 |    4.600963   4.002656    1.15   0.252   -3.307905    12.50983
dy2001 |   (omitted)
dy2002 |   (omitted)
dy2003 |    4.210793   1.701505    2.47   0.014    .8487808    7.572805
dy2004 |   (omitted)
dy2005 |    .364772    2.063236    0.18   0.860   -3.711987    4.441531
dy2006 |   (omitted)
dy2007 |   -4.203056   2.526355   -1.66   0.098   -9.194894    .7887814
 _cons |   -145.8342   87.34749   -1.67   0.097   -318.4245    26.75621
```

The result for nalwacc, established, rating, size, netincome, taxrate, debtshare, chartershare, leasedprev and merger is unchanged, but the variable inflation is now significant on the 5% level. A one percentage point higher inflation is associated with a 5.6 percentage point lower leaseshare.

The spread between BAA and government bonds as well as container demand, harpex, ustransport, the priceindex, the firmsize, the tax rate, debtshare and chartershare still do not show statistical significance.

The newly generated priceindex is not statistically significant (p=15%) even if the collinearity is reduced (mean vif reduced from 25 to 6). Interestingly, the taxrate is not statistically significant (p=55%). One reason for the insignificance of the taxrate might be that most of the lessors are independent firms that cannot use tax shields to reduce the tax burden of other segments of the group. Another reason could be that shipping lines operate on an international level, which offers them other possibilities to reduce taxes.

Debtshare also does not show statistical significance. Therefore, this analysis does neither provide support for the substitution nor the complement theory.

The chartershare is also not statistically significant. Therefore, there seems to be no connection between the buy or lease strategy for ships and containers.

The lease share in a period is strongly dependent on the lease share in the previous period as shown above by the relevance of the variable leasedprev. Unit root tests to measure this autocorrelation do not work without modification because the panel is unbalanced. China Shipping leased share data for the years 1994 to 1998 is missing. To perform the unit root test, it is assumed that China Shipping changed its leased share in the missing years according to the average leaseshare change of the other shipping lines in the panel. The following table shows the result of the unit root test.

Table 4-12 Unit root test results (leasedshare)

```
xtunitroot llc  leasedshare

Levin-Lin-Chu unit-root test for leasedshare
-------------------------------------------
Ho: Panels contain unit roots            Number of panels =      15
Ha: Panels are stationary                Number of periods =     15

AR parameter: Common                     Asymptotics: N/T -> 0
Panel means:  Included
Time trend:   Not included

ADF regressions: 1 lag
LR variance:      Bartlett kernel, 7.00 lags average (chosen by LLC)
----------------------------------------------------------------------------
                     Statistic       p-value
----------------------------------------------------------------------------
Unadjusted t         -4.1717
Adjusted t*          -0.0650         0.4741
----------------------------------------------------------------------------
```

With a probability of 47%, the null hypothesis (there are unit roots) cannot be rejected. Because of this high probability of autocorrelation, a change in change model is presented in the next section. This model type eliminates auto-correlation effects.

4.2 Impact on change in lease share

In this section a different approach based on the same data described previously will be used. The major difference is that the change of each variable between the actual and the previous period instead of the nominal value of the variable is used in the regression. This model type is called change in change. This model is chosen because it eliminates autocorrelation effects which were positively tested in the lease share case described in 4.1 (Greene, 2008; Johanston & DiNardo, 1997; Langbein & Felbinger, 2006).

4.2.1 Hypotheses

The hypotheses are similar to the ones stated in 4.1.1. For the regression analysis, the null hypothesis of all above mentioned independent variables is that they have no impact. The research (alternative) hypothesis regarding all variable changes is as described above.

4.2.2 Data and measurement issues

The data basis for the change in change approach is the same as in the lease share approach. The only difference is that as many variables as possible are defined as change from the previous period's value. The variables inflation and demand were already defined as percent changes. Furthermore, the establishment date of one firm is the same in all years. Therefore, these variables are kept as they were in the last section.

4.2.3 Sample statistics and simple correlations

The following table shows the Stata sample statistics.

Table 4-13 Sample statistics (panel, change in change)

```
. sum
```

Variable	Obs	Mean	Std. Dev.	Min	Max
firmnumber	210	8	4.330818	1	15
year	210	2001.5	4.040761	1995	2008
leasedshare	210	.8538095	7.508605	-20.4	43.4
naldebt	210	-2.635714	244.5355	-874.78	932.49
nalwacc	210	26.12757	212.2345	-827.74	692.34
spread	210	.1928571	.8497066	-.95	2.59
inflation	210	.0914286	.702397	-1.27	1.15
bunkerprice	210	29.83	42.88073	-29.25	129.41
harpex	210	-40.475	410.0503	-768.33	837.94
balticdry	210	538.7857	1581.513	-2047	4304
ustransport	210	.2928572	5.445352	-9.7	7.9
shipprice	210	.5678571	5.02207	-8	8.5
stockindex	210	1.358571	55.90912	-152.3	104.43
rating	210	4.61e-10	.672281	-3.5	3.5
size	210	-.3475238	7.80639	-44.86	31.27
netincome	210	35.64324	429.5385	-1541	4037
taxrate	210	-.168381	37.58654	-222.81	222.12
taxmean	210	-.1475714	6.408011	-24.79	37.17
debtshare	210	.6000953	13.76372	-39.59	96.7
chartershare	210	2.849238	9.982035	-26.48	75.54
demand	210	7.51	1.542056	3.43	9.22
established	210	1925.467	49.10531	1847	1997
merger	210	.0333333	.1799344	0	1
df1	210	.0666667	.2500399	0	1
df2	210	.0666667	.2500399	0	1
df3	210	.0666667	.2500399	0	1
df4	210	.0666667	.2500399	0	1
df5	210	.0666667	.2500399	0	1
df6	210	.0666667	.2500399	0	1
df7	210	.0666667	.2500399	0	1
df8	210	.0666667	.2500399	0	1
df9	210	.0666667	.2500399	0	1
df10	210	.0666667	.2500399	0	1
df11	210	.0666667	.2500399	0	1
df12	210	.0666667	.2500399	0	1

```
-------------+-------------------------------------------------------------
      df13 |        210     .0666667      .2500399            0            1
      df14 |        210     .0666667      .2500399            0            1
    dy1994 |        210            0             0            0            0
    dy1995 |        210     .0714286      .2581548            0            1
    dy1996 |        210     .0714286      .2581548            0            1
-------------+-------------------------------------------------------------
    dy1997 |        210     .0714286      .2581548            0            1
    dy1998 |        210     .0714286      .2581548            0            1
    dy1999 |        210     .0714286      .2581548            0            1
    dy2000 |        210     .0714286      .2581548            0            1
    dy2001 |        210     .0714286      .2581548            0            1
-------------+-------------------------------------------------------------
    dy2002 |        210     .0714286      .2581548            0            1
    dy2003 |        210     .0714286      .2581548            0            1
    dy2004 |        210     .0714286      .2581548            0            1
    dy2005 |        210     .0714286      .2581548            0            1
    dy2006 |        210     .0714286      .2581548            0            1
-------------+-------------------------------------------------------------
    dy2007 |        210     .0714286      .2581548            0            1
```

The share of leased containers changes in one year was between -20 and 43 percentage points in the period from 1995 to 2008.

The correlation matrix (next table) shows the correlation between two variables without taking into account the joint effect of other variables.

Table 4-14 Correlation matrix (panel, change in change)

```
. corr   leasedshare naldebt nalwacc spread inflation bunkerprice harpex balticdry ustransport shipprice
stockindex rating size netincome taxrate debtshare chartershare demand established merger
(obs=210)

             | leased~e  naldebt  nalwacc   spread inflat~n bunker~e    harpex baltic~y ustran~t shippr~e
-------------+------------------------------------------------------------------------------------------
 leasedshare |  1.0000
     naldebt |  0.1181   1.0000
     nalwacc |  0.0789   0.7974   1.0000
      spread |  0.0451   0.0723   0.0747   1.0000
   inflation |  0.0058   0.2600   0.4158  -0.0492   1.0000
 bunkerprice | -0.0544   0.2702   0.3973   0.2441   0.6126   1.0000
      harpex |  0.0854  -0.2315  -0.1670  -0.4831  -0.0683  -0.4025   1.0000
   balticdry |  0.0085   0.1302   0.3618   0.4273   0.3988   0.3844   0.1486   1.0000
  ustransport|  0.0805  -0.4005  -0.4551  -0.3324  -0.5506  -0.5337   0.3084  -0.4033   1.0000
   shipprice | -0.0378   0.0412   0.1652  -0.5036   0.3028   0.2280   0.6233   0.2310  -0.1556   1.0000
  stockindex |  0.0879  -0.1596  -0.1539  -0.6563  -0.1998  -0.4164   0.6815  -0.3654   0.4580   0.5879
      rating |  0.0146  -0.1225  -0.1092   0.1150  -0.0249   0.0531   0.0870   0.1867  -0.0785   0.0640
        size | -0.0523  -0.0169   0.0684   0.0595   0.0622   0.0140   0.0381   0.1289  -0.0461   0.0364
   netincome | -0.0671  -0.0706   0.0566  -0.1898  -0.0170  -0.1669   0.4470   0.2186   0.1620   0.3008
     taxrate | -0.0212   0.0266   0.1252  -0.0459  -0.0537  -0.0387   0.0528  -0.0242   0.0403  -0.0216
   debtshare | -0.0488  -0.3580  -0.4069   0.1130  -0.0637  -0.0229  -0.1567  -0.1205  -0.0185  -0.1454
 chartershare|  0.0208   0.0546   0.0993   0.0011   0.0069  -0.0985   0.0445  -0.0326  -0.0230  -0.0360
      demand | -0.0273  -0.0766  -0.0959  -0.6696   0.0721   0.0712   0.5725  -0.0637   0.0697   0.6505
 established | -0.0588  -0.0187   0.0293   0.0000   0.0000  -0.0000   0.0000   0.0000  -0.0000  -0.0000
      merger |  0.2618   0.0558   0.0252  -0.0282  -0.0193  -0.0069  -0.0370  -0.1424  -0.0442   0.0398
```

```
             | stocki~x   rating     size netinc~e  taxrate debtsh~e charte~e   demand establ~d   merger
-------------+---------------------------------------------------------------------------------------------
  stockindex |  1.0000
      rating | -0.0634   1.0000
        size | -0.0771  -0.0674   1.0000
   netincome |  0.2965   0.0259   0.0833   1.0000
     taxrate |  0.0088  -0.1308   0.0407   0.0523   1.0000
   debtshare | -0.1348   0.0492   0.0019  -0.2237  -0.0943   1.0000
chartershare |  0.0190  -0.0760   0.4174   0.0464   0.0763  -0.0619   1.0000
      demand |  0.3753   0.0554  -0.0345   0.1999   0.0200  -0.1006  -0.0422   1.0000
 established | -0.0000  -0.0325   0.1193  -0.0084   0.0370   0.0504   0.0374   0.0000   1.0000
      merger |  0.1051   0.0198   0.1067  -0.1472   0.0133   0.1072   0.0172   0.0041  -0.0830   1.0000
```

The change of leaseshare is positively correlated with both nalwacc and naldebt as expected. The strongest correlation is between change in leaseshare and the dummy variable merger (positive as expected). The correlation with bunkerprice is negative as expected. The correlation with harpex and ustransport is positive as expected. The correlation with stockindex is positive, which is contrary to expectation. The correlation with size and netincome is negative as expected. The correlation with the establishment year is negative, contrary to expectation. All other correlations are below 5% and therefore very small.

The correlations have to be confirmed by the regression analysis, which shows the joint impact of the variables. The result of a multicollinearity test is shown in the next table.

Table 4-15 VIF test result (panel, change in change)

```
. vif

    Variable |       VIF       1/VIF
-------------+----------------------
  stockindex |     18.12    0.055195
      harpex |     17.11    0.058438
   shipprice |     10.95    0.091337
      demand |     10.03    0.099739
   balticdry |      8.82    0.113405
      spread |      8.30    0.120518
  bunkerprice |     7.03    0.142169
   inflation |      4.94    0.202368
 established |      4.69    0.213129
  ustransport |     4.27    0.234373
      dy2006 |      3.62    0.276447
      dy2007 |      3.11    0.321255
      dy2000 |      2.55    0.392904
     nalwacc |      2.51    0.397692
         df2 |      2.32    0.430123
         df8 |      1.94    0.514233
         df1 |      1.87    0.533469
         df5 |      1.82    0.548821
        df14 |      1.79    0.559517
         df3 |      1.76    0.568717
        df12 |      1.62    0.617838
         df6 |      1.62    0.618902
   debtshare |      1.59    0.626970
         df4 |      1.59    0.628206
```

```
        df13 |     1.57      0.636432
    netincome |     1.54      0.649174
        df10 |     1.54      0.649634
        df11 |     1.51      0.664347
        size |     1.50      0.664911
         df9 |     1.42      0.705455
      merger |     1.37      0.732283
 chartershare |     1.35      0.743253
      dy1996 |     1.28      0.783455
      rating |     1.21      0.827138
     taxrate |     1.19      0.842154
-------------+----------------------
    Mean VIF |     3.98
```

Because the VIF is below 10 for all variables besides stockindex, harpex, shipprice and demand and the average VIF is only 4, relatively low collinearity can be concluded.

To check the functional form, Stata scatter plots for the relationships between the change of lease share and each independent variable are provided below.

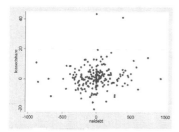

Figure 4-21 Scatter plot: change in lease share and change in naldebt

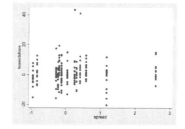

Figure 4-23 Scatter plot: change in lease share and change in interest spread

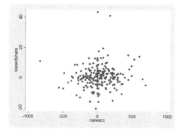

Figure 4-22 Scatter plot: change in lease share and change in nalwacc

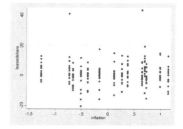

Figure 4-24 Scatter plot: change in lease share and inflation

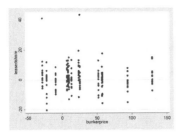

Figure 4-25 Scatter plot: change in lease share and change in bunkerprice

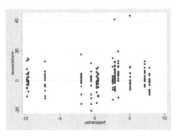

Figure 4-28 Scatter plot: change in lease share and change ustransport

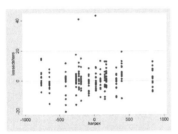

Figure 4-26 Scatter plot: change in lease share and change in harpex

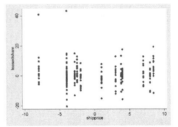

Figure 4-29 Scatter plot: change in lease share and change in shipprice

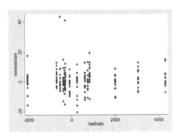

Figure 4-27 Scatter plot: change in lease share and change in Baltic Dry Index

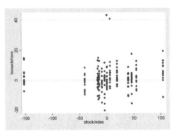

Figure 4-30 Scatter plot: change in lease share and change in stockindex

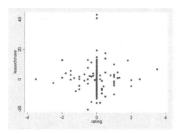

Figure 4-31 Scatter plot: change in lease share and change in rating

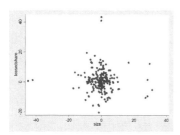

Figure 4-32 Scatter plot: change in lease share and changes in firm size

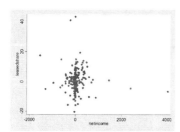

Figure 4-33 Scatter plot: change in lease share and changes in net income

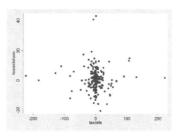

Figure 4-34 Scatter plot: change in lease share and changes in taxrate

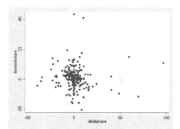

Figure 4-35 Scatter plot: change in lease share and changes in debt share

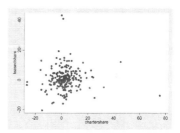

Figure 4-36 Scatter plot: change in lease share and changes in charter share

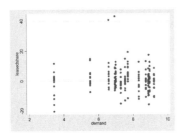
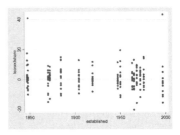

Figure 4-37 Scatter plot: change in lease share and demand

Figure 4-38 Scatter plot: change in lease share and establishment year

Figures 4-21 to 4-38 either show a linear or an unclear relationship between leaseshare and the independent variables. Therefore a linear functional form can be used for regression analysis.

4.2.4 Regression model

A regression analysis is used to find the variables that have a statistically significant impact on the dependent variable. The research design is non-experimental because available time series data and statistical controls are used. No random selection or usage of random effects can be used to construct a randomized field experiment or a quasi-experiment.

The dependent variable is the change in lease share. The following chart shows the histogram of the change in lease share.

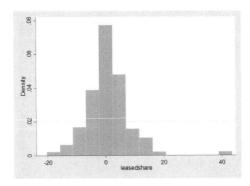

Figure 4-39 Histogram: Change in lease share

Since the histogram looks normally distributed, an OLS panel regression model can be used. The regression equation is

$$\begin{aligned}
\text{leasedshare}_{t_1-t_0} &= \alpha + \beta_1 \text{naldebt}_{t_1-t_0} + \beta_2 \text{spread}_{t_1-t_0} + \beta_3 \text{inflation}_{t_1} + \\
&\quad \beta_4 \text{bunkerprice}_{t_1-t_0} + \beta_5 \text{harpex}_{t_1-t_0} + \beta_6 \text{balticdry}_{t_1-t_0} + \beta_7 \text{ustransport}_{t_1-t_0} + \\
&\quad \beta_8 \text{shipprice}_{t_1-t_0} + \beta_9 \text{stockindex}_{t_1-t_0} + \beta_{10} \text{rating}_{t_1-t_0} + \beta_{11} \text{size}_{t_1-t_0} + \\
&\quad \beta_{12} \text{netincome}_{t_1-t_0} + \beta_{13} \text{taxrate}_{t_1-t_0} + \beta_{14} \text{debtshare}_{t_1-t_0} + \beta_{15} \text{chartershare}_{t_1-t_0} + \\
&\quad \beta_{16} \text{demand}_{t_1} + \beta_{17} \text{established}_{t_1} + \beta_{18} \text{merger}_{t_1} + \sum_{i=1994}^{2007} \gamma_i \text{ dyi} + \\
&\quad \sum_{j=1}^{14} \delta_j \text{ dfj} + \varepsilon_t
\end{aligned}$$

Equation 4-7

where the variables have the above defined meaning, β_i [-] are the coefficients of those variables, γ_i [−] and δ_j [−] are the coefficients of the year- and firm fixed dummy variables, α [-] is a constant and ε_t [-] the error term.

4.2.5 Model estimates

The first table shows the OLS panel regression results using the change in change model described above and robust standard errors.

Table 4-16 OLS regression result (panel, change in change, naldebt, robust)

```
. reg  leasedshare naldebt spread inflation bunkerprice harpex balticdry ustrans-
port  shipprice stockindex rating size netincome taxrate debtshare chartershare
demand established merger df1 df2 df3 df4 df5 df6 df7 df8 df9
df10 df11 df12 df13 df14 dy1994 dy1995 dy1996 dy1997 dy1998 dy1999 dy2000 dy2001
dy2002 dy2003 dy2004 dy2005 dy2006 dy2007, robust
```

```
Linear regression                              Number of obs  =       210
                                               F( 35,   174)  =      2.15
                                               Prob > F       =    0.0006
                                               R-squared      =    0.2485
                                               Root MSE       =    7.1336
```

leasedshare	Coef.	Robust Std. Err.	t	P>|t|	[95% Conf. Interval]	
naldebt	.0068384	.0031542	2.17	0.032	.000613	.0130639
spread	3.585643	1.358194	2.64	0.009	.9049865	6.266299
inflation	1.176815	2.125967	0.55	0.581	-3.019188	5.372818
bunkerprice	.0333006	.0275944	1.21	0.229	-.0211623	.0877635
harpex	.0041311	.006203	0.67	0.506	-.0081117	.0163738
balticdry	-.0001526	.0011195	-0.14	0.892	-.0023622	.002057
ustransport	.0168215	.1619357	0.10	0.917	-.3027896	.3364326
shipprice	-.5994482	.3561203	-1.68	0.094	-1.30232	.1034234
stockindex	.064191	.0431976	1.49	0.139	-.0210677	.1494497
rating	.1616482	.5785473	0.28	0.780	-.9802257	1.303522
size	-.0896976	.0707654	-1.27	0.207	-.2293667	.0499715
netincome	-.0010013	.000761	-1.32	0.190	-.0025032	.0005007
taxrate	-.0060085	.0127855	-0.47	0.639	-.0312431	.019226
debtshare	.0177922	.0623679	0.29	0.776	-.1053028	.1408872
chartershare	.0380777	.0585423	0.65	0.516	-.0774668	.1536222
demand	1.662224	1.176624	1.41	0.160	-.6600683	3.984516
established	-.0059907	.0171774	-0.35	0.728	-.0398935	.0279121
merger	12.99319	4.997125	2.60	0.010	3.130403	22.85597
df1	-.7163709	2.648916	-0.27	0.787	-5.944513	4.511771
df2	-1.000091	4.18305	-0.24	0.811	-9.25614	7.255959
df3	.0238229	2.059671	0.01	0.991	-4.041332	4.088978

```
  df4 |   -.2005697   1.895364   -0.11   0.916   -3.941433   3.540293
  df5 |    .2480312   2.493166    0.10   0.921   -4.672709   5.168772
  df6 |   -1.094924   2.202245   -0.50   0.620   -5.441476   3.251629
  df7 |   (omitted)
  df8 |    .4333586   2.486425    0.17   0.862   -4.474076   5.340794
  df9 |   -.7164927   2.053598   -0.35   0.728   -4.769662   3.336677
 df10 |   -4.134668   1.846581   -2.24   0.026   -7.779249   -.490087
 df11 |    .8372012   2.348532    0.36   0.722   -3.798077   5.472479
 df12 |   -2.936493   1.982106   -1.48   0.140   -6.848559   .9755728
 df13 |   -1.033263    1.87273   -0.55   0.582   -4.729453   2.662927
 df14 |   -2.418236   2.433471   -0.99   0.322   -7.221156   2.384685
dy1994 |   (omitted)
dy1995 |   (omitted)
dy1996 |   -.4798963   2.184915   -0.22   0.826   -4.792243   3.832451
dy1997 |   (omitted)
dy1998 |   (omitted)
dy1999 |   (omitted)
dy2000 |   -5.310427   3.704866   -1.43   0.154   -12.62269   2.001835
dy2001 |   (omitted)
dy2002 |   (omitted)
dy2003 |   (omitted)
dy2004 |   (omitted)
dy2005 |   (omitted)
dy2006 |    -6.43597   3.264088   -1.97   0.050   -12.87827   .0063334
dy2007 |   -5.375007   3.844632   -1.40   0.164   -12.96312   2.21311
 _cons |    .1843951   31.79446    0.01   0.995   -62.56806   62.93685
```

The change in naldebt is significant at the 2% level, and the effect is positive as hypothesized (the p value has to be divided by two because of the one-sided research hypothesis). An increase of 1 USD in naldebt change is associated with a 0.007 percentage point higher leaseshare. In other words, a change of 800 USD in naldebt, which is within the observed range, is associated with a 5.6 percentage point higher leaseshare if all other variables are hold constant. The absolute significance is also given because lease share increases up to 43% in one year.

Furthermore, the spread (interest difference between U.S. government bonds and corporate bonds with a BAA rating) is statistically significant at the 1% level. The effect is positive as hypothesized. A spread increase of one percentage point, which is within the observed range, is associated with an increase of 3.6 percentage points in lease share. This effect also has absolute significance.

In addition, the dummy variable merger shows statistical significance at the 1% level. A merger is associated with a 13 percentage point higher lease share. This effect is also of absolute significance. All other variables are not statistically significant on the 5% level.

The F test result allows rejection of the null hypothesis that all independent variables have no impact on the leased volume at the 1% level. The R squared is 25%. Therefore, the model seems to have a satisfactory fit.

Next, the same model is run with nalwacc instead of naldebt as an independent variable.

Table 4-17 OLS regression result (panel, change in change, nalwacc, robust)

```
. reg  leasedshare nalwacc spread inflation bunkerprice harpex balticdry ustrans-
port  shipprice stockindex rating size netincome taxrate debtshare chartershare
demand established merger df1 df2 df3 df4 df5 df6 df7 df8 df9
df10 df11 df12 df13 df14 dy1994 dy1995 dy1996 dy1997 dy1998 dy1999 dy2000 dy2001
dy2002 dy2003 dy2004 dy2005 dy2006 dy2007, robust
note: df7 omitted because of collinearity
note: dy1994 omitted because of collinearity
note: dy1995 omitted because of collinearity
note: dy1997 omitted because of collinearity
note: dy1998 omitted because of collinearity
note: dy1999 omitted because of collinearity
note: dy2001 omitted because of collinearity
note: dy2002 omitted because of collinearity
note: dy2003 omitted because of collinearity
note: dy2004 omitted because of collinearity
note: dy2005 omitted because of collinearity
```

```
Linear regression                              Number of obs =      210
                                               F( 35,  174) =     2.18
                                               Prob > F      =  0.0005
                                               R-squared     =  0.2400
                                               Root MSE      =  7.1742
```

leasedshare	Coef.	Robust Std. Err.	t	P>|t|	[95% Conf. Interval]	
nalwacc	.0078203	.0046067	1.70	0.091	.0012719	.0169124
spread	3.977558	1.389693	2.86	0.005	1.234734	6.720383
inflation	1.361137	2.203397	0.62	0.538	-2.987688	5.709962
bunkerprice	.0227059	.0284979	0.80	0.427	-.0335401	.0789519
harpex	.0038781	.0062892	0.62	0.538	-.0085349	.016291
balticdry	-.0004562	.0012293	-0.37	0.711	-.0028825	.0019702
ustransport	.0311164	.1709835	0.18	0.856	-.3063522	.3685851
shipprice	-.574551	.3598469	-1.60	0.112	-1.284778	.1356757
stockindex	.059019	.0453411	1.30	0.195	-.0304703	.1485083
rating	.1264323	.5812598	0.22	0.828	-1.020795	1.27366
size	-.0974429	.0748961	-1.30	0.195	-.2452646	.0503789
netincome	-.001247	.0007377	-1.69	0.093	-.0027029	.0002089
taxrate	-.0096177	.0124776	-0.77	0.442	-.0342447	.0150092
debtshare	.0128582	.0678407	0.19	0.850	-.1210383	.1467547
chartershare	.0298394	.0597002	0.50	0.618	-.0879903	.1476691
demand	1.818918	1.185063	1.53	0.127	-.5200312	4.157867
established	-.0057449	.0171366	-0.34	0.738	-.0395673	.0280775
merger	13.06735	5.218443	2.50	0.013	2.767759	23.36695
df1	-1.12368	2.713229	-0.41	0.679	-6.478757	4.231397
df2	-1.567062	4.101138	-0.38	0.703	-9.661443	6.527319
df3	-.5150784	2.138951	-0.24	0.810	-4.736708	3.706551
df4	-.0628135	1.871811	-0.03	0.973	-3.757191	3.631564
df5	-.1496625	2.463933	-0.06	0.952	-5.012706	4.713381

df6	-1.482635	2.231082	-0.66	0.507	-5.886103	2.920832
df7	(omitted)					
df8	.2084714	2.327896	0.09	0.929	-4.386076	4.803019
df9	-.9745617	2.079119	-0.47	0.640	-5.078102	3.128978
df10	-4.565026	1.906828	-2.39	0.018	-8.328516	-.8015352
df11	.453535	2.379258	0.19	0.849	-4.242387	5.149457
df12	-3.195784	1.94659	-1.64	0.102	-7.037752	.6461833
df13	-1.302892	1.850967	-0.70	0.482	-4.95613	2.350346
df14	-2.800416	2.474226	-1.13	0.259	-7.683774	2.082942
dy1994	(omitted)					
dy1995	(omitted)					
dy1996	-.6501871	2.27242	-0.29	0.775	-5.135243	3.834869
dy1997	(omitted)					
dy1998	(omitted)					
dy1999	(omitted)					
dy2000	-4.766526	3.67409	-1.30	0.196	-12.01805	2.484995
dy2001	(omitted)					
dy2002	(omitted)					
dy2003	(omitted)					
dy2004	(omitted)					
dy2005	(omitted)					
dy2006	-6.167335	3.327969	-1.85	0.066	-12.73572	.4010486
dy2007	-4.611605	3.948447	-1.17	0.244	-12.40462	3.181412
_cons	-1.102187	32.07537	-0.03	0.973	-64.40906	62.20469

The nalwacc also shows statistical significance at the 5% level. The direction is positive as expected. An increase of 1 USD in naldebt is associated with a 0.008 percentage point higher leaseshare. The significance of nalwacc (0.008) is slightly higher than naldebt (0.007). The absolute significance of nalwacc is also given because of a change in nalwacc of 800, which is within the observed range and is associated with a change in leaseshare of 6.4 percentage points.

The variables spread and merger are significant as before and show a similar impact. In addition, the variable net income is statistically significant at the 5% level. The effect is negative as hypothesized. An increase of net income by 1 million USD is associated with a 0.001 percentage point lower lease share. In other words, an increase in net income of 4 billion USD, which is within the observed range, is associated with a decrease in lease share of four percentage points. Thus, this effect is also significant on the absolute level.

The other variables do not show significance on the 5% level. In order to check if the average tax rate has a higher impact than the actual tax rate, the model is run again using the average tax rate. This improved the significance of the tax variable from 44% to 24%. However, they both do not show significance on the 5% level.

In order to enhance the significance of further variables, collinearity (as shown in Table 4-18) shall be reduced.

Table 4-18 VIF test result (panel, change in change)

```
. vif
```

Variable	VIF	1/VIF
stockindex	17.72	0.056443
harpex	16.18	0.061813
shipprice	10.93	0.091499
demand	9.89	0.101092
balticdry	8.64	0.115772
spread	8.26	0.121107
bunkerprice	7.00	0.142907
inflation	4.95	0.202208
established	4.74	0.211142
ustransport	4.26	0.234618
dy2006	3.58	0.279121
dy2007	3.11	0.321356
nalwacc	2.49	0.400868
dy2000	2.47	0.404236
df2	2.33	0.430067
df8	1.99	0.503212
df1	1.88	0.531431
df5	1.82	0.548827
df14	1.79	0.559411
df3	1.76	0.568753
debtshare	1.70	0.586838
df12	1.62	0.618101
df6	1.61	0.619312
df4	1.59	0.629030
df13	1.57	0.636424
df10	1.56	0.639389
netincome	1.55	0.646098
size	1.51	0.662091
df11	1.51	0.663828
df9	1.42	0.705522
merger	1.37	0.729611
chartershare	1.34	0.746621
dy1996	1.28	0.783613
taxmean	1.25	0.798144
rating	1.18	0.846155
Mean VIF	3.94	

The variables stockindex, harpex and shipprice are multicolinear. Their correlation is as follows:

Table 4-19 Correlation matrix (panel, change in change, priceindex)

```
. corr  stockindex harpex shipprice (obs=210)
```

	stocki~x	harpex	shippr~e
stockindex	1.0000		
harpex	0.6815	1.0000	
shipprice	0.5879	0.6233	1.0000

Because the correlation matrix shows a high positive correlation, it makes sense to combine these variables in one index. The index called priceindex is generated as follows:

Priceindex = stockindex + harpex/8+ shipprice/8*100   Equation 4-8

The divisions and multiplications are done to streamline the variation of the three variables (target range per variable is about -100/+100).

Next, the same Stata regression is performed as above but the variables stockindex, harpex and shipprice are replaced with the new variable priceindex.

Table 4-20 OLS regression result (panel, change in change, priceindex, robust)

```
reg   leasedshare nalwacc spread inflation   priceindex bunkerprice   balticdry us-
transport    rating size netincome   taxmean debtshare chartershare    demand estab-
lished merger df1 df2 df3 df4 df5 df6 df7 df8 df9 df10 df11 df12 df13 df14 dy1994
dy1995 dy1996 dy1997 dy1998 dy1999 dy2000 dy2001 dy2002 dy2003 dy2004 dy2005 dy2006
dy2007, robust
```

```
Linear regression                          Number of obs =      210
                                           F( 35,   174) =     2.54
                                           Prob > F      =   0.0000
                                           R-squared     =   0.2445
                                           Root MSE      =   7.1529
```

leasedshare	Coef.	Robust Std. Err.	t	P>|t|	[95% Conf. Interval]	
nalwacc	.0081257	.0043795	1.86	0.065	-.000518	.0167694
spread	3.822972	2.269168	1.68	0.094	-.6556652	8.30161
inflation	5.658495	2.792942	2.03	0.044	.1460894	11.1709
priceindex	.0081705	.009051	0.90	0.368	-.0096934	.0260344
bunkerprice	-.0455474	.0236508	-1.93	0.056	-.0922267	.0011319
balticdry	-.0006544	.0010155	-0.64	0.520	-.0026587	.0013499
ustransport	.2971371	.1861276	1.60	0.112	-.0702212	.6644955
rating	.1728177	.5757351	0.30	0.764	-.9635057	1.309141
size	-.0864759	.0700054	-1.24	0.218	-.224645	.0516932
netincome	-.0011432	.000742	-1.54	0.125	-.0026076	.0003212
taxmean	-.1054545	.089473	-1.18	0.240	-.2820466	.0711376
debtshare	.0259784	.0625781	0.42	0.679	-.0975314	.1494883
chartershare	.0252908	.058599	0.43	0.667	-.0903655	.1409471
demand	1.232041	.7445853	1.65	0.100	-.2375408	2.701622
established	-.0034252	.0177861	-0.19	0.848	-.0385295	.0316791
merger	13.2667	5.165311	2.57	0.011	3.071973	23.46143
df1	-.9394107	2.761807	-0.34	0.734	-6.390366	4.511544
df2	-1.620708	4.109272	-0.39	0.694	-9.731144	6.489727
df3	-.4519149	2.131926	-0.21	0.832	-4.65968	3.75585
df4	.1719449	1.881306	0.09	0.927	-3.541172	3.885062
df5	-.142536	2.498906	-0.06	0.955	-5.074606	4.789534
df6	-1.495814	2.240568	-0.67	0.505	-5.918004	2.926376

```
    df7  |  (omitted)
    df8  |  -.2423177   2.316806   -0.10   0.917   -4.814979    4.330343
    df9  |  -.9502415    2.09382   -0.45   0.651   -5.082797    3.182314
   df10  |  -4.190397   1.952241   -2.15   0.033   -8.043517    -.337276
   df11  |   .5232982   2.328535    0.22   0.822   -4.072512    5.119108
   df12  |  -3.163262   1.968207   -1.61   0.110   -7.047895     .721371
   df13  |  -1.290309   1.857095   -0.69   0.488   -4.955641    2.375024
   df14  |  -2.879136   2.523844   -1.14   0.256   -7.860425    2.102152
 dy1994  |  (omitted)
 dy1995  |  (omitted)
 dy1996  |  -.6340933   2.350756   -0.27   0.788    -5.27376    4.005573
 dy1997  |  (omitted)
 dy1998  |   4.866743   2.851431    1.71   0.090    -.7611019   10.49459
 dy1999  |  (omitted)
 dy2000  |  -6.069565   3.266213   -1.86   0.065   -12.51606     .3769327
 dy2001  |  (omitted)
 dy2002  |   6.980293   2.712562    2.57   0.011    1.626532    12.33405
 dy2003  |  -1.348329   4.245094   -0.32   0.751   -9.726835    7.030177
 dy2004  |  (omitted)
 dy2005  |  (omitted)
 dy2006  |  -1.782451   3.321183   -0.54   0.592   -8.337442     4.77254
 dy2007  |  (omitted)
  _cons  |   -1.24124   34.16428   -0.04   0.971   -68.67099    66.18851
------------------------------------------------------------------------------
```

The introduction of the priceindex reduced the multicolinearity as desired. The VIF of all independent variables is below 10 now (see Table 4-21).

Table 4-21 VIF test result (panel, change in change, priceindex)

```
. vif

     Variable |       VIF       1/VIF
--------------+----------------------
       spread |      8.07    0.123958
   priceindex |      7.27    0.137486
    inflation |      6.91    0.144728
    balticdry |      6.08    0.164522
  established |      4.74    0.211142
  bunkerprice |      4.64    0.215583
       demand |      3.81    0.262275
       dy2006 |      3.38    0.296292
       dy2003 |      3.06    0.327198
  ustransport |      3.05    0.327836
      nalwacc |      2.49    0.400868
       dy2002 |      2.46    0.405707
          df2 |      2.33    0.430067
       dy2000 |      2.24    0.446294
          df8 |      1.99    0.503212
          df1 |      1.88    0.531431
          df5 |      1.82    0.548827
       dy1998 |      1.80    0.555098
         df14 |      1.79    0.559411
          df3 |      1.76    0.568753
```

```
   debtshare |     1.70    0.586838
        df12 |     1.62    0.618101
         df6 |     1.61    0.619312
         df4 |     1.59    0.629030
        df13 |     1.57    0.636424
        df10 |     1.56    0.639389
   netincome |     1.55    0.646098
        size |     1.51    0.662091
        df11 |     1.51    0.663828
         df9 |     1.42    0.705522
      merger |     1.37    0.729611
chartershare |     1.34    0.746621
      dy1996 |     1.33    0.753195
     taxmean |     1.25    0.798144
      rating |     1.18    0.846155
-------------+---------------------
    Mean VIF |     2.68
```

The regression result regarding the variables nalwacc, spread and merger are similar to the result before introducing the variable priceindex. The priceindex is not statistically significant, but the independent variable inflation becomes significant on the 5% level. A one percentage point higher inflation is associated with a 5.7 percentage point higher lease share if all other variables hold constant. In addition, the bunkerprice is statistically significant at the 5% level. The impact is negative as hypothesized. A one USD higher bunkerprice is associated with a 0.05 percentage point lower lease share. This effect also has absolute importance, because a 100 USD higher bunkerprice (in the observed range) is associated with a 5 percentage point lower lease share.

The U.S. Transportation Index is statistically significant at the 10% level. The impact is positive as hypothesized. An increase of one point on the index is associated with an increase of 0.3 percentage points in lease share. The absolute relevance is limited because the transportation index varies only up to 8 points (effect on lease share = 2.4 percentage points).

The statistical significance of netincome slightly reduced from the 5% to the 7% level. The negative impact stayed in the same range.

The variable demand shows statistical significance at the 10% level. An increase in demand (index of world GDP and trade growth, seatrade volume, container handling volume, total number of container slots) of one percentage point is associated with an increase in lease share of 1.2 percentage points. This effect also has absolute significance because demand changes up to 9 percentage points (effect on lease share = 10.8 percentage points).

No other variable shows significance at the 10% level.

4.3 Summary of microeconomic analysis and lessons learned

The empirical analysis performed in this chapter shows a statistical and absolute significant positive impact of the NPV advantage of leasing. This result is independent of the usage of the after tax debt interests or the WACC as the discount rate. The positive impact was confirmed using the change in change model. This empirical analysis confirms the relevance of the NPV advantage of leasing calculation for the first time on the microeconomic level.

In both models, the nalwacc showed a slightly higher impact. Therefore, it can be concluded that in practice the WACC has a higher importance than the after tax debt rate as a discount factor in the NPV advantage of leasing calculation. This will be verified by the survey described in chapter 6.

In addition, the variables netincome and merger showed statistical significance in both models. A rising net income is associated with lowering lease share, whereas a merger has a positive association. Both effects are as hypothesized.

The variable inflation is statistically significant in both models, but the impact is in the opposite direction. In the nominal model, the impact is negative whereas the impact in the change in change model is positive.

The variables spread, bunker price, demand, ustransport, rating and established only show statistical significance in one of the two models. Their impact is as hypothesized: spread (positive), bunker price (negative), demand (positive), ustransport (positive), rating (positive) and establishment year (positive).

One reason for the insignificance of some of the other independent variables (priceindex, size, taxrate, debtshare, chartershare) could be the low number of observed firms (15) that belong to the top 25 shipping lines.

The existing theory suggests using NAL analysis for the buy or leasing decision (see chapter 2.1). The empirical literature only shows the effect of the variables net income and rating using regression analysis of non industry specific data (see chapter 2.2). The analysis above confirms the negative effect of the net income on the lease share. It also confirms the effect of rating: The better the rating, the lower the lease share.

The analysis presented in this chapter provides empirical evidence with statistical significance for the relevance of the variables merger, spread, bunker, demand, ustransport and establishment year for the first time.

All variables that show a statistically significant effect on the lease share in the analysis above (net income, merger, spread, bunker, demand, ustransport, rating and establishment year) besides NAL are not included in the existing theoretical evaluation model. Their integration will be discussed in chapter 6.2.

The survey presented in the following chapter will provide further knowledge about the buy or lease decision process at the microeconomic level.

5 Shipping line survey

The focus of this chapter is on the design and result analysis of a shipping line survey conducted in April/May 2010. The target of the survey was to get additional insights into the buy or lease decision process of shipping lines. The survey results will be analyzed to measure how important variables mentioned in the previous literature are for the buy or lease decision. Furthermore, this chapter will question the shipping lines' strategies. The results will be compared with the latest general buy or lease survey from Mukherjee (1991) and the only existing industry- specific survey from Temple (1987).

5.1 Survey design

The survey was sent to as many shipping lines as possible to get a representative picture of the industry. To organize this international survey in an efficient way, the Internet based tool surveymonkey.com was used. A personalized email containing a link to the survey (see 5.1.2) was sent to industry practitioners. This method kept the costs and administrative workload low.

The survey design followed the recommendations of Langbein & Felbinger (2006), Converse & Stanley (1986) and Mangione (1995). Langbein & Felbinger mention that a good design needs to achieve three goals. First, surveyors should aim for the best possible response rate at a given survey budget. Second, unbiased and informative responses are targeted. Last, the responses have to be turned into useful information.

The response rate is important because a high number of non-respondents could lead to results that are not representative. In order to get a high response rate, the answering time was kept to a target below 20 minutes; no additional cost for the respondents was necessary, as they responded via the Internet; the survey was completely anonymous, and several follow up emails were sent to all practitioners approximately every two weeks. Furthermore the respondents were more likely to cooperate because the introductory letter provided explanations, the survey used specific, short, "straightforward language" (Converse & Stanley, 1986, p. 11) and the survey was easy to read and answer (multiple-choice). To prevent respondents from early termination, more confidential statistical questions were asked at the end.

Mangione (1995) suggest using rewards to improve the response rate. In this case no monetary rewards were provided because they are not appropriate in this business setting and because of budget limitations. Furthermore the shipping lines are spread around the globe and the survey was conducted using the Internet, which would make a money transfer complicated. As an incentive, it was offered to provide a free summary of the survey results after completion if the respondent expressed interested in this. This does not contradict anonymity and allows reducing reminders to participants.

The target was to receive at least 30 completed questionnaires. This would facilitate the planned regression analysis. More than 120 responses would be optimal because this would allow more statistical significant results.

To achieve unbiased and informative responses, double barreled questions (combination of two topics in one question) were avoided, balanced questions (question does not force to one direction) and mutually exclusive precise response categories were provided and "agree/disagree" questions (double negatives) were avoided. Furthermore the category "not known" was used when appropriate. In addition, most of the questions offered seven answer categories to measure the intensity of the response:

not important at all						extremely important
□	□	□	□	□	□	□
-3	-2	-1	0	1	2	3

To check the necessary time for the survey and the appropriateness of the questions and answers, some industry experts assisted with a pretest. To turn the responses into useful information, numerical codes were used for response categories. The results were then analyzed using regression techniques.

5.1.1 Participants

As stated above, the target was to get responses from as many as possible shipping lines. The AXS Alphaliner top 400 shipping lines table (Alphaliner, 2010) was used as a basis for this. Contact information included email addresses obtained from industry practitioners and the Internet. Only one contact person per shipping line (if possible, the person responsible for container management) was selected to avoid unbalanced data. In total 357 shipping lines were contacted. Only contacts with email addresses were used. Sixty four of the initially used email addresses were generic (i.e., they did not contain the name of a contact person). It was expected that the response rate regarding these generic email addresses would be very low.

If an email address was no longer valid or no response was received within two weeks, another contact at the same shipping line was selected, and a new invitation was sent out.

5.1.2 Invitation letters and reminders

Several invitation emails as well as reminders were sent out. The following table provides an overview:

Table 5-1 Survey letters

Message Subject	Send Date	Sent	Type
Container buy or lease decision	Mailed on May 13, 2010 11:45 AM	68	invitation
Container buy or lease decision	Mailed on May 13, 2010 11:27 AM	377	Final re-minder
Container buy or lease decision	Mailed on May 10, 2010 8:52 AM	2	invitation
Container buy or lease decision	Mailed on May 6, 2010 9:53 AM	419	reminder
Container buy or lease decision	Mailed on May 6, 2010 9:52 AM	14	invitation
Container buy or lease decision	Mailed on April 29, 2010 9:55 AM	2	invitation
Container buy or lease decision	Mailed on April 28, 2010 4:39 PM	198	reminder
Container buy or lease decision	Mailed on April 26, 2010 12:53 PM	293	invitation
Container survey – the buy or lease decision	Mailed on April 22, 2010 9:14 AM	2	invitation
Container survey – the buy or lease decision	Mailed on April 16, 2010 10:20 AM	3	invitation
Container survey – the buy or lease decision	Mailed on April 15, 2010 8:02 AM	1	invitation
Container survey – the buy or lease decision	Mailed on April 13, 2010 1:54 PM	3	invitation
Container survey – the buy or lease decision	Mailed on April 13, 2010 9:35 AM	3	invitation
Container survey – the buy or lease decision	Mailed on April 12, 2010 5:17 PM	7	invitation
Container survey – the buy or lease decision	Mailed on April 12, 2010 4:32 PM	48	invitation
Container survey – the buy or lease decision	Mailed on April 12, 2010 12:48 PM	357	invitation

Table 5-1 shows that invitations were sent out on many days. Often automated messages were received that the email address is no longer valid or other persons are in charge of container management. As previously described, a new email was sent to another contact person when invitations failed.

In Appendix 1, invitation emails and reminders are provided. An initial invitation letter was sent to all initially chosen contacts by email.

After two weeks, 20 questionnaires were fully completed and six were partially completed. In order to get further responses, a reminder was sent to all contacts who did not reply within two weeks (295 email addresses).

One week later, a second reminder was sent out to the shipping lines that did not respond. The text of the reminder was similar. About one week after the second reminder, the third and final reminder was sent out.

5.1.3 Response rate

In total, 512 contacts at 357 shipping lines received email messages. Sixty nine persons (13.5%) responded. Eighteen finished only parts of the survey, whereas 51 completed it (73%). Four hundred and forty three persons did not respond.

The response rate of 13.5% is not good but explainable because Internet surveys in general get low response rates. The high work load and email inflow of the contacted managers is an additional reason for the low response rate.

The minimum goal of more than 30 completed surveys was reached. The 51 completed questionnaires allow an econometrical analysis.

5.1.4 Questionnaire and summarized responses

The main target of the questionnaire was to get information about the importance of criteria that might affect the container buy or lease decision. The questions were developed based on the criteria mentioned in previous literature (see section 2.3) including the survey from Temple (1987).

Furthermore, some areas, like NPV calculation, the impression of how expensive leasing is, and repair costs were questioned more in detail. The existing and future strategy regarding leasing was another important section of the survey. Last, statistical background questions were asked. These include the share of leased containers—the dependent variable of the analysis.

Each participant received the same questions, with the exception of question number 10, which depends on the answer to question number 9. In Appendix 2, all survey questions as well as the summarized responses are provided (including incomplete questionnaires).

5.2 Survey response analysis

5.2.1 Decision criteria ranking

The main goal of the survey was to find criteria that have an impact on the container buy or lease decision. Furthermore, it would be helpful to know how important these criteria are.

Table 5-2 provides an overview of the surveyed criteria with two different ranking methods. The first ranking is based on the weighted average importance (sum of -3, -2, -1, 0, 1, 2 and 3 multiplied by the percentage it was selected). The second ranking is based on the percent of positive (1, 2 and 3 selected) answers.

Table 5-2 Importance of decision criteria

Question number	criteria	weighted average importance	% of possitive answers
8	Net present value	1.90	83%
1	Flexibility	1.78	83%
19	Future container prices	1.78	88%
21	Profitability	1.73	83%
4	Offsetting imbalances	1.67	86%
11	Internal rate of return	1.60	89%
5	Length of lease period	1.45	78%
23	Expenditure controls	1.40	74%
14	Leasing drop off costs	1.36	81%
22	Purchase options	1.28	79%
2	Buffer stock function	1.16	75%
15	Saving cash	1.14	71%
20	Off balance sheet financing	1.02	75%
7	Inhouse admin costs	0.83	65%
3	Availability in remote locations	0.63	61%
17	Inflation expectations	0.44	52%
6	Hedging new equipment risk	0.22	51%
16	Tax effects	-0.34	36%

Table 5-2 shows that the NPV analysis has the highest importance for the buy or lease decision. Furthermore, equipment flexibility, the expected future container price and the current profitability are of high importance. Interestingly, IRR calculations are also of importance (highest percentage of positive answers). Shipping lines seem to use both calculation methods: NPV and IRR.

Several criteria are of medium importance: length of lease period, expenditure controls, drop off costs, purchase options, buffer stock function of leasing, saving cash and off balance sheet financing.

Of minor importance are in-house administration costs, availability in remote locations, inflation expectations and hedging new equipment risk. Tax effects play no role in most container buy or lease decisions.

The ranking according to the weighted average importance does not differ much from the ranking according to the percentage of positive answers. Because the weighted average importance takes into account how important a criterion is whereas the percentage of positive answers does not reflect the intensity, the weighted average importance ranking method is preferred.

It has to be stressed that the NPV analysis has a high importance. However, many other decision criteria also have a very high importance. It can be concluded that a combination of financial analysis and other decision criteria is appropriate. This will be reflected in the proposed container buy or lease evaluation model in section 6.2.2.

The criteria ranking does not take simultaneous effects into account. To analyze simultaneous effects, an econometrical analysis is performed in section 5.3.

5.2.2 NPV analysis and cost of leasing

As stated in section 5.2.1, the NPV analysis is the most important driver of the buy or lease decision regarding containers. Survey questions 9 and 10 provided further insights into how the NPV analysis is performed in practice.

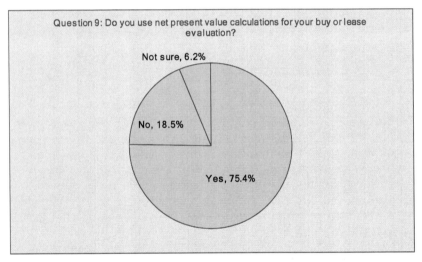

Figure 5-1 Usage of NPV analysis

Figure 5-1 shows that 75.4% of the survey participants use a NPV analysis, whereas 18.5% do not use it and 6.2% are not sure if their company uses it. One good reason for corporations not to use NPV analysis might be the lack of alternatives to leasing if they do not have access to bank financing. Another reason could be the strategic decision to either preferably use leasing or purchasing. To check these hypotheses, the data of questionnaires with a "no" response in question 9 are selected. Three out of eight participants stated that their bank loan access is either not limited or that they have no access at all. Furthermore, they all have either a very high share of leasing (above 80%) or a very low share of leasing (below 15%). Because of the low number of responses, the conclusion that the hypotheses cannot be rejected is not statistically significant. Nevertheless, this discussion shows that for some firms, a NPV analysis might not be appropriate.

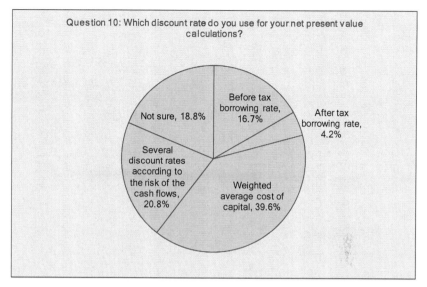

Figure 5-2 NPV calculation discount rate

Figure 5-2 shows that industry practitioners use several different discount rates to calculate the NPV. There seemed to be a good deal of uncertainty regarding discount rate is appropriate because 18.8% chose "not sure". The WACC was most often used (39.6%), followed by several discount rates according to the risk of the cash flows (20.8%) and the before-tax borrowing rate (16.7%). The after-tax borrowing rate (4.2%) was used not often. This is remarkable because the existing general as well as container specific buy or lease theory suggests using the after-tax borrowing rate (see chapter 2.1). In chapter 6, the appropriate discount rate and an extended evaluation model will be discussed.

In survey question 12, participants were asked about their impression of whether leasing or owning is more expensive. The answer does not necessarily have to be the result of an NPV analysis—it could be a gut feeling.

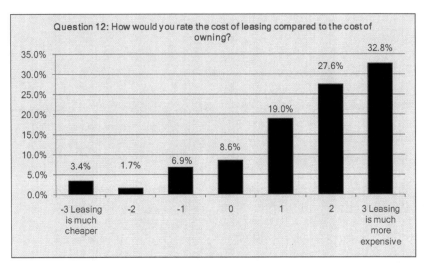

Figure 5-3 Cost of leasing

Figure 5-3 shows that most of the shipping lines (79.3%) have the impression that leasing is more expensive. The weighted average response is 1.5, signaling that this impression is rather significant. One reason for the impression of higher costs of leasing is given by the responses to question 13.

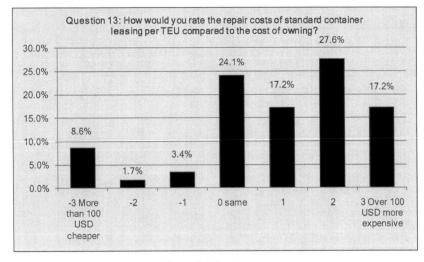

Figure 5-4 Repair costs

Figure 5-4 shows that many respondents (62%) find repair costs of leased containers higher than repair costs of owned equipment. The weighted average response is 0.9. If it is assumed that that categories represent -3=-150; -2=-100; -1=-50; 0=0; 1=50; 2=100; 3=150 USD higher repair costs of leasing, the weighted average repair costs of leased equipment are 46 USD higher than of owned equipment. Repair costs will be discussed in more detail in chapter 6.2.

5.2.3 Inflation

Table 5-3 shows that survey participants did not select inflation as an important criterion for the buy or lease decision. Survey question 18 asks how an expected inflation rise would affect the buy or lease decision.

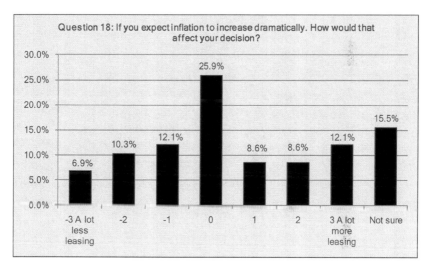

Figure 5-5 Effect of inflation

Figure 5-5 shows that for most practitioners (25.9%), an expected higher inflation would not affect their buy or lease decision. An additional 15.5% were not sure about the impact of a higher inflation. The remaining responses were relatively equally distributed. The weighted average response is 0.1, which also signals that there is no clear direction. Looking at the data of the shipping lines which find inflation very important for their decision does not provide a clear picture regarding the direction of the effect.

5.2.4 Leasing strategy

The questionnaire included questions about the current leasing status and the future strategy. Question 31 was about the fleet split.

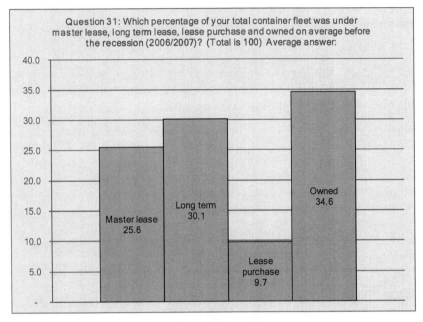

Figure 5-6 Fleet split

Figure 5-6 showed that the survey participants have on average 25.6% on master lease and 30.1% on long-term lease. The total leasing share of 55.7% is well above the industry-wide share of about 40% (see chapter 1: Introduction). The industry share is mainly dependent on decisions of the top 20 shipping lines because their container shipping capacity accounts for more than 85% of the market (see chapter 1). The container shipping capacity is a very good indicator of the container volume because about 2 TEU containers are needed per TEU ship capacity (see Figure 4-1). The top 20 shipping lines operate more than 200,000 TEU (leased and owned) each. According to the responses to question 32, this group represents only 27.4% of the survey participants (see Table 5-3). This means that the top 20 shipping lines are underrepresented in the survey in terms of market share.

Table 5-3 Fleet size and lease share

Size of fleet	% of participants	average lease share
Less than 249 TEU	2.0%	100.0%
250 to 999 TEU	5.9%	93.3%
1000 to 9,999 TEU	27.5%	74.4%
10,000 – 49,999 TEU	23.5%	44.4%
50,000 – 199,999 TEU	13.7%	51.7%
200,000 to 699,999 TEU	17.6%	35.9%
More than 700,000 TEU	9.8%	40.0%

Table 5-3 shows a reducing lease share with the size of the total fleet. Because the top 20 shipping lines are underrepresented in the survey and smaller shipping lines lease more, the survey respondents' overall average leasing share is higher than the market average.

Question 24 asks participants about their leasing share target for the next two years.

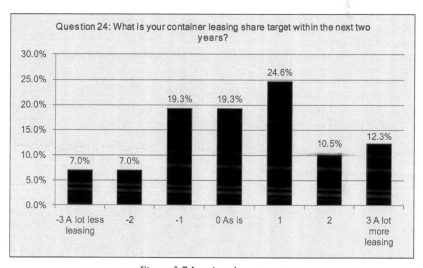

Figure 5-7 Leasing share target

Figure 5-7 shows that the leasing share might slightly gain during the next two years. The weighted average answer is 0.3. Forty seven percent of participants wanted to increase their leasing share, whereas only 33% plan a decrease. The global financial crises, which had an impact on access to bank loans, might be a good explanation for the planned increase.

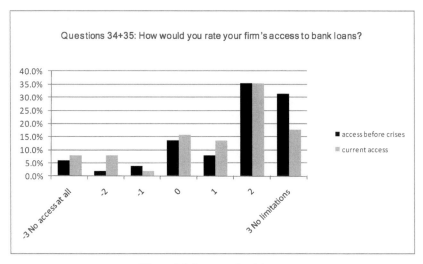

Figure 5-8 Access to bank loans

Figure 5-8 shows that the access to bank loans declined since the start of the financial crises. Furthermore, internal resources of capital tightened because profits reduced.

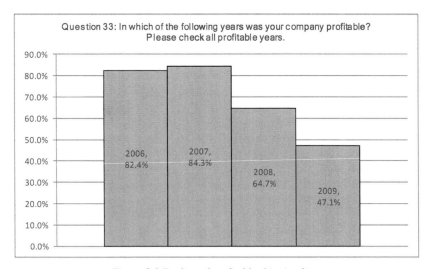

Figure 5-9 Decline of profitable shipping lines

Figure 5-9 shows a decline of participating shipping lines which were profitable from 2006 to 2009. Reducing profits and bank loan access might lead to more leasing.

Question 25 asked participants about their current number of lessors.

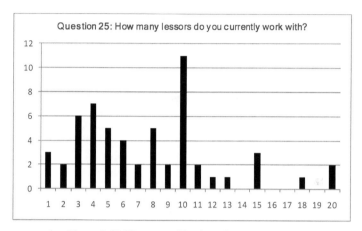

Figure 5-10 Histogram: Number of current lessors

Figure 5-10 shows a diverse picture. Most shipping lines work with 10 or fewer lessors, but some even work with 20 different lessors.

Question 26 asks about the future strategy regarding the number of lessors.

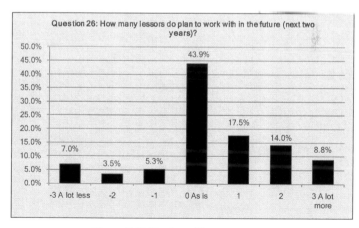

Figure 5-11 Number of lessors strategy

Figure 5-11 shows that many shipping lines (43.9%) do not plan to change the number of lessors they currently work with. The weighted average answer of 0.4 shows a slight tendency to increase the number of lessors. This was also reflected by 40% of participants who plan an increase, whereas only 16% plan a reduction.

Questions 27 and 28 ask about pooling container equipment with other shipping lines.

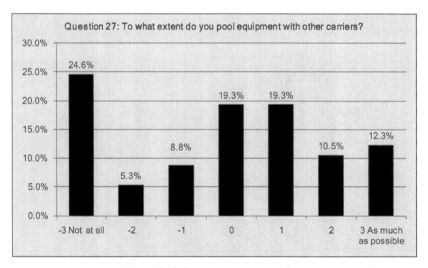

Figure 5-12 Current equipment pooling

Figure 5-12 shows that many shipping lines do not pool equipment at all (24.6%). On the other hand, 42.1% gave a positive answer (1, 2 or 3) which means that they pool equipment to some extent.

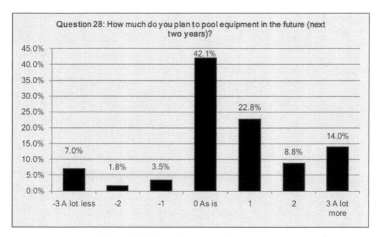

Figure 5-13 Equipment pooling strategy

Figure 5-13 shows that many shipping lines (42.1%) do not plan to change their pooling strategy going forward. The weighted average response of 0.5 as well as 45.6% positive and 12.3% negative answers signal a slightly positive tendency towards increased pooling in the future.

5.2.5 Establishment date and number of employees

Question 29 asks for the establishment date of the shipping line. The hypothesis is that the lease share of younger firms is higher because their access to alternative financing is limited.

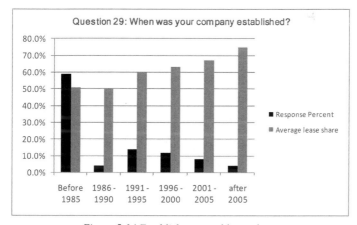

Figure 5-14 Establishment and lease share

Figure 5-14 displays the percent of respondents in each time slot and the respective average lease share. Most participating firms were established before 1985. The participating firms represent all given establishment date slots. The chart shows that younger firms tend to lease more. This conclusion does not take simultaneous effects of other variables into account.

Question 30 is about another important background topic: The number of employees.

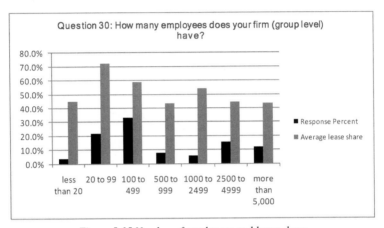

Figure 5-15 Number of employees and lease share

Figure 5-15 shows that the participating firms represent all employee sizes but are not equally distributed. There seems to be a trend towards a lower lease share with a rising firm size (number of employees). Again, this analysis does not take the simultaneous effects of other variables into account.

To analyze the simultaneous effects, an econometric analysis will be performed in section 5.3.

5.3 Econometrical analysis of survey responses

To find the simultaneous effect of the decision criteria described in section 5.1 and other data obtained from the survey on lease share, an econometrical analysis is performed. The results will be used in chapter 6 to enhance the theoretical model for the buy or lease evaluation.

5.3.1 Hypotheses

In this section, for each of the criteria questioned in the survey (variables are underlined below and defined in 5.3.2), a research hypothesis is provided regarding the impact on the lease share (independent variable). The null hypothesis regarding all independent variables is that they have no effect on the lease share.

The research hypothesis regarding increased importance of flexibility is a positive relation to the share of leasing because leasing provides more flexibility (e.g., pick up location, equipment types, redelivery) for the shipping lines. A positive correlation is also expected regarding the importance of bufferstock, remoteloc, imbalances, leasedperiod, obsolescence and admincosts because these criteria were mentioned as leasing advantages in the literature (see section 2.4). Because the NPV disadvantage of leasing in the example calculation in chapter 6.2.3, the hypotheses regarding the effect of the importance of npv and irr on the lease share is negative.

Because of the drop off disadvantage of leasing, a negative relationship between importance of dropoff and leased share is expected (see section 6.2). The importance of cashsaving is expected to have a positive relationship with the share of leased containers. Cashsaving is mentioned in the literature as an argument for leasing (see section 2.4). To the contrary, the importance of tax should have a negative relationship with the lease share because of some tax disadvantages of leasing. Regarding the importance of inflationind, no clear direction is hypothesized. Therefore, the hypothesis regarding inflationind is two-sided. The importance of the future container price does not indicate whether the expected future price is higher or lower than the current level. A high importance could mean that more or less leasing is targeted. Therefore, the hypothesis for futcontprice is two-sided.

If off balance sheet financing is important for a shipping line, leasing is more attractive than buying. Therefore the hypothesis regarding offbalance is a positive relationship with the leased share. Profitable firms have more resources of internal financing. The hypothesis regarding profitindex has, consequentially, a negative relationship with the leasing share. The hypothesis regarding the importance of buyoption is a positive relation to the leased share because only leasing offers the flexibility to buy later. Expenditure controls are often tougher for purchasing than for leasing equipment for a limited time. Therefore, it is expected that the importance of spendcontrol has a positive relationship with the leased share. Because access to other financing sources increases with the age of a firm, it is hypothesized that established has a positive relation to the share of leased containers.

Larger shipping lines are expected to use more purchasing. The employees as well as the fleetsize are therefore hypothesized to have a negative relationship with the leased share. Because profit increases the internal financing resources which make purchasing easier, it is hypothesized that profitindex has a negative impact on the lease share. The hypothesis regarding loanaccess is a negative relationship with the lease share because better access to loans helps to purchase containers.

5.3.2 Data and measurement issues

The data for the econometrical analysis are completely taken from the survey. Several transformations are necessary to analyze the data using Stata software. Unfinished questionnaires as well as questionnaires that include at least one "not sure" answer are not taken into account, because the dependent variable leased (share of leased containers) is missing or the record is incomplete. Only numerical values have to be used.

Table 5-4 below shows a summary of data imported to Stata. The variables have the following meaning:

1. leased [%] is the share of leased containers (sum of master lease and long term lease percentage answered in question 31). Leased is the dependent variable in the analysis. The leased share is between 10 and 100% and on average is 52.4%.
2. flexibility [-] refers to question 1: How important is flexibility (global availability of equipment) for your decision? In general the variables take on a value between -3 and 3 according to the answer chosen if not defined differently.
3. bufferstock [-] refers to question 2: How important is the buffer stock function of leasing for your decision?
4. remoteloc [-] refers to question 3: How important is availability of containers in remote locations for your decision?
5. imbalances [-] refers to question 4: How important is offsetting container flow imbalances for you decision?
6. leasedperiod [-] refers to question 5: How important is the length of the lease period for your decision?
7. obsolescence [-] refers to question 6: How important is hedging the risk of new equipment types for your decision?
8. admincosts [-] refers to question 7: How important are in-house administration costs for container management for you decision?
9. npv [-] refers to question 8: How important are net present value calculations for your buy or lease evaluation?
10. irr [-] refers to question 10: How important are internal rate of return calculations for your buy or lease decision?
11. dropoff [-] refers to question 14: How important are leasing drop off costs for your decision to buy or lease?

12. cashsaving [-] refers to question 15: How important is saving cash (e.g. deferring capital spending, avoiding advances) for your buy or lease decision?
13. tax [-] refers to question 16: How important are tax effects for your buy or lease decision?
14. inflationind [-] refers to question 17 and 18: How important are inflation expectations for your buy or lease decision? If you expect inflation to increase dramatically, how would that affect your decision? An index is generated as multiplication of the two answers. Because both answers are coded from -3 to 3 a simple multiplication would lead to positive results when both answers are negative and positive. To avoid this effect, the answers to question 17 are coded from zero to 6.
15. futcontprice [-] refers to question 19: How important are expected future container prices for your buy or lease decision?
16. offbalance [-] refers to question 20: How important is off balance sheet financing for your buy or lease decision?
17. buyoption [-] refers to question 22: How important are purchase options in a lease contract for your buy or lease decision?
18. spendcontrol [-] refers to question 23: How important are expenditure controls (approvals by higher management when purchasing) for your decision to lease or buy?
19. established [-] refers to question 29: When was your company established? The answers are coded as follows 1=before 1985; 2=1986 to 1990; 3=1991 to 1995; 4=1996 to 2000; 5=2001 to 2005; 6=after 2005.
20. employees [-] refers to question 30: How many employees does your firm (group level) have? The answers are coded as follows: 1=less than 20; 2=20 to 99; 3=100 to 499; 4=500 to 999; 5=1000 to 2499; 6=2500 to 4999; 7=more than 5000.
21. fleetsize [-] refers to question 32: What was the average size of your total container fleet before the recession (2006/2007)? The answers are coded as follows: 1=less than 249 TEU; 2=250 to 999 TEU; 3=1000 to 9,999 TEU; 4=10,000 to 49,999 TEU; 5=50,000 to 199,999 TEU; 6=200,000 to 699,999 TEU, 7=more than 700,000 TEU.
22. profitindex [-] refers to question 21 and question 33: How important is the current profitability of your firm for your buy or lease decision? In which of the following years was your company profitable? Please check all profitable years. An index is generated using the following formula: profitindex = (profit2006 + profit2007 + profit2008) * answer to question 33. If there is a profit in 2006 the variable profit2006 equals 1 otherwise 0. The profit 2009 was not taken into account because the analysis refers

to the period before the financial crises. A transformation of the answers to question 33 to positive values is not necessary in this case because profitability in the years 2006 to 2008 can only lead to values of zero and more.

23. loanaccess [-] refers to question 34: How would you rate your firm's average access to bank loans before the recession (2006/2007)?
24. The variables lp [%], owned [%], masterlease [%] and longterm [%] are alternative dependant variables which will be used to analyze these financing types.

5.3.3 Sample statistics and simple correlations

Table 5-4 shows the sample statistics of the dataset.

Table 5-4 Survey data

. sum

Variable	Obs	Mean	Std. Dev.	Min	Max
leased	34	52.70588	28.70596	10	100
flexibility	34	1.852941	1.328758	-2	3
bufferstock	34	1.470588	1.502227	-3	3
remoteloc	34	.7941176	1.838633	-3	3
imbalances	34	1.735294	1.657103	-3	3
leaseperiod	34	1.352941	1.368085	-3	3
obsolescence	34	.4411765	1.861755	-3	3
admincosts	34	.6176471	2.059931	-3	3
npv	34	2	1.154701	-1	3
irr	34	1.705882	1.142284	-1	3
dropoff	34	1.411765	1.373287	-3	3
cashsaving	34	.8529412	1.956068	-3	3
tax	34	-.4117647	2.244423	-3	3
inflationind	34	-1.647059	7.991975	-18	18
futcontprice	34	1.735294	1.399325	-2	3
offbalance	34	.6764706	1.934074	-3	3
buyoption	34	1.470588	1.691965	-3	3
spendcontrol	34	1.470588	1.796213	-3	3
established	34	2.205882	1.610184	1	6
employees	34	3.764706	1.810053	1	7
fleetsize	34	4.294118	1.567268	1	7
profitindex	34	3.705882	4.115966	-9	9
loanaccess	34	1.470588	1.829643	-3	3
lp	34	8.794118	16.0412	0	80
owned	34	38.5	26.10149	0	80
masterlease	34	28.08824	23.03932	0	80
longterm	34	24.61765	28.64412	0	100

The share of leased containers of the analyzed participants varies between 10% and 100%, with an average of 52.7%. The standard deviation of 28.7% signals that there is much variation regarding the lease strategy. As expected, most variables take on values between -3 and 3. The inflationindex varies between -18 and 18 and the profitindex between -9 and 9. The share of lease purchase is between 0% and 80%, with an average of 8.8%. This is much lower than the average owned share of 38.5% even if owned varies also between 0 and 80%. Again, masterlease varies between 0% and 80% but with an average of 28%. The share of long term leasing is between 0% and 100% with an average of 24.6%. The standard deviation is 28.6%, which is almost as high as the standard deviation of leased.

Table 5-5 provides simple Stata correlations between the share of leased containers (variable leased) and the other variables.

Table 5-5 Simple correlations of survey variables

```
. corr
(obs=34)
```

	leased	flexib~y	buffer~k	remote~c	imbala~s	leasep~d	obsole~e	adminc~s	npv	irr
leased	1.0000									
flexibility	0.1077	1.0000								
bufferstock	0.0096	0.3242	1.0000							
remoteloc	0.0648	0.3593	0.1239	1.0000						
imbalances	-0.0259	0.3809	0.1489	0.5584	1.0000					
leaseperiod	0.1825	0.4462	0.3296	0.2105	0.3098	1.0000				
obsolescence	0.3467	0.4190	0.1727	0.2309	0.4221	0.3177	1.0000			
admincosts	0.1774	0.5767	0.2656	0.5306	0.5110	0.5440	0.6221	1.0000		
npv	-0.1298	-0.0000	0.2795	-0.1856	0.0158	0.2110	0.0282	0.1529	1.0000	
irr	0.0638	0.2102	-0.1112	0.1867	0.1657	0.3205	0.0059	0.1826	0.3446	1.0000
dropoff	0.1723	-0.0821	0.1089	0.3466	0.2358	-0.2410	-0.0732	0.1430	0.1147	0.0216
cashsaving	0.2593	0.4345	0.1996	0.4295	0.1092	0.5975	0.0433	0.4970	0.1073	0.4819
tax	0.4040	-0.0311	0.1131	0.0963	0.1165	0.2067	0.2696	0.4041	0.0818	0.1995
inflationind	0.1800	0.0878	-0.0799	0.0175	0.0096	0.1241	-0.1024	-0.0136	-0.1576	0.0416
futcontprice	0.0206	0.3370	0.1043	0.4022	0.0734	-0.0130	0.0927	0.2687	0.1125	0.3479
offbalance	0.3170	0.2757	0.2209	0.4494	0.1237	0.4109	0.0998	0.4092	-0.0950	0.3671
buyoption	-0.0763	0.5035	0.1964	0.3828	0.2836	0.3712	0.1534	0.2271	0.0776	0.3090
spendcontrol	-0.0407	0.4869	0.3197	-0.0432	0.0024	0.4236	0.2623	0.5333	0.2192	0.0252
established	0.3954	0.2412	0.0590	0.1273	0.1119	0.3099	0.1811	0.3351	-0.0163	0.3634
employees	-0.2446	-0.2164	-0.0363	0.0120	0.2003	-0.2714	-0.3819	-0.5206	0.1595	-0.0052
fleetsize	-0.6170	-0.1678	0.0295	-0.2938	-0.0275	-0.2195	-0.1393	-0.2175	-0.0167	-0.2718
profitindex	-0.2144	0.1470	-0.0455	-0.1124	-0.0784	-0.2178	0.1084	0.0364	0.2550	-0.0190
loanaccess	-0.3048	0.0543	-0.0279	-0.2586	-0.0176	0.0164	0.0529	0.1135	0.2295	-0.0913
lp	-0.4344	0.1123	0.2330	0.1413	0.0549	0.1912	-0.3175	0.0782	0.0638	0.0694
owned	-0.8328	-0.1874	-0.1538	-0.1582	-0.0053	-0.3182	-0.1861	-0.2432	0.1036	-0.1128
masterlease	0.4040	0.3409	0.2500	0.2522	0.2943	0.2451	0.3050	0.1955	-0.1572	-0.0876
longterm	0.6772	-0.1663	-0.1915	-0.1379	-0.2627	-0.0142	0.1021	0.0206	-0.0037	0.1345

	dropoff	cashsa~g	tax	inflat~d	futcon~e	offbal~e	buyopt~n	spendc~l	establ~d	employ~s
dropoff	1.0000									
cashsaving	-0.0219	1.0000								
tax	0.2828	0.3309	1.0000							
inflationind	0.1796	0.0751	-0.0271	1.0000						
futcontprice	0.2950	0.2843	0.0511	-0.1648	1.0000					
offbalance	0.0631	0.8041	0.3942	0.0507	0.3817	1.0000				
buyoption	0.0315	0.3878	-0.0831	0.2226	0.4126	0.4183	1.0000			
spendcontrol	-0.1915	0.3567	0.1397	-0.1681	0.3163	0.1673	0.1742	1.0000		
established	0.3853	0.4332	0.5692	0.1637	0.3342	0.4988	0.3082	0.3322	1.0000	
employees	-0.2768	-0.1812	-0.4870	-0.0213	-0.2646	-0.3773	-0.0320	-0.1606	-0.4404	1.0000
fleetsize	-0.0580	-0.2622	-0.3350	-0.0134	-0.2121	-0.3176	0.0148	0.0570	-0.2168	0.4631
profitindex	-0.1495	-0.2539	0.0226	-0.2501	0.2070	-0.2788	0.0770	0.2693	-0.1003	0.1328
loanaccess	-0.1639	-0.2256	-0.3056	0.0878	-0.1037	-0.2725	-0.0248	0.1703	-0.4453	0.1168
lp	0.0232	0.0676	-0.3231	0.2736	0.1608	0.0789	0.3330	0.2759	0.0639	0.0098
owned	-0.2037	-0.3267	-0.2457	-0.3661	-0.1215	-0.3971	-0.1208	-0.1247	-0.4741	0.2630
masterlease	0.2507	0.0245	0.0019	-0.0579	-0.0481	-0.0218	-0.0260	-0.0413	0.1596	-0.1724
longterm	-0.0290	0.2402	0.4033	0.2270	0.0594	0.3352	-0.0556	-0.0076	0.2678	-0.1064

```
             | fleets~e profit~x loanac~s      lp   owned master~e longterm
-------------+------------------------------------------------------------------
   fleetsize |   1.0000
 profitindex |   0.0420   1.0000
  loanaccess |   0.1722   0.2926   1.0000
          lp |   0.2592  -0.0863   0.0643   1.0000
       owned |   0.5193   0.2888   0.2957  -0.1368   1.0000
 masterlease |  -0.2701  -0.3004  -0.2620  -0.3018  -0.2588   1.0000
    longterm |  -0.4011   0.0268  -0.0948  -0.1926  -0.6264  -0.3995   1.0000
```

These simple correlations do not take simultaneous effects into account. Therefore, the analysis is limited to the highest correlations to leased. Fleetsize has the highest correlation with leased (-62%). A negative relationship between fleetsize and leased was expected.

The importance of tax shows a high correlation to leased (40%). This is surprising because taxes are ranked as the least important decision variable. Furthermore, a negative relationship to leased is hypothesized whereas the correlation is positive. The positive correlation to established (40%) was hypothesized. The high correlation of obsolescence (35%) is surprising, because it is not one of the highest rated variables. The positive relation to leasing was expected.

To check for multi collinearity a Stata VIF test is performed.

Table 5-6 Survey data VIF test

```
. vif

        Variable |       VIF       1/VIF
-------------+----------------------
      remoteloc |     12.04    0.083041
    established |     11.74    0.085191
      cashsaving |     11.58    0.086333
      admincosts |     10.17    0.098367
         dropoff |      9.22    0.108455
       offbalance |      8.29    0.120576
    spendcontrol |      6.30    0.158815
      flexibility |      5.27    0.189895
             npv |      4.94    0.202310
     leaseperiod |      4.77    0.209635
      loanaccess |      4.76    0.209904
             tax |      4.71    0.212389
             irr |      3.85    0.259779
    futcontprice |      3.72    0.268951
       buyoption |      3.63    0.275615
      profitindex |      3.57    0.279818
       employees |      3.20    0.312824
     obsolescence |      2.90    0.344583
       imbalances |      2.89    0.345640
      bufferstock |      2.57    0.388836
        fleetsize |      2.29    0.437295
      inflationind |      1.67    0.600165
-------------+----------------------
        Mean VIF |      5.64
```

Table 5-6 shows that multicollinearity is not a big problem in this case because the average VIF is below 10. Only the variables remoteloc, cashsaving, established and admincosts have a VIF slightly above 10. In this case, creating an index containing these variables does not make sense because their meaning is very different.

To check the functional form of the regression, Stata scatter plots are provided below:

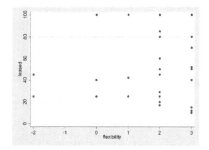

Figure 5-16 Scatter plot: leased and flexibility

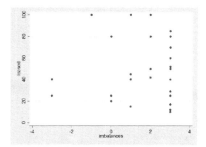

Figure 5-19 Scatter plot: leased and imbalances

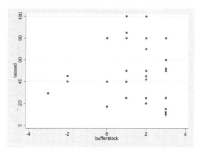

Figure 5-17 Scatter plot: leased and bufferstock

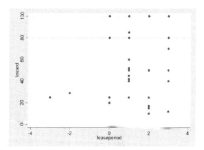

Figure 5-20 Scatter plot: leased and leaseperiod

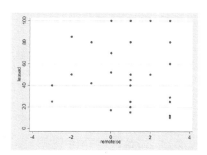

Figure 5-18 Scatter plot: leased and remoteloc

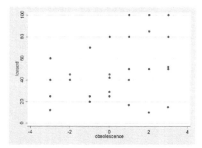

Figure 5-21 Scatter plot: leased and obsolescence

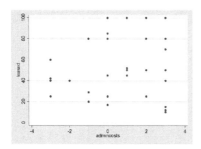

Figure 5-22 Scatter plot: leased and admincosts

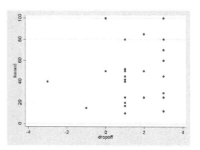

Figure 5-25 Scatter plot: leased and drop-off

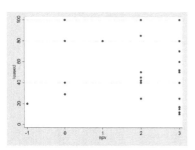

Figure 5-23 Scatter plot: leased and npv

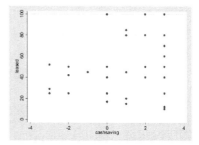

Figure 5-26 Scatter plot: leased and cash-saving

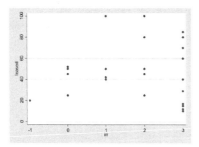

Figure 5-24 Scatter plot: leased and irr

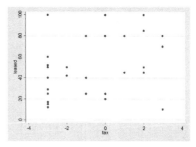

Figure 5-27 Scatter plot: leased and tax

142

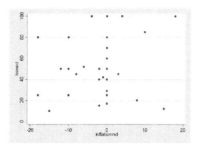

*Figure 5-28 Sactter plot: leased and infla-
tionind*

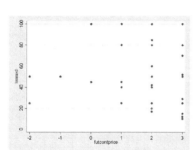

*Figure 5-29 Scatter plot: leased and fut-
contprice*

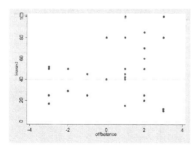

*Figure 5-30 Scatter plot: leased and off-
balance*

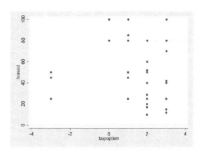

*Figure 5-31 Scatter plot: leased and
buyoption*

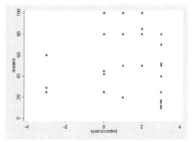

*Figure 5-32 Scatter plot: leased and
spendcontrol*

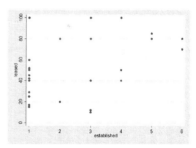

*Figure 5-33 Scatter plot: leased and estab-
lished*

143

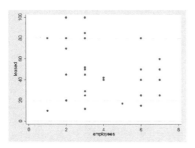

Figure 5-34 Scatter plot: leased and employees

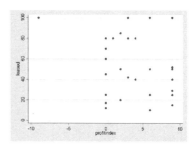

Figure 5-36 Scatter plot: leased and profit-index

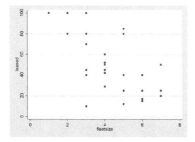

Figure 5-35 Scatter plot: leased and fleet-size

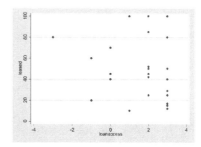

Figure 5-37 Scatter plot: leased and loanaccess

The scatter plots in Figures 5-16 to 5-37 either show a linear or unclear relationship to leased. Therefore, a linear econometric model seems to be appropriate.

5.3.4 Regression model

A regression analysis is used to find the variables that have a statistical significant impact on the dependent variable. Regression analysis in general takes simultaneous effects of several variables into account. The research design is non-experimental because survey data including statistical controls are used. No random selection or usage of random effects can be used to construct a randomized field experiment or a quasi-experiment. The number of shipping lines is too low to randomly select shipping lines that are invited. Even inviting as many shipping lines as possible and sending several reminders did not lead to the optimal 120 completed surveys.

The dependent variable is the lease share (variable: leased). The following chart shows the histogram of leased.

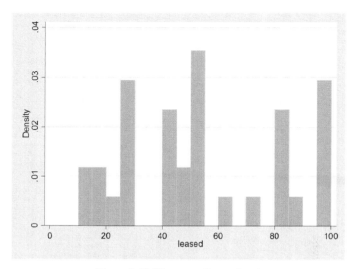

Figure 5-38 Histogram (lease share)

Because of the low number of observations (34), the shape of the histogram does not look like a perfect normal distribution. Nevertheless the assumption of a normal distribution seems to be appropriate. Therefore, an OLS panel regression model can be used. As discussed in section 5.3.3 above, a linear econometric model will be used for the analysis.

The regression equation is

leased =
$\alpha + \beta_1$flexibility $+ \beta_2$bufferstock $+ \beta_3$remoteloc $+ \beta_4$imbalances +
$\beta_5$leasedperiod $+ \beta_6$obsolescence $+ \beta_7$admincosts $+ \beta_8$npv $+ \beta_9$irr +
β_{10}dropoff $+ \beta_{11}$cashsaving $+ \beta_{12}$tax $+ \beta_{13}$inflationind $+ \beta_{14}$futcontprice +
β_{15}offbalance $+ \beta_{16}$buyoption$+\beta_{17}$spendcontrol +
β_{18}established $+\beta_{18}$employees $+ \beta_{20}$fleetsize$+\beta_{21}$profitindex $+ \beta_{22}$loanaccess +
ε

Equation 5-1

where the variables have the above (see section 5.3.2) defined meaning, β_i [-] are the coefficients of those variables, α[-] is a constant and ε [-] the error term.

5.3.5 Model estimates

Table 5-7 shows the OLS panel regression results with the **lease share** as dependent variable using the model described above and robust standard errors.

Table 5-7 Survey: robust OLS regression result (lease share)

```
reg leased flexibility bufferstock remoteloc imbalances leaseperiod obsolescence
admincosts npv irr dropoff cashsaving tax inflationind futcontprice offbalance
buyoption spendcontrol established employees fleetsize profitindex loanaccess, ro-
bust
```

```
Linear regression                                    Number of obs =      34
                                                     F( 22,   11) =   46.38
                                                     Prob > F      =  0.0000
                                                     R-squared     =  0.9047
                                                     Root MSE      =  15.345
```

leased	Coef.	Robust Std. Err.	t	P>|t|	[95% Conf. Interval]	
flexibility	-5.313542	3.573435	-1.49	0.165	-13.17862	2.551535
bufferstock	-1.514235	2.613759	-0.58	0.574	-7.267079	4.23861
remoteloc	-16.03848	4.33829	-3.70	0.004	-25.58699	-6.489972
imbalances	2.202035	2.323256	0.95	0.364	-2.911416	7.315487
leaseperiod	6.079423	4.081015	1.49	0.164	-2.902831	15.06168
obsolescence	10.84989	1.407708	7.71	0.000	7.751546	13.94824
admincosts	1.691877	3.644273	0.46	0.652	-6.329113	9.712868
npv	-13.37784	4.183142	-3.20	0.008	-22.58488	-4.170811
irr	-1.480468	3.895862	-0.38	0.711	-10.0552	7.094266
dropoff	19.54221	6.26151	3.12	0.010	5.760723	33.32371
cashsaving	7.051061	4.071369	1.73	0.111	-1.909962	16.01208
tax	-3.576358	2.445306	-1.46	0.172	-8.958439	1.805724
inflationind	.4870575	.3071849	1.59	0.141	-.189052	1.163167
futcontprice	-.6100325	2.633669	-0.23	0.821	-6.4067	5.186635
offbalance	4.650476	4.504609	1.03	0.324	-5.264101	14.56505
buyoption	-.7027219	1.450161	-0.48	0.637	-3.894504	2.489061
spendcontrol	1.700635	3.067187	0.55	0.590	-5.050198	8.451469
established	-7.678746	5.416804	-1.42	0.184	-19.60105	4.243559
employees	6.939994	2.727229	2.54	0.027	.9374034	12.94258
fleetsize	-15.5007	3.153458	-4.92	0.000	-22.44141	-8.559983
profitindex	1.846532	.8799121	2.10	0.060	-.0901416	3.783205
loanaccess	-6.933118	2.363162	-2.93	0.014	-12.1344	-1.731834
_cons	111.8156	21.63198	5.17	0.000	64.2039	159.4272

Several variables have a statistically significant effect on the lease share at the 10% level, even though the number of observations is very low (34). A low number of observations in general leads to lower statistical significance.

Availability of containers at remote locations (variable: remoteloc) is even significant at the 1% level. The impact is very high (minus 16) and contrary to expectation because a positive effect on the lease share was hypothesized. One explanation could be that shipping lines find the availability of equipment in remote locations important but do not think that lessors can offer this feature in a better way. A selection of a one point higher importance of remoteloc is associated with a 16 percentage point lower lease share if all other variables hold constant (ceteris paribus).

Leaseperiod is significant at the 10% level (p-value has to be divided by two because the hypothesis is one-sided and in the same direction as the result). The impact on the leasedshare is positive as hypothesized. A selection of one point higher importance of leaseperiod is associated with a 6.1 percentage point higher lease share (ceteris paribus).

Obsolescence is statistically significant at the 1% level and has a positive effect on the lease share as expected. A selection of a one point higher importance of obsolescence is associated with a 10.8 percentage point higher lease share (ceteris paribus).

NPV is statistically significant at the 1% level and has a high negative impact on the lease share, as expected. A selection of a one point higher importance of npv is associated with a 13.4 percentage point lower lease share of a shipping line (ceteris paribus).

Dropoff is statistically significant at the 1% level. The positive direction is surprising. A negative effect on the lease share with rising importance of dropoff costs was hypothesized because drop off costs of leased are higher than of owned equipment. A selection of a one point higher importance of dropoff is associated with 19.5 percentage point more leasing (ceteris paribus). This impact is the highest compared to the other variables.

Cashsaving is significant on the 6% level (p-value has to be divided by two). The effect is positive as hypothesized. A selection of a one point higher importance of cashsaving is associated with a 7.1 percentage point higher lease share (ceteris paribus).

Tax is significant at the 10% level (p-value has to be divided by two). The effect is negative as hypothesized. A selection of a one point higher importance of tax is associated with 3.6 percentage points less in lease share (ceteris paribus).

The variable employees is significant at the 3% level. The effect is positive, which is contrary to expectation. It was assumed that bigger firms—measured by the number of employees—lease less. Belonging to a one group higher employee class is associated with a 6.9 percentage point higher lease share (ceteris paribus).

Fleetsize is significant at the 1% level. The impact is negative as expected. Belonging to a one group higher fleetsize class is associated with a 15.5 percentage point lower lease share (ceteris paribus).

Profitindex is significant at the 6% level. The positive relationship to leased is contrary to the hypothesis. The more years between 2006 and 2008 are profitable and the higher the importance of profit the more containers are leased.

Loanaccess is significant at the 1% level. The negative impact on the lease share was expected. A selection of a one point better access to loan financing is associated with a 6.9 percentage point lower lease share (ceteris paribus).

The remaining variables (flexibility, bufferstock, imbalances, admincosts, irr, inflationind, futcontprice, offbalance, buyoption, spendcontrol and established) do not show statistical significance at the 10% level.

This analysis confirms the relevance of the npv calculation that is suggested theoretically (see chapter 2.1.2). On the other hand, it shows that other reasons for leasing are also very important in practice. These include access to bank loans, profitability, firm size, taxes, cash saving, obsolescence, the lease period and industry-specific reasons such as equipment availability at remote locations and drop off costs. These additional criteria will be integrated in an evaluation model in chapter 6.2. Interestingly, cash saving, which was not rated as a sensible reason for leasing by Brealey (2008), is one of the criteria that show statistical significance. There are two possible conclusions. Either the list of sensible reasons from Brealey should be extended, or shipping lines do not decide based on optimal criteria. In chapter 5.3, the impact of the financial crises on profits and bank loan access with their impact on the leasing strategy is described. Saving cash is an important goal if internal and loan financing is limited. Therefore, it is suggested to add cash saving to the list of sensible reasons for leasing.

The following table shows the OLS regression result with the **master lease** share as the dependent variable. All other aspects of the regression remain unchanged. Because master leases are a portion of the total leases, the hypotheses regarding the impact of the variables are the same as in the case described previously.

Table 5-8 Survey regression result (master lease)

```
reg    masterlease flexibility bufferstock remoteloc imbalances leaseperiod obsoles-
cence admincosts npv irr dropoff cashsaving tax inflationind futcontprice offbal-
ance buyoption spendcontrol established employees fleetsize profitindex loanaccess,
robust
```

```
Linear regression                                  Number of obs =       34
                                                   F( 22,    11) =     5.41
                                                   Prob > F      =   0.0030
                                                   R-squared     =   0.7430
                                                   Root MSE      =   20.229
```

masterlease	Coef.	Robust Std. Err.	t	P>|t|	[95% Conf. Interval]	
flexibility	7.46002	5.500843	1.36	0.202	-4.647253	19.56729
bufferstock	.7666291	3.829787	0.20	0.845	-7.662675	9.195934
remoteloc	-3.427078	6.524133	-0.53	0.610	-17.7866	10.93244
imbalances	-.2521433	3.473437	-0.07	0.943	-7.897127	7.39284
leaseperiod	10.1899	5.304479	1.92	0.081	-1.485176	21.86498
obsolescence	3.709089	3.565849	1.04	0.321	-4.139291	11.55747
admincosts	-.3826724	4.896323	-0.08	0.939	-11.15941	10.39406
npv	-7.75705	5.885438	-1.32	0.214	-20.71081	5.196712
irr	-.0786026	5.736611	-0.01	0.989	-12.7048	12.54759
dropoff	14.0298	7.631892	1.84	0.093	-2.767885	30.82747
cashsaving	-1.831818	5.433202	-0.34	0.742	-13.79021	10.12658
tax	-2.944429	3.925845	-0.75	0.469	-11.58516	5.696298
inflationind	-.9031583	.6363462	-1.42	0.184	-2.303747	.4974302
futcontprice	-2.876523	4.61921	-0.62	0.546	-13.04334	7.29029
offbalance	-.3432619	4.601221	-0.07	0.942	-10.47048	9.783956
buyoption	-1.983431	3.248456	-0.61	0.554	-9.133235	5.166372
spendcontrol	-.4714237	4.260467	-0.11	0.914	-9.848648	8.905801
established	-2.012525	6.374588	-0.32	0.758	-16.0429	12.01785
employees	3.677315	3.086122	1.19	0.259	-3.115193	10.46982
fleetsize	-5.412968	3.26206	-1.66	0.125	-12.59271	1.766778
profitindex	-.4869311	1.523732	-0.32	0.755	-3.840643	2.86678
loanaccess	-3.488152	4.346387	-0.80	0.439	-13.05448	6.07818
_cons	25.4218	26.93334	0.94	0.366	-33.85807	84.70167

The regression result shows only a few variables with statistical significance at the 10% level.

Flexibility is significant at the 10% level (p-value has to be divided by two). As expected, the direction of the effect is positive. A selection of a one point higher importance of flexibility is associated with a 7.5 percentage point higher master lease share (ceteris paribus). This effect is significant in absolute terms.

Leaseperiod is significant at the 4% level. The direction of the effect is positive as hypothesized. A selection of a one point higher importance of leaseperiod is associated with 10.2 percentage point higher lease share (ceteris paribus). This is also significant in absolute terms.

Dropoff is significant at the 9% level. The effect is positive, which is contrary to expectations as in the case of the total lease share. A selection of a one point higher importance of dropoff is associated with a 14 percentage point higher lease share (ceteris paribus).

Fleetsize is significant at the 6% level. The effect is negative as expected. Belonging to a one group higher fleetsize class is associated with a 5.4 percentage point lower lease share (ceteris paribus).

The other variables do not show statistical significance. This might be due to the low number of observations.

It can be concluded that regarding the master lease share, the variables flexibility, lease period, drop off costs and fleet size are important, whereas financial calculations like npv are of less importance for the shipping lines. This makes sense because master leases have a duration of about one year and therefore provide a good deal of flexibility. Drop off costs play an important role here because they are a major cost driver. The fleet size matters because the larger shipping lines are able to optimize their equipment management on a global basis. Smaller shipping lines tend to use a higher portion of master leases to outsource (part of) the equipment management problem.

The following table presents the results of a regression analysis with the share of *long term* leasing as a dependent variable. The other variables remain unchanged. Because long term leasing is part of the overall lease share, the hypotheses are the same as described above in section 5.3.1.

Table 5-9 Survey regression result (long term)

```
reg longterm flexibility bufferstock remoteloc imbalances leaseperiod obsolescence
admincosts npv irr dropoff cashsaving tax inflationind futcontprice offbalance
buyoption spendcontrol established employees fleetsize profitindex loanaccess, ro-
bust
```

```
Linear regression                          Number of obs =        34
                                           F ( 22,   11) =      6.65
                                           Prob > F      =    0.0012
                                           R-squared     =    0.7068
                                           Root MSE      =    26.865
```

longterm	Coef.	Robust Std. Err.	t	P>|t|	[95% Conf. Interval]	
flexibility	-12.77356	6.057323	-2.11	0.059	-26.10564	.5585172
bufferstock	-2.280864	5.680806	-0.40	0.696	-14.78423	10.22251
remoteloc	-12.61141	5.746202	-2.19	0.051	-25.25871	.035901
imbalances	2.454179	4.154258	0.59	0.567	-6.689282	11.59764
leaseperiod	-4.11048	5.918278	-0.69	0.502	-17.13652	8.915563
obsolescence	7.140801	3.495975	2.04	0.066	-.5537882	14.83539
admincosts	2.07455	6.022084	0.34	0.737	-11.17997	15.32907
npv	-5.620794	6.298512	-0.89	0.391	-19.48373	8.242137
irr	-1.401865	8.164798	-0.17	0.867	-19.37246	16.56873
dropoff	5.512419	8.932666	0.62	0.550	-14.14825	25.17308
cashsaving	8.882879	7.289429	1.22	0.248	-7.161047	24.9268
tax	-.6319287	4.493907	-0.14	0.891	-10.52295	9.259094
inflationind	1.390216	.5537249	2.51	0.029	.1714754	2.608956
futcontprice	2.266491	4.762765	0.48	0.643	-8.216284	12.74927
offbalance	4.993738	7.395782	0.68	0.513	-11.28427	21.27174
buyoption	1.28071	3.126007	0.41	0.690	-5.599586	8.161006
spendcontrol	2.172059	5.335624	0.41	0.692	-9.57157	13.91569
established	-5.666221	9.051339	-0.63	0.544	-25.58808	14.25564
employees	3.262679	4.240235	0.77	0.458	-6.070014	12.59537
fleetsize	-10.08773	4.787745	-2.11	0.059	-20.62548	.4500282
profitindex	2.333463	1.415026	1.65	0.127	-.7809888	5.447915
loanaccess	-3.444966	4.542556	-0.76	0.464	-13.44307	6.553134
_cons	86.39376	36.0677	? 34	0.039	5.248502	167.539

Again, in Table 5-9, fewer variables than in the total lease share case show statistical significance at the 10% level.

Flexibility is significant at the 6% level. The effect is negative, which is opposite to the hypothesis and the impact in the master lease case. A selection of a one point higher importance of flexibility is associated with a 12.8 percentage point lower long term lease share (ceteris paribus). This makes sense because long term leases (with 3 to 5 years duration) are less flexible than master leases.

Remoteloc is significant at the 5% level. The effect is negative, which is opposite to expectation as in the total lease share case. A selection of a one point higher importance of remoteloc is associated with a 12.6 percentage point less long term lease share (ceteris paribus).

Obsolescence is significant at the 3% level. The effect is positive as hypothesized. A selection of a one point higher importance of obsolescence is associated with a 7.1 percentage point higher long term lease share (ceteris paribus).

Inflationind shows significance at the 3% level. Infaltionind is neither significant in the general lease share case nor in the master lease case. The effect is positive, which makes sense, because long term leases provide a certain hedge against inflation (fixed per diem rate for three to five years). A selection of a one point higher importance of inflationind is associated with a 1.4 percentage point higher long term lease share (ceteris paribus). This is significant in absolute terms because the range of inflationindex is from -9 to +9 because of the multiplication of importance and direction.

Fleetsize is significant at the 3% level. The effect is negative as expected. Belonging to a one group higher fleetsize class is associated with a 10.1 percentage point lower long term lease share (ceteris paribus).

No other variables show statistical significance at the 10% level. Interestingly, this includes npv and irr, which should have a significant impact according to theory (see chapter 2).

The following table presents the results of a regression analysis with the share of *lease purchase* as dependent variable. The other variables remain unchanged. Because lease purchase is seen as part of the purchase share, the hypotheses are opposite to the lease share case (see section 5.3.1).

Table 5-10 Survey regression result (lease purchase)

```
reg lp flexibility bufferstock remoteloc imbalances leaseperiod obsolescence admin-
costs npv irr dropoff cashsaving tax inflationind futcontprice offbalance buyoption
spendcontrol established employees fleetsize profitindex loanaccess, robust
```

Linear regression

Number of obs = 34
$F(22, 11)$ = 3.03
Prob > F = 0.0304
R-squared = 0.8081
Root MSE = 12.171

lp	Coef.	Robust Std. Err.	t	P>|t|	[95% Conf. Interval]	
flexibility	-1.925132	3.685005	-0.52	0.612	-10.03577	6.185508
bufferstock	2.312962	1.720205	1.34	0.206	-1.473183	6.099108
remoteloc	3.602825	4.127173	0.87	0.401	-5.481021	12.68667
imbalances	-1.280639	2.439499	-0.52	0.610	-6.649939	4.088661
leaseperiod	.3311488	2.662065	0.12	0.903	-5.528017	6.190315
obsolescence	-6.211151	2.844508	-2.18	0.052	-12.47187	.0495682
admincosts	3.79759	3.677619	1.03	0.324	-4.296794	11.89197
npv	2.213352	2.998156	0.74	0.476	-4.385544	8.812248
irr	4.523343	2.875536	1.57	0.144	-1.80567	10.85236
dropoff	-3.025472	3.390913	-0.89	0.391	-10.48882	4.437877
cashsaving	-7.502655	3.882033	-1.93	0.079	-16.04695	1.041642
tax	-2.601969	2.570017	-1.01	0.333	-8.258538	3.054599
inflationind	.6514331	.3779685	1.72	0.113	-.1804699	1.483336
futcontprice	-1.492917	3.118888	-0.48	0.642	-8.357542	5.371708
offbalance	2.466046	2.934169	0.84	0.419	-3.992016	8.924108
buyoption	1.93461	1.864583	1.04	0.322	-2.169309	6.038529
spendcontrol	4.517956	2.451464	1.84	0.092	-.8776793	9.913592
established	.5635011	3.063441	0.18	0.857	-6.179087	7.30609
employees	-2.259975	1.942162	-1.16	0.269	-6.534644	2.014695
fleetsize	2.849071	2.042307	1.40	0.191	-1.646017	7.344159
profitindex	-.4759505	.9063905	-0.53	0.610	-2.470903	1.519002
loanaccess	-1.760918	2.235718	-0.79	0.448	-6.681701	3.159865
_cons	-2.385519	12.36354	-0.19	0.851	-29.59749	24.82646

Obsolescence shows significance at the 3% level. The direction of the impact is negative, which is as hypothesized (positive in the case of lease share). A selection of a one point higher importance of obsolescence is associated with a 6.2 percentage point less lease purchase share (ceteris paribus).

Irr is significant at the 7% level. The direction is positive as expected (negative in the case of lease share). A selection of a one point higher importance is associated with a 3.9 percentage point higher lease purchase share. It is worth mentioning that in this case, npv is not statistically significant. This leads to the conclusion that practitioners tend to use irr to evaluate lease purchase opportunities.

Cashsaving is significant at the 4% level, and the impact is negative as hypothesized. A selection of a one point higher importance of cashsaving is associated with a 7.5 percentage point lower lease purchase share.

Spendcontrol is statistically significant at the 9% level. The effect is positive, which is contrary to expectation. A selection of a one point higher importance of spendcontrol is associated with a 4.5 percentage point higher lease purchase share. A possible conclusion could be that it is easier to get management approval for lease purchases than for instant purchases.

Fleetsize shows statistical significance at the 10% level. The effect is positive as expected. Belonging to a one group higher fleetsize class is associated with a 2.8 percentage point higher long term lease share (ceteris paribus).

All other variables do not show statistical significance.

Last, the share of *owned* (dependent variable) equipment is analyzed using regression. The other variables remain unchanged. The hypotheses are opposite to the lease share case (see section 5.3.1).

Table 5-11 Survey regression result (owned)

```
reg owned flexibility bufferstock remoteloc imbalances leaseperiod obsolescence ad-
mincosts npv irr dropoff cashsaving tax inflationind futcontprice offbalance buyop-
tion spendcontrol established employees fleetsize profitindex loanaccess, robust

Linear regression                                    Number of obs =        34
                                                     F( 22,    11) =      9.90
                                                     Prob > F      =    0.0002
                                                     R-squared     =    0.7804
                                                     Root MSE      =    21.185
```

owned	Coef.	Robust Std. Err.	t	P>|t|	[95% Conf. Interval]	
flexibility	7.238674	5.126922	1.41	0.186	-4.045605	18.52295
bufferstock	-.7987279	3.697006	-0.22	0.833	-8.935783	7.338328
remoteloc	12.43566	5.534543	2.25	0.046	.2542103	24.6171
imbalances	-.9213962	3.291323	-0.28	0.785	-8.16555	6.322758
leaseperiod	-6.410572	4.893794	-1.31	0.217	-17.18174	4.360596
obsolescence	-4.638739	2.999517	-1.55	0.150	-11.24063	1.963154
admincosts	-5.489468	5.436926	-1.01	0.334	-17.45606	6.477125
npv	11.16449	4.762785	2.34	0.039	.6816741	21.64731
irr	-3.042876	5.514573	-0.55	0.592	-15.18037	9.094618
dropoff	-16.51674	7.516016	-2.20	0.050	-33.05938	.0258963
cashsaving	.4515941	6.269582	0.07	0.944	-13.34766	14.25085
tax	6.178327	3.889881	1.59	0.141	-2.383243	14.7399
inflationind	-1.138491	.4223086	-2.70	0.021	-2.067986	-.2089955
futcontprice	2.102949	4.393365	0.48	0.642	-7.566781	11.77268
offbalance	-7.116522	6.333287	-1.12	0.285	-21.05599	6.822948
buyoption	-1.231888	2.438927	-0.51	0.623	-6.59993	4.136154
spendcontrol	-6.218592	4.500251	-1.38	0.194	-16.12358	3.686394
established	7.115245	7.42218	0.96	0.358	-9.220862	23.45135
employees	-4.680019	3.803589	-1.23	0.244	-13.05166	3.691624
fleetsize	12.65163	4.227596	2.99	0.012	3.34675	21.9565
profitindex	-1.370581	1.208224	-1.13	0.281	-4.029863	1.288701
loanaccess	8.694036	3.404412	2.55	0.027	1.200976	16.1871
_cons	-9.430036	27.80205	-0.34	0.741	-70.62193	51.76186

Remoteloc shows statistical significance at the 5% level. The effect is positive, which is opposite to the hypothesis. A selection of a one point higher importance of remoteloc is associated with a 12.4 percentage point higher share of owned equipment (ceteris paribus). Shipping lines seem to serve remote locations with owned containers.

Obsolescence is significant at the 8% level. The direction of the impact is negative, which is as hypothesized (positive in the case of lease share). A selection of a one point higher importance of obsolescence is associated with a 4.6 percentage point less owned share (ceteris paribus).

Npv shows significance at the 2% level. The direction of the impact is positive as hypothesized. A selection of a one point higher importance of npv is associated with an 11.1 percentage point higher owned share (ceteris paribus).

Dropoff is significant at the 5% level. The effect is negative, which is contrary to expectation, as in the case of the total lease share. A selection of a one point higher importance of dropoff is associated with a 16.5 percentage point higher owned (ceteris paribus).

Tax is significant at the 7% level. The direction is positive as hypothesized. A selection of a one point higher importance of tax is associated with a 6.2 percentage point higher owned share (ceteris paribus).

Inflationind is significant at the 2% level. The effect is negative. A selection of a one point higher importance of inflationind is associated with a 1.3 percentage point lower owned share (ceteris paribus). This effect is rather small compared to the other coefficients. Therefore, the absolute significance is low.

Spendcontrol is statistically significant at the 10% level. The effect is negative, which was expected. A selection of a one point higher importance of spendcontrol is associated with a 6.2 percentage point lower owned share (ceteris paribus).

Fleetsize shows statistical significance at the 1% level. The effect is positive as expected. Belonging to a one group higher fleetsize class is associated with a 12.7 percentage point higher long term lease share (ceteris paribus).

No other variable shows statistical significance regarding their impact on the share of owned equipment. Due to the low number of observations, it is not possible to analyze the effects in subgroups (for example, large shipping lines) using regression analysis.

5.3.6 Conclusion of econometrical analysis of survey data

The econometrical analysis of the survey data confirms the relevance of the NAL calculation for the buy or lease decision regarding container equipment in practice. A higher importance of NAL is associated with a lower lease share. In addition the importance of access to bank loans (negative), profitability (positive), fleet size (negative), taxes (negative), cash saving (positive), obsolescence (positive), the lease period (positive) as well as industry specific reasons such as equipment availability at remote locations (positive) and drop off (positive) costs show a statistically significant impact on the lease share. These additional criteria will be integrated in an extended evaluation model in chapter 6.2.

Regarding master leases, flexibility, lease period, drop off costs and fleet size are important, whereas financial calculations like NAL are of less importance for the shipping lines. For long term leasing decisions, the criteria flexibility, remoteloc, obsolescence, inflationind and fleetsize are important. For lease purchase decisions, obsolescence, irr, cashsaving, spendcontrol and fleetsize are taken into account.

5.4 Comparison with past surveys

5.4.1 Comparison with Temple's 1987 survey

In 1987, Temple surveyed 15 container shipping lines regarding their buy or lease decision. In this section, the results of Temple's survey are compared with the survey results considered in this thesis. Comparability is limited because only 15 shipping lines were surveyed in 1987, whereas 51 completed questionnaires were received in 2010. Furthermore, the original set of questions from 1987 is no longer available. Therefore, the 2010 survey questions differ to some extent, even if they attempted to match the question topics from the earlier survey.

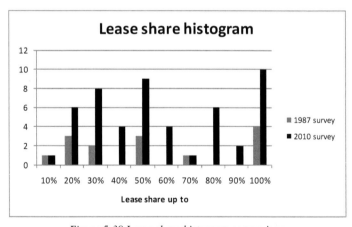

Figure 5-39 Lease share histogram comparison

Figure 5-39 shows the participants' lease share distribution for both surveys. Some similarity can be seen. Shipping lines still have very different leasing strategies. All surveyed liners use leasing. The leasing share in 2010 and 1987 survey ranges from about 10% to 100%.

The average survey lease share increased from 51.7% in 1987 to 55.7% in 2010. During this period, the total market share of leased equipment dropped from 47% to 41% (figures calculated based on Foxcroft (2008, 2009b)). This can be explained by the firm size of the participants. In the 2010 survey, big shipping lines are underrepresented in terms of market share whereas they are overrepresented in the 1987 survey.

Both surveys show a declining lease share with the size of the total container fleet.

Table 5-12 Survey result comparison with Temple

Criteria	2010 Survey % of positive responses	1987 Temple survey % of responses
IRR	89%	n.a.
Future container prices	88%	n.a.
Offsetting imbalances	86%	31%
NPV	83%	n.a.
Profitability	83%	n.a.
Flexibility	83%	82%
Leasing drop off costs	81%	n.a.
Purchase options	79%	n.a.
Length of lease period	78%	n.a.
Buffer stock function	75%	44%
Off balance sheet financing	75%	n.a.
Expenditure controls	74%	n.a.
Saving cash	71%	38%
Inhouse admin costs	65%	19%
Availability in remote locations	61%	7%
Inflation expectations	52%	n.a.
Hedging new equipment risk	51%	25%
Tax effects	36%	n.a.

Table 5-11 compares the importance of several decision criteria in both studies. The 1987 survey only provides a percentage for how often a criterion was mentioned. The 2010 survey provides more detailed information including the intensity of the opinion. To compare both surveys, the percentage of positive responses (answers 1, 2 and 3) from the 2010 survey is calculated. Furthermore several criteria were not analyzed in the 1987 survey (marked with n.a.). This includes the important criterion NPV.

Both surveys find that equipment flexibility is a very important decision criterion (83 versus 82%).

The importance of all other criteria listed in both surveys seems to have increased from 1987 to 2010. Offsetting imbalances is very important in the 2010 survey (86% versus 31%). Taking into account the intensity of the opinion by calculating the weighted average response, its importance in the 2010 survey reduces to rank 5 (see Table 5-2). Offsetting imbalances seems to be most important for medium sized shipping lines with a total container volume of 10,000 to 200,000 TEU. The fleet size of the big players in 1987 was 100,000 TEU, whereas it is now in the range of 1 million TEU and above. If the fleet size of the participants in 1987 is multiplied by 10, nearly all participants appear in the category above 200,000 TEU, where the importance of offsetting imbalances is lower according to the 2010 survey. Therefore the first impression that the importance of offsetting imbalances has drastically increased might be misleading.

The buffer stock function of leasing is more important in the 2010 survey (75% versus 44%). Due to the financial crises, the shipping lines might be more risk adverse. The option to redeliver unused containers as well as the option to increase the container fleet without delay is highly recognized, because it reduces the level of unutilized equipment.

The same argument can be used for the saving cash criterion. Because of the financial crises, cash is more important than before (71% versus 38%).

There is a big difference between the surveys regarding "availability in remote locations" (61% versus 7%). One reason could be the globalization of the business. Also, smaller players need to have access to equipment on a global basis.

A different survey technique (interview versus Internet) as well as different questions might be a reason for the lower importance figures in the 1987 survey in general.

Even if the 2010 survey shows that participating shipping lines highly respect the advantages of leasing, leasing is perceived expensive by more participants than before (79% versus 38%).

Table 5-13 Comparison of leasing strategies

Criteria	2010 Survey % of positive responses	1987 Temple survey % of responses
Number of current lessors	1 to 20	5 to 12
Plan to work with less lessors	16%	46%
Plan to keep the number of lessors	44%	46%
Plan to work with more lessors	40%	8%
Pooling of equipment (1,2,3/Yes)	42%	33%
Pooling of equipment (-3,-2,-1,0/No)	58%	67%

Table 5-12 provides a comparison of leasing strategies in 1997 and 2010. The diversity of the used number of lessors has increased. This could be due to the fact that more firms of all sizes were surveyed. The 2010 average number of lessors a firm works with is 7.6. This figure is not available for 1987, but from the range of 5 to 12 lessors, an average of about 8 can be estimated. It looks like shipping lines did not realize their plan to reduce the number of lessors they work with (1987: 46%). Currently there is a tendency to increase the number of lessors.

There survey results regarding pooling are similar. Both surveys show a majority that does not plan to pool equipment.

5.4.2 Comparison with Muhherjee's survey in 1991

Mukherjee (1991) surveyed Fortune top 500 firms from many industries regarding their buy or lease decision, whereas the 2010 survey focuses exclusively on container shipping.

Table 5-14 NPV discount factor comparison

	2010 survey	1991 Mukherjee survey
Before tax borrowing rate	20.5%	6.3%
After tax borrowing rate	5.1%	75.0%
WACC	48.7%	12.5%
Several discount rates according to the risk of the cash flows	25.6%	6.3%

Table 5-13 compares the discount factors used by the participants of the 1991 and the 2010 survey. Because the used categories are not identical, similar categories are summarized to make the surveys comparable. Interestingly, 75% of the participating Fortune 500 firms in 1991 use the after tax borrowing rate as suggested by theory (see chapter 2.1.2). In 2010, only 5.1% of the participating shipping lines follow the theoretical advice. Instead, many practitioners in shipping (48.7%) use the WACC, which should be used to evaluate an investment decision rather than a financing decision.

The category "several discount factors according to the risk of the cash flows" was chosen by 25.6% in 2010 and 6.3% in 1991. The two Fortune 500 firms working with several discount factors use the after tax borrowing costs for the yearly costs and the WACC for the residual value. The appropriate discount rate will be discussed in chapter 6.

Table 5-15 Comparison of reasons for leasing with 1991 survey

Reasons for leasing	2010 survey	1991 Mukherjee survey
Avoiding risk of obsolescence	51%	82%
Leasing is cheaper than borrowing	12%	57%
Length of lease period	78%	5%
Taxes	36%	5%
Off balance sheet financing	75%	3%
Avoidance of capital expenditure controls	74%	2%

Table 5-14 shows some interesting differences between the 1991 and 2010 survey. Avoiding the risk of obsolescence (hedging the risk of new equipment types) seems to be less important for the shipping industry (51% versus 82%). A majority of the participating Fortune 500 firms perceive leasing as cheaper than borrowing (12% versus 57%). The length of the lease period, off balance sheet financing and expenditure controls are much more important in shipping. Taxes seem to be neither very important for the decision in shipping nor for the Fortune top 500 firms.

5.5 Summary of survey and lessons learned

The shipping line survey conducted in 2010 that is presented in this chapter delivers some interesting insights on the decision process in practice. It updates the survey conducted by Temple in 1987 and provides information regarding additional decision criteria (including NPV analysis) for the first time.

First, shipping lines take many decision criteria into account. The analysis shows that the NPV calculation result is one important criterion. But other criteria, like flexibility, future container prices and profitability also have a very high importance. Furthermore these criteria include "not sensible" reasons for leasing as Brealey et al. (2008) describes them: saving cash and off balance sheet financing (see chapter 2.1.1).

Shipping lines seem to be uncertain which discount rate should be used for the NPV analysis because many practitioners either are not sure or choose a not recommended interest rate (after tax borrowing rate). The comparison to the survey conducted by Mukherje (1991) shows that the recommended discount rate is used by most of the Fortune 500 firms. In chapter 6.2.2, a model for the container buy or lease decision is developed, which can improve the situation in the future.

The respondents perceive leasing as more expensive compared to owning. One component of the leasing cost is repair. They also have the impression that repair costs of leased equipment are higher than for owned containers.

There is much of uncertainty regarding inflation. Practitioners have very different views of the importance of inflation as well as the direction of an impact of higher expected inflation on the lease share.

The leasing strategy of most shipping lines remains unchanged. There is only a slight tendency towards usage of more lessors, more equipment pooling and a higher lease share. This could be the result of the financial crises, which reduced bank loan access and profits.

The econometrical analysis of the survey data confirms the impact of some criteria with statistical significance taking simultaneous effects into account. This is the first econometrical analysis of survey data performed regarding the container buy or lease decision of shipping lines. The importance of npv, tax, fleetsize and loanaccess have a significant negative impact on the lease share as hypothesized. The importance of the lease period, obsolescence and cashsaving have a significant positive impact as hypothesized. The variables remoteloc (negative), dropoff (positive), employees (positive) and profitindex (positive) show a statistically significant impact contrary to expectation. Again, this analysis shows that there are a number of important criteria besides the NPV analysis. These criteria will be used to extend the existing evaluation model in chapter 6.

The analysis also shows differences between master lease and long term lease decisions. The importance of flexibility, leaseperiod and fleetsize has a significant positive impact on the master lease share as hypothesized. Furthermore, dropoff costs have a significant positive impact on the masterlease share, which is contrary to expectation. Only two of these variables also have a significant effect on the long term lease share: flexibility and fleetsize. However, their impact is negative, which is contrary to expectation and the master lease case. Furthermore, the variables obsolescence and inflationind have a positive impact on the long term lease share as expected. Last, the variable remoteloc has a negative association to the long term leasing share, which is contrary to expectation. It is worth mentioning that several variables show statistical significance in the total lease share case whereas they are neither significant in the master nor in the long term lease case: npv, cashsaving, tax, employees, profitindex and loanaccess. The fact that npv is not significant in the long term case whereas several other variables show statistical significance confirms the hypothesis of the relevance of many criteria for the decision.

The comparison with the container buy or lease survey conducted by Temple (1987) shows that shipping lines still have very different leasing strategies. All surveyed liners use leasing, but the leased share ranges in both surveys from about 10% to 100%. The npv criterion was not analyzed in 1987. Flexibility was regarded as very important in both surveys. The other criteria (offsetting imbalances, buffer stock function, cash saving, inhouse administration costs, availability in remote locations and hedging new equipment risk) show an increased importance in the 2010 survey.

Shipping lines seem to have improved their container management since 1987 by taking many factors into account when deciding to lease or to buy.

6 Enhanced theoretical model

In this chapter, the existing theoretical model will be enhanced based on the decision criteria suggested in previous literature (chapter 2), the conclusions of the macroeconomic (chapter 3) as well as the microeconomic (chapter 4) empirical analysis and the survey results (chapter 5).

6.1 General buy or lease evaluation concept

As a starting point for the improvement of the general theoretical model, the formula presented in the standard corporate finance and academic literature as discussed in the section 2.1.1 is chosen:

$$\mathbf{NAL} = \mathbf{D_0} + \sum_{t=1}^{N} \frac{-L_t(1-T)-D_t T+O_t(1-T)}{[1+r_d(1-T)]^t} - \frac{S_N}{[1+r_d(1-T)]^N} \qquad \textbf{Equation 6-1}$$

Where:

NAL	= net advantage of leasing [currency]
D_0	= initial financing provided (debt amount received) in t_0 [currency]
N	= length of the lease in years [-]
L_t	= lease payment in period t [currency]
T	= marginal corporate tax rate [%]
D_t	= depreciation in period t [currency]
O_t	= operative costs incl. in lease (e.g. maintenance, insurance) [currency]
S_N	= lessee's after tax salvage value (terminal value) at time N [currency]
$r_d(1-T)$	= discount rate (risk equivalent opportunity costs/after tax cost of debt) [%]

If NAL is positive, the firm should lease; otherwise the firm should buy and borrow the asset.

Based on the decision criteria listed below the model will be enhanced.

6.1.1 General decision criteria

The following table gives an overview of the decision criteria suggested in previous literature (chapter 2) and the empirical analysis (chapters 3 to 5) which are important for the general (non industry specific) evaluation model. Furthermore, it is stated if they are included in the suggested theoretical model presented in 2.1. The table first lists the criteria that are included in the existing formula (see section 6.1) and thereafter the criteria that are not included. Decision criteria will be included in the enhanced general model they show statistical significance in one of the empirical analyses (with no contradicting impact) or a weighted average importance of more than one in the survey. Container industry-specific reasons will be analyzed in section 6.2.

Table 6-1 Decision criteria for general buy or lease decisions

Decision criteria	Source chapter	Included in existing theoretical model	Enhanced model integration
Tax rate	2, 4, 5	yes	yes
Valuable options	2	yes - model extensions	yes
NPV advantage	2, 3, 4, 5	yes	yes
Availability of low-cost credit	2, 4, 5	yes	yes
Financial constraints (100%financing)/ asymmetric information / loan access	2, 4, 5	no	yes
Establishment year	2, 4, 5	no	yes
Rating	2, 4, 5	no	yes
Current profitability / After-tax profit	2, 4, 5	no	yes
Debt share / charter share	2, 4	no	no – not significant
Agency costs (future collateral and interest costs increase if leasing is used)	2	no	no – not analyzed
Off-balance sheet financing / debt ratio	2, 5	no	yes
Deposits / advances / saving cash	2, 5	no	yes
Inflation	2, 3, 4, 5	no	no – contradicting effects
Better acquisition or sale price of lessor	2	no	yes
Expected inflation / inflationindex	2, 5	no	no – contradicting effects
Avoid loan restrictions	2	no	no – not analyzed
Transaction and Information costs - avoid purchase and disposal transaction - avoid capital expenditure approval - reduce record keeping/administration - faster than purchasing and negotiating loans (standardized) - right equipment, condition and location - flexible and convenient - no ownership dilution	2, 5	no	yes

Decision criteria	Source chapter	Included in existing theoretical model	Enhanced model integration
Risk sharing - avoid sale and residual risk - short term usage - protect against obsolescence - hedge of business risk if lease rate is tied to usage - reduced responsibility - hedge against a loss of tax shields in the case of declining profits	2, 5	no	yes
Degree of lessor competition	2	no	no – not analyzed
Merger with other shipping line	4	no	no – merger affects lease share without strategic decision

Table 6-1 shows that several decision criteria are not included in the general buy or lease model. Their integration will be discussed in section 6.1.2.

6.1.2 Enhanced general buy or lease evaluation model

To integrate all decision criteria mentioned in Table 3-1, a two-step approach to the buy or lease decision is suggested.

In the **first step** firms analyze a number of simple criteria without the necessity of a comparing calculation:

First, if a company is financially constrained, cash plays an important role. Often credit lines are exhausted and no further bank loans are available. The establishment year of the company plays a role because a longer track record builds up confidence of banks and internal funds. A better credit rating helps to get additional funds. Leasing is the preferred alternative in the case of financial constrains / limited track record / lower rating because up to 100% of the asset costs are financed.

Second, profitability might have two effects. On one hand, leasing and debt affect the profitability differently. Leasing reduces the profit less than loan financing in the first years and more in the later years. This effect might be interesting for some firms and lead to their decision to lease. On the other hand, a high profitability is often associated with a high liquidity level. This could lead to the decision to buy (see the pecking order theory of Myers & Majluf (1984)).

Third, off balance sheet financing might be appealing for firms that want to retain their current debt share to keep their existing rating / debt financing conditions. Leasing offers a simple way to generate off balance sheet financing. Leasing does not change the balance sheet, but agency costs have to be taken into account. Banks might increase the future interest or collateral level even if the balance sheet is unchanged.

Fourth, firms might choose to lease equipment to avoid transaction and information costs. For example, if a firm does not have connections to a supplier of an equipment type which is only produced in a different country whereas it is available at its location for lease, the lease alternative might be very attractive. Leasing avoids the purchase and disposal transaction, capital expenditure approvals, reduces record keeping, is faster than purchasing and negotiating loans, is flexible and avoids ownership dilution.

Fifth, risk sharing can be a reason to choose leasing. For example, leasing can be used to avoid the residual risk, the risk of obsolescence of equipment or if the equipment is only needed for a short period (e.g. a few days or weeks).

In **step two**, firms, that have not decided based on one of the criteria listed in step one, decide based on the following NAL calculation. A better purchase or sales price of the lessor is taken care of in the new formula by using the purchase price of the lessor and the salvage value of the lessee. All other criteria to be integrated according to Table 6-1 with the exception of deposits and advances have been taken into account either in step one or the general formula presented in section 6.1. On one hand, loan financing requires in most cases that the firms pay for a certain share of the acquisition cost using equity (often 20 to 40% of acquisition costs). On the other hand, lessors sometimes require lessees to pay a deposit (for example, two monthly rentals). Deposits are in general lower than advances.

To simplify the integration of deposits and advances the general formula presented in section 3.1 is split into two NPV calculations. The NPV of the loan alternative is calculated as follows:

$$NPV_D = -A_0 + D_0 - \sum_{t=1}^{N} \frac{R_t + I_t(1-T)}{[1+r_d(1-T)]^t} + \sum_{t=1}^{N} \frac{D_t T}{[1+r_d(1-T)]^t} + \frac{S_N}{[1+r_d(1-T)]^N} \qquad \text{Equation 6-2}$$

Where the variables have the same meaning as in section 6.1 and
A_0 = lessor's acquisition cost of asset in t_0 [currency]
R_t = repayment in period t [currency]
I_t = interests in period t [currency]

The term $-A_0 + D_0$ represents the advance (equity share) that the firm has to provide for acquiring the asset. Schallheim (1994, p. 116) shows that the term

$$\sum_{t=1}^{N} \frac{R_t + I_t(1-T)}{[1+r_d(1-T)]^t}$$

equals to the debt amount if the discount rate is the after tax cost of debt. Since this is the case, the formula reduces to

$$NPV_D = -A_0 + \sum_{t=1}^{N} \frac{D_t T}{[1+r_d(1-T)]^t} + \frac{S_N}{[1+r_d(1-T)]^N} \qquad \text{Equation 6-3}$$

The NPV of the leasing alternative is calculated as follows:

$$NPV_L = -Dep_0 + \sum_{t=1}^{N} \frac{-L_t(1-T)+O_t(1-T)}{[1+r_d(1-T)]^t} + \frac{Dep_0}{[1+r_d(1-T)]^N} \qquad \text{Equation 6-4}$$

The variables have the same meaning as in section 6.1 and
Dep_0 = Deposit provided to the lessor in t_0 [currency]

It is assumed that the deposit is not carrying interests as it is often the case in practice.

Next, the two formulas can be assembled to the NAL:

$$NAL = NPV_L - NPV_D = A_0 - Dep_0 + \sum_{t=1}^{N} \frac{-L_t(1-T)-D_t T+O_t(1-T)}{[1+r_d(1-T)]^t} - \frac{S_N}{[1+r_d(1-T)]^N} +$$
$$\frac{Dep_0}{[1+r_d(1-T)]^N} \qquad \text{Equation 6-5}$$

There are three differences to the formula presented in 6.1. First, Brealey (2008) does not differentiate between the cost of the asset and the debt amount, because it is assumed that the total acquisition price is financed ($A_0 = D_0$). Second, the initial deposit paid to the lessor (Dep_0) is now included. Third, the last term describes the discounted repayment of the deposit.

The discount factor has been controversially discussed by many authors. The after- tax cost of debt has a prominent role in the literature. The WACC is also emphasized by some authors (see section 3.1.1). The after-tax cost of debt makes sense for the term

$$\sum_{t=1}^{N} \frac{-L_t(1-T)-D_t T+O_t(1-T)}{[1+r_d(1-T)]^t}$$

because the riskiness of the lease cash flow is comparable to the loan cash flow. Also the tax and operative cash flows can be estimated to be in the same risk class. Regarding the salvage value the risk can be higher, which would require a higher discount rate like the WACC. This depends on the type of asset and the market conditions. Schallheim (1994, p. 159) proposes a method to calculate an appropriate discount rate (see section 3.1.1). Regarding the repayment of the deposit, the after tax debt rate should be applied, too, because the counterparty is the same as for the lease cash flows.

6.2 Container buy or lease evaluation theory

The evaluation of the container buy or lease decision is similar to the general approach, but has to be extended by some industry-specific issues. The existing container-related literature lists many reasons to lease or to buy (see section 3.1.2). In addition Tan (1983) and Temple (1987) developed NPV models that are comparable with Brealey (2008). But, their models neither provide a complete decision theory that includes all criteria, nor the correct handling of advances and deposits. The target of this section is to provide a more complete decision theory.

6.2.1 Additional container-specific decision criteria

In addition to the general decision criteria listed in Table 3-1, there are several relevant decision criteria for the container buy or lease decision. Table 6-2 provides an overview, which shows that all of them are **not** integrated in the existing general decision model presented in 6.1.2.

Table 6-2 Additional decision criteria for container buy or lease decisions

Decision criteria	Source chapter	Included in existing theoretical model	Enhanced model integration
Fleet size	5	no	yes
Expected future container price	2, 5	no	yes
Repair costs	2, 5	no	yes
Redelivery costs (drop off charges)	2, 5	no	yes
Pick up time extensions must be negotiated	2	no	yes
Industry condition (oil prices, charter rates, world trade/GDP growth, us transportation index, balticdry, shipprice)	2, 3, 4	no	yes
Industry condition (harpex, stockindex)	2, 3, 4	no	no – not significant
Additional ship (slot) capacity	2	no	yes
Avoid repositioning / offsetting container flow imbalances	2, 5	no	yes
Buffer stock function of leasing	2, 5	no	yes
Global availability of equipment / flexibility	2, 5	no	yes
Availability of containers in remote locations	2, 5	no	yes

Before developing an enhanced buy or lease decision model, container repair and redelivery costs are analyzed in detail, because detailed knowledge is necessary for their integration.

6.2.1.1 Repair costs

There are three major standards used for inspecting and repairing a container (WCN, 2008):

First, IICL5 is defined by the Institute of International Container Lessors. IICL5 is the highest container inspection/repair standard.

Second, the Common Interchange Criteria (CIC) are published by the Container Owners Association (COA) to standardize container inspection/repair. The CIC standard is below IICL5.

Last, the Unified Container Inspection and Repair Criteria (UCIRC) are most commonly used by shipping lines as in-service inspection standard. UCIRC is the lowest of the three mentioned standards. If an in-service container (leased or owned) needs to be repaired according to the UCIRC inspection, shipping lines either use UCIRC or a higher standard (IICL5 or CIC) as a basis for the repair.

The following table provides an overview over estimated average repair costs according to the three standards (COA, 2009):

Table 6-3 Average repair costs according to different standards

Repair costs in USD				
	IICL	CIC	Weight	UCIRC (estimated as 50% of CIC)
Americas	234.00	203.00	14.70%	
Europe	504.00	458.00	16.60%	
Asia	194.00	165.00	68.70%	
Weighted average	251.34	219.22		109.61
Difference to IICL	-	32.12		141.72

Weight represents the global offhire distribution

Some shipping lines try to optimize their repair costs by repairing containers at cheaper locations (with lower wages). For example, damaged containers will be first repositioned to China and repaired there.

Leasing contracts include a section on the redelivery of a container. It is defined at which condition containers have to be returned. Some lessors use IICL5, others CIC in their contracts. Obviously CIC is less expensive for the lessee. The cost difference between repairs according to IICL5 and CIC has been analyzed by a number of shipping lines in cooperation with COA. They found repairs according to IICL5 to be on average 32 USD per container more expensive than repairs according to CIC. There has been no study about the cost difference between IICL5 and UCIRC but it is expected to be in the range of 140 USD.

Based on the survey responses another estimate for the repair disadvantage of leasing is calculated (see section 5.2.2). The calculated weighted average higher repair costs of leased equipment are 46 USD. This number is substantially lower than the 140 USD mentioned above. This could be for two reasons. First, survey participants underestimate the repair costs of leased equipment (negative and zero responses account for 38% of answers). They might not take into account that leased equipment has to be returned according to a higher repair standard compared to own boxes. Second, the estimate for UCIRC repair costs above is very rough and might overestimate the average repair cost disadvantage of leasing.

Because leased containers need to be repaired according to IICL or CIC at redelivery whereas owned containers in a depot are only inspected according to UCIRC the buy or lease calculation is affected. This effect will be integrated in the evaluation formula below.

One further aspect regarding repair has to be mentioned. In most cases container repair is organized by the lessors at redelivery. The lessee pays the estimated repair costs to the lessor. But the lessor does not necessarily repair the container, because it might be beneficial to sell the container (especially if it is old) in *"as is"* condition or repair it according to the very low *"wind and watertight"* standard before selling. This makes sense, because secondhand containers are mainly used for storage or inland transportation where requirements are lower. In this case lessors can make a profit of approximately the difference between the wind and watertight standard and the IICL5/CIC standard because buyers are not willing to pay much more for an IICL/CIC container than a *wind and watertight* container. Shipping lines also make use of this effect for their own equipment. By choosing to lease equipment, shipping lines lose this option. Figure 6-1 provides an overview of the different repair costs.

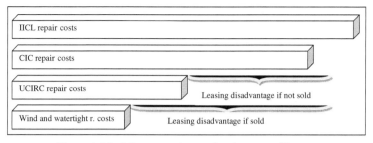

Figure 6-1 Redelivery repair cost disadvantage of leasing

The total redelivery repair disadvantage of leasing is difficult to estimate because sufficient data for a complete statistical analysis is not available. In the case of a continued use of a container the analysis above results in a leasing disadvantage of 140 USD if a container is repaired according to IICL whereas an owned container would be repaired according to UCIRC. If the leasing contract used CIC the disadvantage reduces by 32 USD. The calculation based on the survey results in a disadvantage of 46 USD. In the case where the container is sold in the second hand market, the average disadvantage increases to more than 140 USD because only the wind and watertight standard is required. In total a disadvantage of leasing regarding repair at redelivery of about 140 USD is estimated.

6.2.1.2 Redelivery costs

In addition to the repair costs, the lessee eventually has to pay redelivery charges to the lessor. Those charges depend on the location of the redelivery. The following example makes clear why redelivery charges are included in container leasing contracts. Almost all containers are produced in China today. This is also the location where most products are produced and a high demand for containers exists. But there are also locations, like in the United States or Africa, where not that many empty containers are needed. In order to balance this global mismatch, shipping lines as well as lessors either sell or reposition empty containers to locations with excess demand for containers like China. If shipping lines want to drop off leased containers at a *"bad"* location with low demand, they have to pay redelivery charges. The redelivery charges make sure that lessors do not suffer a loss in the volume of the repositioning costs. Many contracts also limit the number of containers that are allowed to be redelivered at certain locations within a timeframe.

Owned equipment in bad locations either needs to be repositioned or sold. Leased equipment can be repositioned to a better location (without or lower redelivery charges) or redelivered to the lessor right away. There is only a small disadvantage compared to owned equipment, because leased containers cannot be sold at the bad location. This disadvantage is estimated at 20 USD on average.

6.2.2 Enhanced container buy or lease evaluation model

Comparable to the general buy or lease decision model introduced in chapter 4.1 a two-step model for the container specific decision is suggested. The first five points in step one are exactly the same as described in section 6.1.2. In order to provide a complete model they are repeated here.

In the **first step**, firms analyze a number of criteria without the necessity of a comparing calculation:

First, if a company is financially constrained, cash plays an important role. Often, credit lines are exhausted, and no further bank loans are available. The establishment year of the company plays a role because a longer track record builds up the confidence of banks and internal funds. A better credit rating helps to get additional funds. Leasing is the preferred alternative in the case of financial constraints / limited track record / lower rating because up to 100% of the asset costs are financed.

Second, profitability might have two impacts. On one hand, leasing and debt affect profitability differently. Leasing reduces the profit less than loan financing in the first years and more in the later years. This effect might be interesting for some firms and lead to their decision to lease. On the other hand, a high profitability is often associated with a high liquidity level. This could lead to the decision to buy (see the pecking order theory of Myers & Majluf (1984)).

Third, off balance sheet financing might be appearling for firms that want to retain their current debt share to keep their existing rating / debt financing conditions. Leasing offers a simple way to generate off balance sheet financing. Leasing does not change the balance sheet, but agency costs have to be taken into account. Banks might increase the future interest or collateral level even if the balance sheet is unchanged.

Fourth, firms might choose to lease equipment to avoid transaction and information costs. For example, if a firm does not have connections to a supplier of an equipment type that is only produced in a different country whereas it is available at its location for lease, the lease alternative might be very attractive. Leasing avoids the purchase and disposal transaction, capital expenditure approvals, reduces record keeping, is faster than purchasing and negotiating loans, is flexible and avoids ownership dilution.

Fifth, risk sharing can be a reason to choose leasing. For example, leasing can be used to avoid the residual risk, the risk of obsolescence of equipment or if the equipment is only needed for a short period (e.g., a few days or weeks).

In addition to the five standard decision criteria, the following container specific can be added:

Sixth, with increasing fleet size the share of leased containers which are more flexible can be reduced. Therefore larger firms might choose to purchase to adjust the targeted lease share.

Seventh, the expected future container price might influence the buy or lease decision. If the container price is expected to increase a large amount, it might be beneficial to purchase equipment whereas an expected price reduction could make leasing attractive.

Eighth, additional transaction costs have to be taken into account. If there are delays in shipping demand, containers might be needed later than expected. Because pick up times are defined in the leasing contract, lessees need to negotiate pick up time extensions with the lessor. Those negotiations are unnecessary in the case of owned equipment.

Ninth, the industry condition (oil prices, charter rates, world trade/GDP growth, US transportation index, balticdry, shipprices) might have an impact on the buy or lease decision. Shipping lines could decide to lease or buy more or less depending on the status of the industry.

Tenth, additional ship capacity might have an impact on the buy or lease decision. About 2 TEU additional containers are needed for one additional container slot.

Eleventh, shipping lines might use leasing to avoid repositioning / offsetting container flow imbalances.

Twelfth, shippers might lease because it is cheaper than holding an owned container buffer stock.

Thirteenth, some container shipping lines might decide to purchase equipment because they need equipment in remote locations where lessors do not provide equipment.

In **step two**, firms that have not decided based on one of the criteria listed in step one, decide based on the following net advantage of leasing calculation. All criteria mentioned in Table 6-1 with the exception of repair and redelivery costs have been taken into account either in step one or the general formula presented in section 4.2.

The following formula integrates the two remaining issues:

$$NAL = A_0 - Dep_0 + \sum_{t=1}^{N} \frac{-L_t(1-T)-D_tT+O_t(1-T)}{[1+r_d(1-T)]^t} - \frac{S_N}{[1+r_s(1-T)]^N} + \frac{Dep_0}{[1+r_d(1-T)]^N} - \frac{Rep_N + Red_N}{[1+r_s(1-T)]^N}$$

Equation 6-6

Where the variables have the same meaning as defined in section 6.2 and

Rep_N = cost advantage of owning regarding redelivery repair costs [currency]

Red_N = cost advantage of owning regarding redelivery charges [currency]

Regarding repair and redelivery costs it is suggested that they use the same discount factor as in the case of the salvage value (r_S) because repair and redelivery have a comparable risk. In the following this discount rate will be analyzed in more detail.

6.2.2.1 Discount rate for the residual

As described in chapter 2.1.1, Schallheim (1994, p. 159) suggests using the following discount rate for the residual:

$$r_S = r_f + \beta(r_m - r_f)$$
Equation 6-7

Where:

r_S = discount rate for the residual [%]

r_f = risk-free rate (on government bonds) [%]

r_m = market return [%]

β = beta, measure of systematic risk [-]

The following table provides an overview over U.S. government bond interests with five-year maturity.

Table 6-4 Five-year U.S. Treasury interests, 1995 to 2008

Year	Five-year U.S. Treasury yield
1995	6.38%
1996	6.18%
1997	6.22%
1998	5.15%
1999	5.55%
2000	6.16%
2001	4.56%
2002	3.82%
2003	2.97%
2004	3.43%
2005	4.05%
2006	4.75%
2007	4.43%
2008	2.80%
Average	**4.75%**

Source: U.S. Federal Reserve

Based on this table it is assumed, that r_f = 4.75%. To calculate the beta, Schallheim (1994, p. 159) proposes:

"Measure a time series of prices for used equipment, and then correlate the returns from this time series with the time series of returns from a market wide index".

The following table lists secondhand prices as well as stock index data:

Table 6-5 Container resale prices and stock indexes

Year	Resale price of 20 foot standard container	% change	Dow Jones (average of 1st day of month closing)	% change	Standard & Poors (average of 1st day of month closing)	% change		
1995	980		4 534		547			
1996	860	-12%	5 780	27%	675	23%		
1997	780	-9%	7 438	29%	876	30%		
1998	750	-4%	8 610	16%	1 088	24%		
1999	700	-7%	10 475	22%	1 331	22%		
2000	680	-3%	10 688	2%	1 420	7%		
2001	570	-16%	10 140	-5%	1 186	-16%		
2002	620	9%	9 181	-9%	989	-17%		
2003	660	6%	9 018	-2%	968	-2%		
2004	900	36%	10 326	15%	1 134	17%		
2005	850	-6%	10 529	2%	1 208	7%		
2006	900	6%	11 472	9%	1 318	9%		
2007	920	2%	13 198	15%	1 478	12%		
2008	950	3%	11 224	-15%	1 215	-18%		
2009	800	-16%	8 888	-21%	949	-22%	Average	
Average Market return		-0.68%		6.00%		5.46%	5.73%	

Source: Andrew Foxcroft, Containerization International and Thomson Reuters
*=prices applicable to used containers of 12-13 approximate age and do not include cost of repairs/modification or customisation

| Correlation to Resale change | | | 0.042 | | 0.095 | 0.069 | | |

175

Based on the average market return and the correlation to the resale price change stated in Table 6-5, it is assumed, that $r_m = 5.7\%$ and $\beta = 0.07$. Consequently, the estimated discount rate for the residual (before tax) is

$$r_S = r_f + \beta(r_m - r_f) = 4.75\% + 0.07 * (5.7\% - 4.75\%) = 4.82\% \qquad \textbf{Equation 6-8}$$

Because of the low correlation between the residual value and the stock market index returns r_S is below r_m. It is also below the average BAA corporate bond rate of 7.4% (FED, 2010b). A lower discount factor for the residual and repair costs does not seem appropriate. Therefore the after tax bond rate is suggested for discounting the residual, repair and redelivery costs, too. This reduces the NAL formula for the container leasing case to

$$\textbf{NAL} = \textbf{A}_0 - \textbf{Dep}_0 + \sum_{t=1}^{N} \frac{-L_t(1-T) - D_t T + O_t(1-T)}{[1 + r_d(1-T)]^t} + \frac{Dep_0 - S_N - Rep_N - Red_N}{[1 + r_d(1-T)]^N} \qquad \textbf{Equation 6-9}$$

6.2.3 Numerical example

In this section a numerical example for the second step of the model developed in section 3.2.2 is provided because this calculation is suggested for most shipping lines. It is assumed that a firm did not decide to lease or buy according to the criteria listed in the first step.

In order to calculate the NAL, a number of assumptions are necessary. The following table summarizes the assumptions used by Tan (1983) and Temple (1987) and provides a set of assumptions that is updated based on Foxcroft (2009b).

Table 6-6 NPV calculation assumptions

Assumption	Tan, 1983	Temple, 1987	Foxcroft, 2009b
20 foot container cost (new standard dry van)	USD 2500	USD 1700	USD 2050
Economic life in shipping	10 years	More than 7 years	About 12 years
Lease duration	10 years	5 years	5 years (long term)
Residual value	Zero	USD 500 after 7 years	USD 800 (after 12-13 years, see above)
Lease rental (per diem)	USD 1.45	USD 1.00	USD 0.65
Reduced rental (per di-	Not covered	Not relevant	10% reduction from year 6 (de-

em) after first lease term			pending on market conditions at renewal)
Before tax borrowing rate	14%	10%	7.4% (average 2008 BAA bond rate,(FED, 2010b))
Corporate tax rate	52%	34% / 0%	25% (depends on tax regulations of country)
Capital allow-ance/depreciation	100% in first year	Decreasing over 5 years	10% of original costs over 10 years (depends on tax regulations of country)
Tax lag	24 months	none	none (taxes often have to be paid in advance, depends on tax proce-dure of country, it is assumed that the firm is profitable and there-fore can make use of allowances)
Assumption	**Tan, 1983**	**Temple, 1987**	**Foxcroft, 2009b**
Lease payment	At beginning of year in advance	In same period	End of month
Redelivery repair costs disadvantage of leasing	Not covered	Not covered	Average 140 USD (see 4.2.1)
Redelivery cost disadvan-tage of leasing	Not covered	Not covered	Average 20 USD (see 4.2.1)
In-service repair and oth-er operation costs	Not covered	Not covered	Same as owned
Discount rate	Net of tax borrowing rate	15%	After tax cost of debt (7.4%*[1-25%] = 5.6%)
Deposit to lessor	Not covered	Not covered	Two monthly rental amounts
Advance rate for bank financing (equity share of container investment)	Not covered	Not covered	75% (25% equity share)

Using the assumptions provided in Table 6-6 the NAL calculation can be performed. To simplify the presentation here, the cash flow is calculated on a yearly basis. To be more precise a monthly calculation should be performed.

$$NAL = A_0 - Dep_0 + \sum_{t=1}^{N} \frac{-L_t(1-T) - D_t T + O_t(1-T)}{[1 + r_d(1-T)]^t} + \frac{Dep_0 - S_N - Rep_N - Red_N}{[1 + r_d(1-T)]^N} \qquad \textbf{Equation 6-10}$$

$$NAL = 2050 - 60 * 0.65 + \sum_{t=1}^{5} \frac{-0.65 * 365 * (1 - 25\%) - 205 * 25\% + 0}{[1 + 5.6\%]^t} +$$

$$\sum_{t=6}^{10} \frac{-0.65 * (1 - 10\%) * 365 * (1 - 25\%) - 205 * 25\%}{[1 + 5.6\%]^t} +$$

$$\sum_{t=11}^{12} \frac{-0.65 * 0.9 * 365 * (1 - 25\%)}{[1 + 5.6\%]^t} +$$

$$\frac{60 * 0.65 - 800 * (1 - 25\%) - 140 - 20}{[1 + 5.6\%]^{12}}$$

$$\textbf{Equation 6-11}$$

$$NAL = 2011 + \sum_{t=1}^{5} \frac{-229.19}{[1 + 5.6\%]^t} + \sum_{t=6}^{10} \frac{-211.39}{[1 + 5.6\%]^t} + \sum_{t=11}^{12} \frac{-160.14}{[1 + 5.6\%]^t} + \frac{-721}{[1 + 5.6\%]^{12}}$$

$$\textbf{Equation 6-12}$$

The cash flow is summarized in the following table:

Table 6-7 NAL example calculation

t	0	1	2	3	4	5	6	7	8	9	10	11	12
Initial cash flow	$2,011.00												
Rental etc.		-$229.19	-$229.19	-$229.19	-$229.19	-$229.19	-$211.39	-$211.39	-$211.39	-$211.39	-$211.39	-$160.14	-$160.14
Residual etc.													-$721.00
Total	$2,011.00	-$229.19	-$229.19	-$229.19	-$229.19	-$229.19	-$211.39	-$211.39	-$211.39	-$211.39	-$211.39	-$160.14	-$881.14
NAL	-$196.73												

Based on the assumptions made, the NAL is -197 USD. The more precise calculation on monthly bases does not change the result fundamentally (NAL = USD -243). Consequently, a firm should rather buy than lease containers, if it plans to use containers for 12 years.

If the lifetime is extended to 15 years, the NAL turns positive to 178 USD. Under this assumption leasing becomes the better alternative.

Since the market prices and other assumptions change over time, it is recommended that the NAL analysis is performed frequently. It has to be mentioned, that leasing or purchasing can also make sense, if one of the criteria mentioned in 6.2.2 (step one) is of importance.

6.3 Summary of enhanced theoretical concept and lessons learned

Based on the existing standard model for buy or lease evaluation described by Brealey et al. (2008) and others, an enhanced theoretical concept is developed. Decision criteria which show statistical significance in the empirical macroeconomic, the microeconomic, the survey model or a weighted average importance of more than one in the survey analysis are integrated in the formula. First, a general enhanced model is developed.

In the **first step** firms analyze a number of criteria without the necessity of a comparing calculation:

First, if a company is financially constrained, is very young or has a low credit rating leasing is the preferred alternative.

Second, profitability might lead to more leasing to increase profits. But high profits can also be used to purchase equipment.

Third, off balance sheet financing in the form of leasing might be interesting for firms, which want to retain their current debt share to keep their existing rating / debt financing conditions.

Fourth, firms might choose to lease equipment to avoid transaction and information costs (e.g. purchase and disposal transaction, expenditure controls).

Fifth, risk sharing can be a reason to choose leasing (e.g. avoiding the residual risk, the risk of obsolescence of equipment or if equipment is only needed for a short period.

If a shipping line has not decided based on one of these criteria, a NAL calculation is performed in the **second step**. Compared to the existing literature the formula now includes deposits and advances as well as purchase and salvage cost advantages of lessors.

$$\mathbf{NAL} = \mathbf{NPV_L} - \mathbf{NPV_D} = \mathbf{A_0} - \mathbf{Dep_0} + \sum_{t=1}^{N} \frac{-L_t(1-T) - D_t T + O_t(1-T)}{[1+r_d(1-T)]^t} - \frac{S_N}{[1+r_d(1-T)]^N} +$$
$$\frac{Dep_0}{[1+r_d(1-T)]^N} \qquad \textbf{Equation 6-13}$$

Where:

NAL	= net advantage of leasing [currency]
A_0	= lessor's acquisition cost of asset in t_0 [currency]
Dep_0	= deposit provided to the lessor in t_0 [currency]
N	= length of the lease in years [-]
L_t	= lease payment in period t [currency]
T	= marginal corporate tax rate [%]
D_t	= depreciation in period t [currency]

O_t = operative costs incl. in lease (e.g. maintenance, insurance) [currency]

S_N = lessee's after tax salvage value (terminal value) at time N [currency]

$r_d(1-T)$ = discount rate (risk equivalent opportunity costs/after tax cost of debt) [%]

If the calculated NAL is positive equipment should be leased, otherwise purchased and financed by debt.

For the **container-specific decision** model, the following criteria can be added to the general **step one**:

Sixth, with increasing fleet size the share of leased containers which are more flexible can be reduced.

Seventh, the expected future container price might influence the buy or lease decision.

Eighth, additional transaction cost (e.g. negotiate extended pick up times) have to be taken into account.

Ninth, the industry condition (oil prices, charter rates, world trade/GDP growth, US transportation index, balticdry, shipprices) might have an impact on the buy or lease decision.

Tenth, additional ship capacity might have an impact on the buy or lease decision.

Eleventh, shipping lines might use leasing to avoid repositioning / offsetting container flow imbalances.

Twelfth, shippers might lease because it is cheaper than holding an owned container buffer stock.

Thirteenth, some container shipping lines might decide to purchase equipment because they need equipment in remote locations where lessors do not provide equipment.

In **step two**, firms that have not decided based on one of the criteria listed in step one, decide based on the following net advantage of leasing calculation. The general formula presented above is extended by integration of repair and redelivery costs:

$$NAL = A_0 - Dep_0 + \sum_{t=1}^{N} \frac{-L_t(1-T) - D_t T + O_t(1-T)}{[1+r_d(1-T)]^t} + \frac{Dep_0 - S_N - Rep_N - Red_N}{[1+r_d(1-T)]^N} \qquad \textbf{Equation 6-14}$$

Where the variables have the same meaning as above and

Rep_N = cost advantage of owning regarding redelivery repair costs [currency]

Red_N = cost advantage of owning regarding redelivery charges [currency].

7   Overall summary and future research suggestions

In chapter 2, the existing theoretical and empirical literature regarding the buy or lease decision in general and with focus on containers is summarized. Most corporate finance textbooks as well as academic theory literature suggest computing the NAL. If the NAL is greater than zero, leasing should be chosen. The proposed NAL calculation does not take many decision criteria into account that are mentioned in the literature.

The theoretical literature coverage of the buy or lease decision regarding shipping containers is very limited. The industry-specific models for containers from Tan (1983) and Temple (1987) also use a NAL calculation. The assumptions made do not reflect the current situation on the market and many decision criteria are not taken into account.

The existing general empirical studies analyze the effect of several variables on the lease share of companies using a regression analysis. Surveys from O'Brien & Nunnally (1983) and Mukherjee (1991) show that large corporations widely use the NAL calculation for decision preparation. None of the existing empirical studies examines the effect of NAL calculations with a regression model.

Container specific empirical literature is even more limited. No regression analysis of industry data exists. Only one survey was conducted by Temple (1987) which does not cover many relevant decision criteria including the NAL and does not use regression methods for analysis.

To get a better overview a summary of all decision criteria mentioned in the existing literature with their effect on the buy or lease decision is provided. Furthermore the literature gap is worked out.

In chapter 3, an empirical macroeconomic regression analysis is presented. Based on an aggregated dataset of containers purchased by shipping lines and lessors as well as other industry and macroeconomic data a simplified NAL variable is calculated to run a regression analysis. This analysis confirms the empirical relevance of the NAL calculation with statistical significance for the first time. A change in NAL is positively associated with a change in lease share. Furthermore a change in freight index shows a statistically significant positive effect on the lease share change.

In chapter 4 an empirical analysis on the microeconomic level is presented. Based on a unique dataset for the global top 25 shipping lines over 15 years the impact of the NAL as well as other criteria is analyzed with regression methods. The results show a statistical and absolute significant positive impact of the

NAL of leasing. It confirms the relevance of the NAL calculation for the first time on the microeconomic level.

The analysis confirms the negative effect of net income on the lease share. It also affirms the effect of rating: The better the rating, the lower the lease share.

Furthermore empirical evidence with statistical significance is provided for the relevance of the variables merger (positive), spread (positive), bunker price (negative), demand (positive), ustransport (positive) and establishment year (positive) for the first time.

In chapter 5. a shipping line survey conducted in 2010 that delivers some interesting insights on the decision process in practice is presented. It updates the survey conducted by Temple in 1987 and provides information regarding additional decision criteria (incl. NAL analysis) for the first time. The analysis shows that the NAL calculation result is one important criterion. But other criteria, like flexibility, future container prices and profitability also have a very high importance. Furthermore these criteria include "not sensible" reasons for leasing as Brealey et al. (2008) describes them—saving cash and off balance sheet financing.

Shipping lines seem to be uncertain which discount rate to use for the npv analysis, because many practitioners either are not sure or choose not the recommended interest rate (after tax borrowing rate). The comparison to the survey conducted by Mukherje (1991) shows that the recommended discount rate is used by most of the fortune 500 firms.

The respondents perceive leasing as more expensive compared to owning. One component of the leasing cost is repair. They also have the impression that repair costs of leased equipment are higher than for owned containers.

There is much uncertainty regarding inflation. Practitioners have very different views of the importance of inflation as well as the direction of an impact of higher expected inflation on the lease share.

The leasing strategy of most shipping lines remains unchanged. There is only a slight tendency towards usage of more lessors, more equipment pooling and a higher lease share. This could be the result of the financial crises which reduced bank loan access and profits.

The econometrical analysis of the survey data confirms the impact of some criteria with statistical significance. This is the first regression analysis of survey data performed regarding the container buy or lease decision made by shipping lines. The importance of npv, tax, fleetsize and loanaccess have a significant negative impact on the lease share as hypothesized. The importance of the lease period, obsolescence and cashsaving have a significant positive impact as hypothesized. The variables remote loc (negative), dropoff (positive), employees (positive) and profitindex (positive) show a statistically significant impact contrary to expectation.

The comparison with the container buy or lease survey conducted by Temple (1987) shows that shipping lines still have very different leasing strategies. All surveyed liners use leasing but the lease share ranges in both surveys from about 10 to 100%. The npv criterion was not analyzed in 1987. Flexibility was regarded as very important in both surveys. The other criteria (offsetting imbalances, buffer stock function, cash saving, inhouse administration costs, availability in remote locations and hedging new equipment risk) show an increased importance in the 2010 survey.

Shipping lines seem to have improved their container management since 1987 by taking many factors into account when deciding to lease or to buy.

In chapter 6, an enhanced theoretical decision model is developed based on the existing standard model for buy or lease evaluation described by Brealey (2008) and others. Decision criteria which show statistical significance in the empirical macroeconomic (chapter 3), the microeconomic (chapter 4), the survey model or a weighted average importance of more than one in the survey analysis (chapter 5) are integrated in the formula. The presented container specific model can be used by shipping lines to improve their decisions in the future.

Further research is suggested in several areas. On the microeconomic level, it would be interesting to include smaller shipping lines in the analysis to get a more complete and representative result for the industry. The additional observation could lead to further statistically significant decision criteria. To confirm the empirical relevance of the NAL calculation in general, it would be important to extend the analysis to other industries. This also applies to the analysis of survey data. A non industry specific survey should be performed and analyzed with regression techniques to confirm the relevance of NAL calculations and other criteria. Finally, based on the suggested empirical analyses the theoretical model can be updated by integrating further relevant criteria.

Appendix 1: Survey invitation letters and reminders

1. Initial invitation letter:

To: participant@email.com

From: michael.wehrheim@web.de

Subject: Container survey – the buy or lease decision

Body: Dear Mr. xy

We are sending this online academic survey to benefit from your professional experience regarding container equipment! If you are not responsible for container matters, please reply with the name and email address of your colleague who is in charge of container buy or lease decisions.

Previously I served as Vice President Finance for Capital Lease. Currently I am working on my doctor thesis: "The buy or lease decision of shipping lines regarding containers". Prof. Hans-Dietrich Haasis of the Institute of Shipping Economics and Logistics, Bremen University, Germany, is advising my doctoral thesis.

A key part to my dissertation is this survey to analyze the buy or lease decision process of shipping lines. The goal is a better understanding of the process for both theory and practice. The results may help to optimize your buy or lease decisions in the future. By filling out the survey you will receive a free summary of the results.

The internet based survey will take no longer than 10 minutes of your valuable time. Your input is highly appreciated to achieve a good representation of all shipping lines in the survey.

The survey responses are completely anonymous. It is not possible to find out who enters which data. Please click on this link to participate: http://www.surveymonkey.com/s.aspx

We would appreciate to receive your responses by April 24th 2010.

If you have any questions or comments, please do not hesitate to contact me.
Thank you for your help!

Best regards,

Michael Wehrheim
5711 Overlea Rd.
Bethesda, MD 20816
USA
+1 240 743 4711
Michael.wehrheim@web.de

Please note: If you do not wish to receive further emails from us, please click the link below, and you will be automatically removed from our mailing list.
http://www.surveymonkey.com/optout.aspx

2. First and second reminder:

To: participant@email.com
From: michael.wehrheim@web.de

Subject: Container buy or lease decision Body: Dear Dear Mr. Lam

Did you complete our survey regarding the container buy or lease decision? It is not too late! Please take a few minutes of your valuable time to learn about buy or lease optimization and help us achieving a representative result.

Here is a link to the survey:
http://www.surveymonkey.com/s.aspx

Thanks for your participation!

Best regards,

Michael Wehrheim

Please note: If you do not wish to receive further emails from us, please click the link below, and you will be automatically removed from our mailing list.
http://www.surveymonkey.com/optout.aspx

3. Final reminder

To: participant@email.com
From: michael.wehrheim@web.de

Subject: Container buy or lease decision Body: [CustomValue]

Did you complete our survey regarding the container buy or lease decision?

This is your last chance to participate and get a free summary of the survey results! The survey will be closed on Friday May 21.

Your responses are anonymous - there is no confidentiality risk!

Here is a link to the survey:
http://www.surveymonkey.com/s.aspx

Thanks for your participation!

Best regards,

Michael Wehrheim

Please note: If you do not wish to receive further emails from us, please click the link below, and you will be automatically removed from our mailing list.
http://www.surveymonkey.com/optout.aspx

Appendix 2: Survey questionnaire and answers

Container buy or lease survey

Recognizing the impact of the global recession, please answer the following questions based on your average container buy or lease decision before the recession (2006/2007).
All questions in this section relate to your buy or lease decisions.

Operational Questions

1) How important is flexibility (global availability of equipment) for your decision?

Not important at all						Extremely important
□	□	□	□	□	□	□
-3	-2	-1	0	1	2	3
1.4%	2.9%	2.9%	10.1%	8.7%	39.1%	34.8%

2) How important is the buffer stock function of leasing for your decision?

Not important at all						Extremely important
□	□	□	□	□	□	□
-3	-2	-1	0	1	2	3
5.8%	2.9%	2.9%	13.0%	26.1%	31.9%	17.4%

3) How important is availability of containers in remote locations for your decision?

Not important at all						Extremely important
□	□	□	□	□	□	□
-3	-2	-1	0	1	2	3
10.1%	5.8%	5.8%	17.4%	29.0%	14.5%	17.4%

4) How important is offsetting container flow imbalances for you decision?

Not important at all						Extremely important
□	□	□	□	□	□	□
-3	-2	-1	0	1	2	3
4.3%	1.4%	1.4%	7.2%	21.7%	29.0%	34.8%

5) How important is the length of the lease period for your decision?

Not important at all						Extremely important
□	□	□	□	□	□	□
-3	-2	-1	0	1	2	3
2.9%	2.9%	1.4%	14.5%	21.7%	30.4%	26.1%

6) How important is hedging the risk of new equipment types for your decision?

Not important at all						Extremely important
□	□	□	□	□	□	□
-3	-2	-1	0	1	2	3
14.5%	7.2%	8.7%	18.8%	23.2%	17.4%	10.1%

7) How important are in-house administration costs for container management for you decision?

Not important at all						Extremely important
□	□	□	□	□	□	□
-3	-2	-1	0	1	2	3
14.5%	2.9%	7.2%	10.1%	17.4%	21.7%	26.1%

Financial Questions

8) How important are net present value calculations for your buy or lease evaluation?

Not important at all   Extremely important   not sure

□	□	□	□	□	□	□	□
-3	-2	-1	0	1	2	3	not sure
0.0%	3.1%	1.5%	10.8%	6.2%	35.4%	35.4%	7.7%

9) Do you use net present value calculations for your buy or lease evaluation?

Yes	□	75.4%	continues with question 10
No	□	18.5%	continues with question 11
Not sure	□	6.2%	continues with question 11

10) Which discount rate do you use?

□	Before tax borrowing rate	16.7%
□	After tax borrowing rate	4.2%
□	Weighted average cost of capital	39.6%
□	Several discount rates according to the risk of the cash flows	20.8%
□	Not sure	18.8%
□	Other (please specify) _____	0.0%

11) How important are internal rate of return calculations for your buy or lease decision?

Not important at all   Extremely important   Not sure

□	□	□	□	□	□	□	□
-3	-2	-1	0	1	2	3	
3.4%	0.0%	3.4%	8.6%	17.2%	32.8%	25.9%	8.6%

12) How would you rate the cost of leasing compared to the cost of owning?

Leasing is much cheaper   Leasing is much more expensive

□	□	□	□	□	□	□
-3	-2	-1	0	1	2	3
3.4%	1.7%	6.9%	8.6%	19.0%	27.6%	32.8%

13) How would you rate the repair costs of standard container leasing per TEU compared to the cost of owning?

More than 100 USD cheaper   same   Over 100 USD more expensive

□	□	□	□	□	□	□
-3	-2	-1	0	1	2	3
8.6%	1.7%	3.4%	24.1%	17.2%	27.6%	17.2%

14) How important are leasing drop off costs for your decision to buy or lease?

Not important at all   Extremely important

□	□	□	□	□	□	□
-3	-2	-1	0	1	2	3
3.4%	0.0%	3.4%	12.1%	37.9%	17.2%	25.9%

15) How important is saving cash (e.g. deferring capital spending, avoiding advances) for your buy or lease decision?

Not important at all   Extremely important

□	□	□	□	□	□	□
-3	-2	-1	0	1	2	3
6.9%	8.6%	3.4%	10.3%	17.2%	22.4%	31.0%

16) How important are tax effects for your buy or lease decision?

Not important at all   Extremely important   Not sure

☐	☐	☐	☐	☐	☐	☐		☐
-3	-2	-1	0	1	2	3		
25.9%	3.4%	10.3%	19.0%	6.9%	20.7%	5.2%		8.6%

17) How important are inflation expectations for your buy or lease decision?

Not important at all   Extremely important   Not sure

☐	☐	☐	☐	☐	☐	☐		☐
-3	-2	-1	0	1	2	3		
8.6%	8.6%	6.9%	17.2%	13.8%	19.0%	12.1%		13.8%

18) If you expect inflation to increase dramatically. How would that affect your decision?

A lot less leasing   A lot more leasing   Not sure

☐	☐	☐	☐	☐	☐	☐		☐
-3	-2	-1	0	1	2	3		
6.9%	10.3%	12.1%	25.9%	8.6%	8.6%	12.1%		15.5%

19) How important are expected future container prices for your buy or lease decision?

Not important at all   Extremely important

☐	☐	☐	☐	☐	☐	☐
-3	-2	-1	0	1	2	3
1.7%	5.2%	1.7%	3.4%	19.0%	31.0%	37.9%

20) How important is off balance sheet financing for your buy or lease decision?

Not important at all   Extremely important   Not sure

☐	☐	☐	☐	☐	☐	☐		☐
-3	-2	-1	0	1	2	3		
8.6%	3.4%	5.2%	6.9%	27.6%	25.9%	19.0%		3.4%

21) How important is the current profitability of your firm for your buy or lease decision?

Not important at all   Extremely important

☐	☐	☐	☐	☐	☐	☐
-3	-2	-1	0	1	2	3
3.4%	0.0%	1.7%	12.1%	20.7%	22.4%	39.7%

22) How important are purchase options in a lease contract for your buy or lease decision?

Not important at all   Extremely important

☐	☐	☐	☐	☐	☐	☐
-3	-2	-1	0	1	2	3
10.3%	0.0%	1.7%	8.6%	24.1%	29.3%	25.9%

23) How important are expenditure controls (approvals by higher management when purchasing) for your decision to lease or buy?

Not important at all   Extremely important

☐	☐	☐	☐	☐	☐	☐
-3	-2	-1	0	1	2	3
6.9%	3.4%	3.4%	12.1%	13.8%	24.1%	36.2%

Leasing strategy questions

24) What is your container leasing share target within the next two years?

A lot less leasing			As is			A lot more leasing
☐	☐	☐	☐	☐	☐	☐
-3	-2	-1	0	1	2	3
7.0%	7.0%	19.3%	19.3%	24.6%	10.5%	12.3%

25) How many lessors do you currently work with?

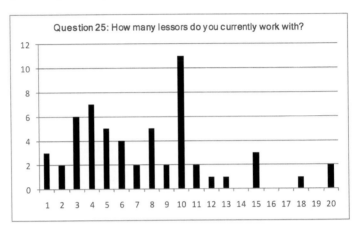

Figure A-1 Number of current lessors histogram

The average number of lessors shipping lines works with is 7.6.

26) How many lessors do plan to work with in the future (next two years)?

A lot less			As is			A lot more
☐	☐	☐	☐	☐	☐	☐
-3	-2	-1	0	1	2	3
7.0%	3.5%	5.3%	43.9%	17.5%	14.0%	8.8%

27) To what extent do you pool equipment with other carriers?

Not at all						As much as possible
☐	☐	☐	☐	☐	☐	☐
-3	-2	-1	0	1	2	3
24.6%	5.3%	8.8%	19.3%	19.3%	10.5%	12.3%

28) How much do you plan to pool equipment in the future (next two years)?

A lot less			As is			A lot more
☐	☐	☐	☐	☐	☐	☐
-3	-2	-1	0	1	2	3
7.0%	1.8%	3.5%	42.1%	22.8%	8.8%	14.0%

Background Questions

Please answer also the following questions about your firm. The answers are necessary for the analysis to compare groups of shipping lines in different situations. Your answers are anonymous and all the information will be handled confidentially.

29) When was your company established?

Before 1985	1986 to 1990	1991 to 1995	1996 to 2000	2001 to 2005	after 2005	Not sure
□	□	□	□	□	□	□
58.8%	3.9%	13.7%	11.8%	7.8%	3.9%	0.0%

30) How many employees does your firm have?

< 20	20 to 99	100 to 499	500 to 999	1000 to 2499	2500 to 4999	> 5,000
□	□	□	□	□	□	□
3.9%	21.6%	33.3%	7.8%	5.9%	15.7%	11.8%

31) Which percentage of your total container fleet was under master lease, long term lease, lease purchase and owned on average before the recession (2006/2007)?   (Total is 100)

Master lease (incl. one way and short term) 25.6% (average)

Long term lease (incl. flexible long term) 30.1% (average)

Lease purchase (incl. optional lease purchase) 9.7% (average)

Owned (incl. bank financed) 34.6% (average)

If lease purchase is added to the owned side as Andrew Foxcroft defines it regarding the industry overview tables for Containerization International, on average 55.7% are leased and 44.3% are owned.

32) What was the average size of your total container fleet before the recession (2006/2007)?

□	Less than 249 TEU	2.0%
□	250 to 999 TEU	5.9%
□	1000 to 9,999 TEU	27.5%
□	10,000 – 49,999 TEU	23.5%
□	50,000 – 199,999 TEU	13.7%
□	200,000 to 699,999 TEU	17.6%
□	More than 700,000 TEU	9.8%

33) In which of the following years was your company profitable? Please check all profitable years.

2006	2007	2008	2009	Not sure
□	□	□	□	□
82.4%	84.3%	64.7%	47.1%	5.9%

34) How would you rate your firm's average access to bank loans before the recession (2006/2007)?

No access at all   No limitations

□	□	□	□	□	□	□
-3	-2	-1	0	1	2	3
5.9%	2.0%	3.9%	13.7%	7.8%	35.3%	31.4%

35) How would you rate your firm's current access to bank loans?

No access at all   No limitations

□	□	□	□	□	□	□
-3	-2	-1	0	1	2	3
7.8%	7.8%	2.0%	15.7%	13.7%	35.3%	17.6%

36) Please provide comments about the survey and additional information about your buy or lease decision here:

_____

Thank you for completing the survey!

If you would like to get a free survey results summary please send a blank email to michael.wehrheim@web.de.
If you have any questions please do not hesitate to contact me at the same email address.
Best regards, Michael Wehrheim

References

Adams, M., & Hardwick, P. (1998). Determinants of the leasing decision in United Kingdom listed companies. [Article]. Applied Financial Economics, 8(5), 487-494.

Adedeji, A., & Stapleton, R. C. (1996). Leases, debt and taxable capacity. [Article]. Applied Financial Economics, 6(1), 71-83.

Alphaliner. (2010). Alphaliner Top 100 shipping lines. Retrieved May 26 2010: http://www.axs-alphaliner.com/top100/index.php

Anderson, P. F., & Martin, J. D. (1977). Lease vs. Purchase Decisions: A Survey of Current Practice. Financial Management, 6(1), 41-47.

Ang, J., & Peterson, P. P. (1984). The Leasing Puzzle. The Journal of Finance, 39(4), 1055-1065.

Baker, G. P., & Hubbard, T. N. (2003). Make Versus Buy in Trucking:Asset Ownership, Job Design, and Information. American Economic Review, 93(3), 551-572.

Bamberg, P. D. G., & Baur, D. F. (1991). Statistik (7th Edition ed.). Muenchen: Olsenbourg.

Bayless, M. E., & Diltz, J. D. (1986). An Empirical Study of the Debt Displacement Effects of Leasing. Financial Management, 15(4), 53-60.

BEA. (2009). U.S. Price Indexes for Gross Domestic Product Retrieved 11/15/2009, from Bureau of Economic Analysis: http://www.bea.gov /national/nipaweb/TableView.asp?SelectedTable=4&ViewSeries=NO&Ja va=no&Request3Place=N&3Place=N&FromView=YES&Freq=Year&Fir stYear=1977&LastYear=2009&3Place=N&Update=Update&JavaBox=no #Mid

Bloomberg. (2010). Baltic Dry Index. Retrieved 10 June 2010:

BLS. (2009). U.S. Inflation: CPI deflator. Retrieved 11/15/2009, from U.S. Department of Labor - Bureau of Labor Statistics: ftp://ftp.bls.gov/pub/ special.requests/cpi/cpiai.txt

Bower, R. S. (1973). Issues in Lease Financing. Financial Management, 2(4), 25-34.

Brealey, Myers, & Allen. (2008). Principles of corporate finance (Vol. 9th edition). New York: McGraw-Hill.

Brealey, R. A., & Myers, S. C. (1991). Principles of Corporate Finance (Fourth Edition ed.).

Brigham, E. F., & Gapenski, L. C. (1990). Intermediate financial management. Chicago: Dryden Press.

Chemmanur, T. J., & Yan, A. (2000). Equilibrium Leasing Contracts Under Double-sided Asymmetric Information. SSRN eLibrary.

COA. (2009, 24 August 2009). COA Common Interchange Criteria project: Comparative CIC/IICL-5 Off-hire inspection criteria Survey Now Completed. Retrieved June 10 2010, 2010, from http://www.containerowners association.org/9.html

Containerdatabase, I. b. o. M. T. (2009). Shipping line capacity development 1994-2009

Converse, J. M., & Stanley, P. (1986). Survey Questions - Handcrafting the standardized questionaire (Vol. 63). Newbury Park: SAGE Publications.

Copeland, T. E., & Weston, J. F. (1982). A Note on the Evaluation of Cancellable Operating Leases. Financial Management, 11(2), 60-67.

Dasgupta, S. (2007). To Lease or to Buy? A Structural Model of a Consumer's Vehicle and Contract Choice Decisions. Journal of marketing research, 490 - 502.

De Bodt, E., Filareto, M.-C., & Lobez, F. (2001). Leasing Decision, Banking Debt and Moral Hazard. Retrieved March 18, 2009, from http://ssrn.com /paper=264593

Deloof, M., Lagaert, I., & Verschueren, I. (2007). Leases and Debt: Complements or Substitutes? Evidence from Belgian SMEs. Journal of Small Business Management, 45(4), 491.

Deziel, L. B. (1981). Market Equilibrium for transportation equipment leases. Dissertation at Stanford University, 1 -175.

Dietel, B., & Heinen, E. (1991). Industriebetriebslehre: Entscheidungen im Industriebetrieb (Vol. 9. Auflage). Wiesbaden: Gabler.

DoT. (2009). U.S. Transportation Index (TSI) Retrieved Nov 2009, from U.S. Department of Transportation - Bureau of Transportation Statistics: www.bts.gov

Drewry. (2002). Leasing is an attractive option. Container Leasing - Seeking out the opportunities, 18-19.

Dynamar. (2007). Top 25 container liner operators trading profiles 2007. Unpublished manuscript.

Eades, K. M., & Marston, F. C. (2002). Incentives for Leasing: Evidence from the Largest U.S. Lessees and Lessors.

EIA (Cartographer). (2009). Crude oil price history.

Eisfeldt, R. (2007). Leasing, ability to repossess, and debt capacity. Review of Financial Studies - Soc Financial Studies.

Engelhardt, G. V. (1996). Consumption, Down Payments, and Liquidity Constraints. Journal of Money, Credit and Banking, 28(2), 255-271.

FED. (2010a). Market yield on U.S. Treasury securities at 5-year constant maturity, quoted on investment basis. Retrieved June 10 2010, 2010, from http://www.federalreserve.gov/releases/h15/data/Annual/H15_TCMNOM_Y5.txt

FED. (2010b). MOODY'S YIELD ON SEASONED CORPORATE BONDS - ALL INDUSTRIES, BAA. Retrieved June 10 2010, 2010, from http://www.federalreserve.gov/releases/h15/data/Annual/H15_BAA_NA.txt

Flath. (1980). The economics of Short-term Leasing. Economic Inquiry, 18(4), 247-250.

Foxcroft, A. (2008). Market Analysis - Container Leasing Market 2008. London: Containerization International.

Foxcroft, A. (2009a). Containerization International Market Analysis: World Container Census 2009. Containerization International, 2009, 28.

Foxcroft, A. (2009b). Market Analysis - Container Leasing Market 2009. London: Containerization International.

Foxcroft, A. (2009c). Share of owned and leased containers of top 25 shipping lines Containerization International.

Franks, J. R., & Hodges, S. D. (1978). Valuation of Financial Lease Contracts: A Note. The Journal of Finance, 33(2), 657-669.

Franks, J. R., & Hodges, S. D. (1987). Lease Valuation when Taxable Earnings are a Scarce Resource. The Journal of Finance, 42(4), 987-1005.

Graham, J. R., Lemmon, M. L., & Schallheim, J. S. (1998). Debt, Leases, Taxes, and the Endogeneity of Corporate Tax Status. The Journal of Finance, 53(1), 131 162.

Greene, W. H. (2008). Econometric Analysis (sixth Edition ed.). New York.

Grenadier, S. R. (1995). Valuing lease contracts A real-options approach. [doi: DOI: 10.1016/0304-405X(94)00820-Q]. Journal of Financial Economics, 38(3), 297-331.

Harper, P. C., shipbroker. (2009). Harpex. Retrieved 4 Nov. 2009, from Harper Peterson & Co.: www.harperpetersen.com/harpex

Hartmann-Wendels, T., Pfingsten, A., & Weber, M. (2007). Bnkbetriebslehre (Vol. 4. Auflage). Berlin: Springer Verlag.

Hendel, I., & Lizzeri, A. (2002). The Role of Leasing under Adverse Selection. The Journal of Political Economy, 110(1), 113-143.

IMF. (2009). World Economic Outlook. October 2009.

ISL. (2007). Lage und Aussichten des Marktes für Container im Winter 2007/08.

ISL. (2008). Shipping Statistics Yearbook 2008: Institue of Shipping Economics and Logistics.

ISL. (2009). Shipping line capacity development 1994-2009

ISL based on Lloyd's List, v. i. (2009). Monthly bunker market prices 2003 - 2006 (mid of month, in US $): Institute of Shipping Economics and Logistics.

Johanston, J., & DiNardo, J. (1997). Econometric Methods (Fourth Edition ed.). Irvin, California, USA.

Johnson, J. P., & Waldman, M. (2003). Leasing, Lemons, and Buybacks. The RAND Journal of Economics, 34(2), 247-265.

Klein, B., Crawford, R. G., & Alchian, A. A. (1978). Vertical integration, appropriable rents, and the competitive contracting process. Journal of Law and Economics, 21(2), 297-326.

Krishnan, V. S., & Moyer, R. C. (1994). Bankruptcy Costs and the Financial Leasing Decision. Financial Management, 23(2), 31-42.

Kruschwitz, L. (2010a). Finanzierung und Investition. Muenchen: Oldenbourg.

Kruschwitz, L. (2010b). Finanzmathematik: Lehrbuch der Zins-, Renten-, Tilgungs-, Kurs- und Renditeberechnung (Vol. 5. Auflage). Muenchen: Oldenbourg.

Langbein, L., & Felbinger, C. (2006). Public Program Evaluation - A statistical quide. Armonk, New York: M.E. Sharpe.

Leiner, P. D. B. (1995). Grundlagen statistischer Methoden. Muenchen: Oldenbourg.

Lemper, B. (2007). Erfolgsmodell mit Standardmassen. THB Sonderbeilage Container, 1-2.

Lemper, B. (2008). Containermarkt - erste Zeichen der konjunkturellen Abkuehlung. THB Sonderbeilage Container, 4-5.

Lemper, P. D. B. (2008). Containermarkt - erste Zeichen der konjunkturellen Abkuehlung. THB Sonderbeilage Container, 4-5.

Lewellen, W. G., Long, M. S., & McConnell, J. J. (1976). Asset Leasing in Competitive Capital Markets. The Journal of Finance, 31(3), 787-798.

Lewis, C. M., & Schallheim, J. S. (1992). Are Debt and Leases Substitutes? The Journal of Financial and Quantitative Analysis, 27(4), 497-511.

Lim, S. C., Mann, S. C., & Mihov, V. T. (2003). Market evaluation of off-balance sheet financing: You can run but you can't hide. SSRN eLibrary, 47.

Lloyd's. (1989). To lease or not to lease. Lloyd's Shipping Economist August, 14-18.

Mangione, T. W. (1995). Mail Surveys - Improving the quality (Vol. 40). Thousand Oaks, California: SAGE Publications.

Miller, M., H. and Upton, Charles W. (1976). Leasing, Buying, and the Cost of Capital Services. The Journal of Finance, 31(3), 761-786.

Mukherjee, T. K. (1991). A Survey of Corporate Leasing Analysis. Financial Management, 20(3), 96-107.

Myers, C. S., & Majluf, N. S. (1984). Corporate Financing and Investment Decisions When Firms Have InformationThat Investors Do Not Have. Journal of Financial Economics, 13(2), 187-221.

Myers, S. C., Dill, D. A., & Bautista, A. J. (1976). Valuation of Financial Lease Contracts. The Journal of Finance, 31(3), 799-819.

Nevitt, P. K., & Fabozzi, F. J. (2000). Equipment leasing. Homewood, Ill.: Dow Jones-Irwin.

O'Brien, T. J., & Nunnally, B. H., Jr. (1983). A 1982 Survey of Corporate Leasing Analysis. Financial Management, 12(2), 30-36.

Olsen, R. A. (1978). Lease vs. Purchase or Lease vs. Borrow: Comment. Financial Management, 7(2), 82-83.

Palmer, C. A. (1991). Container leasing allows efficient management of traffic flows. Asian Shipping March 1991.

Pritchard, R. E., & Hindelang, T. J. (1980). The Lease/Buy Decision: Anacom - A division of American Management Associations.

Rehkugler, H., & Glunz, S. (2007). Grundzuege der Finanzwirtschaft. Muenchen: Oldenbourg.

Reuters. (2009a). Annual Income Statement. Retrieved 15 Dec. 2009, from Thomson Reuters: http://thomsonreuters.com/

Reuters. (2009b). Annual Key Financial Items. Retrieved 15 Dec. 2009, from Thomson Reuters: http://thomsonreuters.com/

Reuters. (2009c). Stock prices of shipping lines. Retrieved 19 Nov. 2009, from Thomson Reuters: http://thomsonreuters.com/

Robichek, A. A. (1965). Optimal financing decisions.

Schallheim, J. S. (1994). Lease or buy? : principles for sound decision making. Boston, Mass.: Harvard Business School Press.

Schierenbeck, P. D. H. (1989). Grundzuege der Betriebswirtschaft (10th Edition ed.). Muenchen: Oldenbourg.

Sharpe, S. A., & Nguyen, H. H. (1995). Capital market imperfections and the incentive to lease. [doi: DOI: 10.1016/0304-405X(95)00830-8]. Journal of Financial Economics, 39(2-3), 271-294.

Smith, C. W., Jr., , Wakeman, L. M., & Hawkins, G. D. (1985). Determinants of Corporate Leasing Policy/Discussion. The Journal of Finance, Vol. 40(Iss. 3), 16.

Sorensen, I. W., & Johnson, R., E. . (1977). Equipment Financial Leasing Practices and Costs: An Empirical Study. Financial Management, 6(1), 33-40.

Stopford, M. (2009). Maritime Economics (third edition ed.). London: Routledge.

Tan, J. O. F. (1983). Containers - The Lease-Buy Decision. ICHCA.

Temple, B. S. (1987). The lease-versus-buy decision for container equipment. Bedford, New York: Institute of Internatonal Container Lessors.

Van Horne, J. C. (1998). Financial management and policy. Upper Saddle River, N.J.: Prentice Hall.

WCN. (2000). Container Industry - Finance lease options on the increase. World Cargo News, May 2000, 41-43.

WCN. (2008). Towards common inspection criteria. World Cargo News(June).

Weingartner, H. M. (1987). Leasing, Asset Lives and Uncertainty: Guides to Decision Making. Financial Management, 16(2), 5-12.

Williamson, O. E. (1985). The economic institutions of capitalism.

Yan, A. (2006). Leasing and Debt Financing: Substitutes or Complements? Journal of Financial and Quantitative Analysis, 41, 709-731.

Wertschöpfungsmanagement
Value-Added Management

Herausgegeben von/ Edited by Hans-Dietrich Haasis

www.peterlang.de

Burkhard Lemper / Manfred Zachcial (eds.)

Trends in Container Shipping

Proceedings of the ISL Maritime Conference 2008
9th and 10th of December, World Trade Center Bremen

Frankfurt am Main, Berlin, Bern, Bruxelles, New York, Oxford, Wien, 2009.
154 pp., num. fig., tab. and graph.
Maritime Logistics. Edited by Frank Arendt, Hans-Dietrich Haasis and
Manfred Zachcial. Vol. 1
ISBN 978-3-631-59780-4 · hardback € 39,80*

In the tradition of the Liner Shipping Conferences in the eighties, the Institute
of Shipping Economics and Logistics organised again a Maritime Conference
in Bremen. The aim of the conference in December 2008 was to analyse
and to forecast the trends and perspectives of the international container
shipping market. The international shipping industry and the global container
shipping market have recently seen some of the most successful years in
history. Excellent employment and high charter rates initiated a very strong
order boom, especially in the highest size classes of 8.000 TEU to 12.000 TEU
vessels and beyond. This development of accelerated fleet expansion met a
cooling down period in global economy as a consequence of the worldwide
financial crisis. The implications for the international trade markets have also
affected the shipping industry and the container shipping market. Against this
background the main topics of the Maritime Conference 2008 were: World
economy, trade and shipping; vessel size development and its implications;
implications of market growth on ports and hinterland; financing and taxation
aspects.

Content: Trends and perspectives of the international container shipping
market against the background of the global economic crisis · World economy,
trade and shipping · Vessel size development and its implications · Implications
of market growth on ports and hinterland · Financing and taxation aspects

Frankfurt am Main · Berlin · Bern · Bruxelles · New York · Oxford · Wien
Distribution: Verlag Peter Lang AG
Moosstr. 1, CH-2542 Pieterlen
Telefax 00 41 (0) 32 / 376 17 27

*The €-price includes German tax rate
Prices are subject to change without notice
Homepage http://www.peterlang.de